Lecture Notes in Economics and Mathematical Systems

Alan Martina

Lectures on the Economic Theory of Taxation

Economic Reform, Socially Optimal Piecemeal Consumption Taxation Structures and Information

Springer-Verlag
Berlin Heidelberg New York
London Paris Tokyo
Hong Kong Barcelona
Budapest

Author

Dr. Alan Martina
Faculty of Economics and Commerce
The Australian National University
ACT 2601
Australia

ISBN 3-540-55538-2 Springer-Verlag Berlin Heidelberg New York
ISBN 0-387-55538-2 Springer-Verlag New York Berlin Heidelberg

Library of Congress Cataloging-in-Publication Data. Martina, Alan. Lectures on the economic theory of taxation : economic reform, socially optimal piecemeal consumption taxation structures, and information / Alan Martina. p. cm. – (Lecture notes in economics and mathematical systems ; 384) Includes bibliographical references. ISBN 0-387-55538-2 (alk. paper). – ISBN 3-540-55538-2 1. Taxation. I. Title. II. Series. HJ2305.M37 1992 336.2–dc20 92-15323

Printed in Germany

Typesetting: Camera ready by author/editor
Printing and binding: Druckhaus Beltz, Hemsbach/Bergstr.
42/3140-543210 - Printed on acid-free paper

To Mary, Kim and William.

'... [D]oubt no less than knowledge is delight.'

Dante Alighieri [1265 - 1321], Inferno, canto XI, 93.

Contents

0. General Introduction.

The present discussion of taxation theory is based upon two basic assumptions. The one is that the community, in which public policy is applied, is concerned about achieving distributive justice among the many heterogeneous individuals to be found in this community. The other assumption is that the economic system is constrained in various ways from operating perfectly efficiently, while the public authorities, in their attempts to apply and implement socially-beneficial taxation policies, are restricted in their use of policy instruments. The imposition of these two general assumptions, in turn, alludes to a third, and more fundamental, assumption that is applied explicitly, or implicitly, throughout the lectures which follow; namely, that economic agents within the community only have access to limited amounts of relevant and accurate information. This latter assumption has a major direct, and indirect, influence on the way in which the argument is developed in these lectures - an assumption which, it seems reasonable to assert, reflects an important and relevant aspect of modern societies,

Perhaps the first to take into account this list of considerations, in a systematic discussion of taxation policy, was Sidgwick in The Principles of Political Economy [1883, 1887, Book III, and particularly Chs. VI, and VII].[1] To begin with

---

[1] Throughout, reference is being made to the second edition of The Principles of Political Economy - which was published in 1887. The first edition of this book was published in 1883.

Sidgwick was well aware of the fact that the operation of a free-market economic system may result in severe inequalities in the distribution of total community income and wealth (Ch VI).[2] In addition, if one accepts the Benthamite utilitarian principles - that the social welfare function is a simple summation of individual utility levels, and that individuals possess identical utility functions which are increasing, but at a diminishing rate, in individual wealth - then there are grounds for believing that the level of well being within this community could be increased by reducing inequalities in the distribution of wealth.[3] In other words, on grounds of distributive justice, there is a *prima facie* case for re-distributing the unequally distributed wealth within the community. But against this argument had to be placed a qualification - a qualification that is best summarised in Sidgwick's words:

> "[W]e have to allow for loss through increased idleness, decreased saving, lessened efficiency of capital, pressure of population, checked growth to culture."[4]

Thus the government is constrained in its use of policy instruments (with which to re-distribute income and wealth) for there are social costs (as well as social benefits) associated with their use. Put slightly differently, Sidgwick was aware that it is

---

[2] This point has recently been re-emphasised by Hammond [1990, pp. 7 - 8].

[3] Sidgwick [1887, p. 519]. Sidgwick did not impose the assumption that individual utility functions are identical. This was an assumption discussed by Pigou [1920], however.

[4] Sidgwick [1887, p.xxii].

unlikely that the public authorities would have access to lump-sum taxes and subsidies - viz. taxes and subsidies which have no influence on individual behaviour.

These fundamental themes in taxation theory, initially sketched out by Sidgwick, were subsequently taken up by Edgeworth [1897]. [5]

Thus, by the turn of this century, Sidgwick and Edgeworth were already strongly alluding to the fact that there were considerable information problems associated with attempting to implement socially-beneficial taxation policies. But perhaps the clearest warning came from Pareto [1913, 1916] - a warning that is to be found in Pareto's general statement of the concept of the social welfare function - a concept which was later independently discovered by Bergson [1938]. [6] In particular in Trattato di Sociologia generale [1916, p.1473] [7] Pareto observed that there are difficulties associated with determining the value of the social weights, or coefficients, that need to be decided upon before changes of individual utility levels can be aggregated into a measure of changes in social welfare. Specifically he stated:

---

5 See Tuomala [1990, pp.1- 3] on this piece of history of economic thought.

6 For an assessment of Pareto's contribution to the development of the theory of social welfare functions see Chipman [1976]. A different, and dissenting, evaluation of Pareto's contribution is to be found in Bergson [1983]. Also see Chipman [1987, p. 379] for further comments on this matter.

7 This book was later translated into English with the new title Mind and Society It was published in 1935.

"Let us imagine a community so situated that a strict choice has to be made between a very wealthy community with large inequalities in income among its members and a poor community with approximately equal incomes. ... Results will depend upon the coefficients that are used in making the heterogeneous utilities of the various social classes homogeneous. The admirer of the 'superman' will assign a coefficient of approximately zero to the utility of the lower classes, and get a point of equilibrium very close to a state where large inequalities prevail. The lover of equality will assign a high coefficient to the utility of the lower classes and get a point of equilibrium very close to the equalitarian condition. There is no criterion save sentiment for choosing between the one and the other."

The problem that Pareto is referring to in this passage is the situation where there is only very limited information available concerning the (total differential) form of the social welfare function for any community. An implication, which arises out of this dearth of relevant information, is that it will be difficult (if not impossible) to know what constitutes socially-beneficial taxation policies.

[In fact it is *exactly* this information problem (concerning the total differential form of the social welfare function) which provides the point of departure for the first set of lectures set out in this book. This general information problem also comes to create considerable difficulties for the analysis set out in the second set of lectures.]

Thus by 1916 some of the essential elements of the information problems, associated with the implementation of socially-beneficial taxation policies, were beginning to be identified in the academic literature. Yet during the period from 1916 to 1971 little more was said - compared to what was to come - about these matters.[8] Only with the publication of the seminal paper by Diamond and Mirrlees [1971], do these information problems come to be discussed far more often, and with growing sophistication.

Nevertheless, reasonable criticisms can be made of the way the theory of taxation has evolved since then - criticisms which are very well stated by Hammond [1990] (although his comments were directed at modern public economics in general, and not just at modern taxation theory). To begin with there has been a tendency to avoid the matter of distributive justice by assuming either that the public authorities can apply lump-sum taxes and transfers, or that there is just a single individual, or many identical individuals, in the community. [It is true that there are certain advantages to be gained by initially applying this latter assumption, so that certain fundamental technical

---

8 There were exceptions to this general statement. For example, Ramsey [1927] - and later Samuelson [1951, 1982, 1986] - alluded to information problems associated with implementing taxation policy in circumstances where the government is constrained in that it can only employ commodity taxes to raise a given amount of revenue. A number of authors - for example Graaff [1957, ch. 5] - also returned to re-consider the sort of information problems which were initially raised by Sidgwick. It was also recognised by Pigou [1947] and Samuelson [1954, 1969] that there were a range of special information problems associated with the satisfactory provision of public goods.

problems can be settled.[9] But once these issues have been resolved, the matter of distributive justice should come to have at least some influence on how taxation theory is developed from this point on.]

The other, not unrelated, general criticism made by Hammond of modern taxation theory (and public economics in general) is the tendency not to take into account the full range of information problems which prevent both market mechanisms from operating perfectly efficiently, and governments from applying certain classes of policy tools. Expressed differently, this particular criticism suggests that modern taxation theory fails to place a realistic set of information constraints upon the operation of market mechanisms and the actions of public authorities.

As indicated by the comments made in the opening paragraph of this introduction, both of these general criticisms of modern taxation theory (and public economics is general), made by Hammond, are explicitly taken into account in the lectures which follow. But combining these two broad issues, within the framework of a single general model, has the potential to cause the subsequent analysis to become comparatively complex.[10] In the attempt to reduce the severity of this problem, only two

---

9 In particular, employing this strategy assists with determining how the analysis of a particular problem in taxation theory (say that of establishing the structure of socially optimal taxation systems) could be satisfactorily developed. Such an approach, in fact, is exploited in the second set of lectures before moving on to consider more complex versions of the problem at hand.

10 A similar point has been made by Hammond [1990].

general classes of problems are considered here: (i) problems that would seem most likely to generate useful and definite results; (ii) problems for which no obviously relatively simple tractable solution is likely to exist. This is essentially the stratagem adopted in these lectures.

The first set of lectures begins with recognising the sort of information problem first alluded to by Pareto in 1916 - namely, that detailed, accurate, information on the form of the swf is not likely to be available. [Recent empirical research, which attempts to determine the exact form of the swf employed by various national governments, only tends to confirm that this is still the current situation.[11]] In these circumstances, the rest of the first set of lectures is concerned with attempting to answer the following question: Under what circumstances would a community gain from reforming a distorted economic system by a small amount and in a particular direction? It turns out that this question can be answered in such a way that comparatively little information is required concerning the form of the social welfare function. Nevertheless, there may still be a wide range of information problems present which indicate that it is still not an easy task to determine if a modern society has gained from some particular change in social states. These various matters are discussed in some detail in the introduction to the first set of lectures.

---

11 See Yitzhaki and Slemrod [1991, p. 480] on this point and the references cited there.

At this point in the discussion it is useful to note, in passing, that Sidgwick was not innocent of the sort of difficulties just alluded to. After discussing a range of factors which cause economic agents to alter their behaviour in response to reforms of (or alterations to) the economic system, he went on to make the prophetic observation:[12]

> "Any estimate of the force of the considerations above given must necessarily be vague; but it seems clear that they apply far more strongly against any sudden sweeping equalization [or economic reform], than they do against a more slow and gradual movement towards this result [or gradual market re-organization] ... ."

Much of the discussion in the first set of lectures implicitly takes cognisance of this remark by considering only, in any detail, small changes in social states. This general point will be expanded upon in the introduction to those lectures.

The next general class of problem, discussed in the second set of lectures, is concerned with demonstrating that there do not seem to be comparatively simple solutions to a wide range of realistic problems in taxation theory. The attempt to demonstrate the veracity of this assertion takes the form of attempting to answer the following question: Under what set of circumstances is it socially optimal to apply piecemeal con-

---

12 See Sidgwick [1887, p. 525].

sumption taxation structures, or systems?[13] The answer arrived at in those lectures is that only in very special circumstances will it be socially optimal to implement such policies - circumstances which seem unlikely to ever be satisfied in reality.

It should be pointed out that, and as explained in the introduction to the second set of lectures, the question posed above is a comparatively general one for it alludes to a wide class of special topics in taxation theory - including, amongst other things, the matters of: (i) under what circumstances it is socially optimal to apply uniform consumption taxation systems and (ii) the socially optimal properties of marginal linear income tax rates.

0.1 A Brief Additional Comment on the Organization of the Lectures.

In the instance of nearly all the varied topics considered in the two sets of lectures, essentially the *same* general equilibrium welfare model is employed to analyse the particular matter being discussed - a model which consists of two basic components: (a) a general specification of the differential form of the social welfare function, and (b) two reduced-form equations (which are the dual of one another) representing changes of individual utility within a highly distorted economic system. By a process of combining these two basic components of the general

[13] The term 'piecemeal taxation structures' is defined at the beginning of the introduction to the second set of lectures.

model, while simultaneously imposing various additional pertinent assumptions (or constraints) as required, it is possible to analyse a wide range of topics in taxation theory.[14] So, for example, by exploiting the general model, it is possible to provide a comparatively general statement of the conditions that need to be satisfied if, as a result of altering the tariff rates on internationally-traded goods, the community gains from more trade. [This topic is covered, in particular, in section 5.] It is also possible to demonstrate, by employing the same general model, the properties of marginal linear income tax rates within comparatively general settings. [This topic is covered in section 13].

These comments imply that there is a common, but clearly visible, thread of ideas running through most of the two sets of lectures. To reflect this fact the term 'section', or 'subsection', is employed - instead of the term 'chapter' - to indicate that ideas are developed over a number of sections in the discussion. Nevertheless, the two sets of lectures are treated as representing two separate set of ideas - although (as indicated above) there is some overlapping of concepts and ideas to be found in the two sets of lectures. For this reason each set of lectures is provided with its own set of references.

The lectures which follow also attempt to take students past what is currently available in the relevant literature.

---

[14] The initial stimulus to employ this analytical approach was provided by a paper by Peter Lloyd [1974]. There it was indicated that much could be achieved, in the theory of taxation reform, by the use of unconstrained (as distinct from the application of Lagrangian) optimising techniques.

Indeed, a good part of these lectures is devoted to attempting to forge new ways of looking at old problems. Having said that, this course of lectures is directed at any student who has completed a course in microeconomics which has covered, for example, the first three parts to be found in Deaton and Muellbauer [1990], and a choice of topics from Gravelle and Rees [1985] and Cowell [1986].

Finally it is hoped that the unity of the analysis and results, striven for throughout these lectures, will assist the student to understand more fully what seem to be some of the central issues at stake in modern taxation theory - and how these various issues relate to one another.

References:

Bergson, A. [1938], "A Reformulation of Certain Aspects of Welfare Economics", Quarterly Journal of Economics, Vol. 52, pp. 310 - 34.

Bergson, A. [1983], "Pareto on Social Welfare", Journal of Economic Literature, Vol. 21, pp. 40 - 6.

Chipman, J. S. [1976], "The Paretian Heritage", Revue Européene des Sciences Sociales et Cahiers Vilfredo Pareto, Vol. 14, pp. 65 - 171.

Chipman, J. R. [1987], "When is a Fixed Income Distribution Optimal?" in Feiwel, G.R. (ed.), Arrow and the Foundations of the Theory of Economic Policy (New York: New York University Press).

Cowell, F. A. [1986], Microeconomic Principles (Oxford: Philip Allen).

Deaton, A. S. and Muellbauer, J. [1980], Economics of Consumer Behaviour (Cambridge: Cambridge University Press).

Diamond, P. A. and Mirrless, J.A. [1971], "Optimal Taxation and Public Production; I - Production Efficiency; II - Tax Rules", American Economic Review, Vol. 61, pp. 8 - 27, pp 261 - 78.

Edgeworth, F. Y. [1897], "The Pure Theory of Taxation", Economic Journal, Vol. 7, pp. 46 - 70, pp. 226 -38, pp. 550 - 71.

Graaff, J. de V. [1957], Theoretical Welfare Economics (Cambridge: Cambridge University Press).

Gravelle, H. and Rees, R. [1981], Microeconomics (London: Longman).

Hammond, P. J. [1990], "Theoretical Progress in Public Economics: A Provocative Assessment", Oxford Economics Papers, Vol. 42, pp. 6 - 33.

Lloyd, P. J. [1974], "A More General Theory of Price Distortions in Open Economies", Journal of International Economics, Vol. 4, pp. 365 - 386.

Pareto, V., [1913], "Il massimo di utilità per una collettività in Soiciologia [A Maximum of Utility for a Community, in

Sociology]", Giornale degli Economisti e Rivista di Statistica, Vol. 46, pp. 337 - 41.

Pareto, V., [1916], Trattato di Sociologia generale (Florence: Barbera). English translation: Mind and Society (New York: Harcourt, Brace and Company, 1935).

Pigou, A. C. [1920], The Economics of Welfare (London: Macmillan).

Pigou, A. C. [1947], A Study in Public Finance: Third Edition (London Macmillan).

Ramsey, F.P. [1927], " A Contribution to the Theory of Taxation", Economic Journal, Vol. 37, pp.47 - 61.

Samuelson, P. A. [1954], "The Pure Theory of Public Expenditure", Review of Economics and Statistics, Vol. 67, pp. 931 - 5.

Samuelson , P. A. [1969], "Pure Theory of Public Expenditures and Taxation", in Margolis, J. and Guitton, H. (eds), Public Economics (London: Macmillan).

Samuelson, P. A. [1951/1986], "The Theory of Optimal Taxation", Journal of Public Economics, Vol. 30, pp. 135 - 142.

Samuelson, P. A. [1982], "A Chapter in the The History of Ramsey's Optimal Feasible Taxation and Optimal Public Utility Prices", in Anderson, S., Laursen, K. *et al.* (ed.), Economic Essays in Honour Jorgen H. Gelting (Danish Economic Association).

Sidgwick, H. [1883, 2nd Edition 1887], Principles of Political Economy (London: Macmillan).

Tuomala, M. [1990], Optimal Income Tax and Redistribution (Oxford: Clarendon Press).

Yitzhaki, S. and Slemrod, J. [1991] , "Welfare Dominance: Application to Commodity Taxation", American Economic Review, Vol. 81, pp. 480 - 496.

The First Set of Lectures

Ranking Reforms of Distorted Economic Systems with Compensated Pareto and Welfare Dominance Criteria

1. Introduction.

In a many-person community, where individuals possess different tastes and economic distortions are widespread throughout the economy, it might be conjectured that there is little likelihood, in reality, of it ever being socially optimal to apply comparatively simple taxation systems - especially when this community is, to some degree, concerned about the matter of distributive justice. For the present this conjecture will be accepted as being valid - although this conjecture is returned to and considered in some detail in the second set of lectures. [The implications of that discussion is that the conjecture made above appears to be a sound assessment of the reality which probably exists in a reasonably complex community. [15]]

Given this presumption, it seems reasonable to go on to argue that, instead of searching for some relatively simple socially optimal taxation-cum-subsidy system, the community should adopt the less demanding social objective of attempting to reform the distorted economic system in a direction which will result in a rise in the level of social welfare. The cogency of this recommendation has been recognised for some time. Consequently a sizable literature, which is concerned with this topic, has been generated. Much of the relevant literature, based

---

[15] The main reason for holding discussion of this conjecture in abeyance is that much of the theoretical framework, required to analyse this particular topic, is essentially that required to analyse the particular problem to be discussed in the present (first) set of lectures.

on the assumption that the economy is closed to international trade, has been surveyed by Auerbach [1985, p. 118 -124], while Corden [1984, pp.86 - 96] and Dixit [1985, pp. 341 - 352] provide surveys of the literature based on the more realistic assumption that the economy is open to international trade. There are, however, two broad weaknesses associated with this literature. The first is that much of it is based upon the assumption that there is just a single individual in the community. The other is that many of the results presented in this literature are based upon special cases which often only generate sufficient conditions - not necessary and sufficient conditions - for an improvement in social states.[16]

As for the first of these weakness, relaxing the assumption that there is just a single individual in the community, by allowing for the presence of many individuals with differing tastes, naturally has the potential for creating considerable demands on information. In particular, to determine the circumstances where it is socially optimal to reform a distorted economy in a particular direction, it may be necessary to know the exact form of the social welfare function (swf) - information which most likely is not available.[17] There are, however, two techniques that may be employed for avoiding, or reducing the extent of, this particular difficulty.

[16] See Lloyd and Schweinberger [1988, p. 292] on this point.
[17] A similar point has been made by Yitzhaki and Slemrod [1991, p.480] in the context of the theory of taxation reform. Also see Hammond [1990].

1.1 Pareto Improvements in Social States.

The technique most widely employed in the relevant literature is to apply the compensated Pareto improvement criterion.[18] In this case any individual, who experiences an economic loss as a result of the implementation of some economic reform, is fully compensated for these losses. The actual compensation provided, in turn, is usually assumed to take the form of providing lump-sum, or non-lump sum, income transfers which are financed by applying non-lump-sum consumption taxes. This is the general approach adopted by, for example, Dixit and Norman [1980, 1986], Lloyd and Schweinberger [1988], Dixit [1987], Diewert, Turunen-Red and Woodland [1989] and Wong [1991] in their particular discussions of aspects of the theory of economic reform.

Certainly the main advantage, associated with applying the compensated Pareto improvement criterion, is that it requires only a minimal amount of information concerning the form of the swf - all that needs to be known is that the swf is increasing in individual utility levels. But against this advantage needs to be set the real possibility that implementing the policy, of actually providing appropriate income compensation, may have to contend with considerable practical difficulties. There are two difficulties that will be emphasised and examined in section 4.1 and 4.2 below. The first is that the provision of compensating personal lump-sum income transfers may create the incen-

---

[18] This criterion is defined at the beginning of section 4.1 below in the main text.

tives for individuals to behave strategically in the attempt to maximize their utility levels. Such behaviour, however, is incompatible with these individuals providing accurate relevant private information - information relating to the individual losses (or gains) experienced during a pertinent change in social states.[19] Yet, without this information being available, it may be impossible, on numerous occasions, to determine whether Pareto-improving changes in social states have actually taken place.

The way out of this difficulty that has been adopted recently in the relevant literature is to assume that income transfer mechanisms, which are not dependent on individuals providing relevant personal information, are employed. This is done by providing general, non-personal, compensating income transfers. (These mechanisms are discussed, in particular, in Dixit and Norman [1986], Dixit [1987] and Diewert *et al.* [1989]. Also see Turunen [1987].) The weakness with providing compensating income transfers in this form, however, is that it is wasteful, or excessive, in the sense that it provides income transfers to all individuals in the community - even though there will be individuals in the community who have experienced a before-transfer gain in utility during the relevant change in social states. Put differently, the compensating income transfer system is not precisely targeted at providing compensation only to those who have experienced a loss of utility as a result of this change in social states.

---

[19] This point has been emphasised by Dixit [1987, p. 148].

This observation brings us to the second difficulty, alluded to above, concerning the payment of compensating income transfers; namely, because the general income transfer system is relatively poorly targeted, the scope to implement compensated Pareto-improving taxation reform may be limited, compared to what could be achieved if transfers could be more precisely directed at those who do need to be compensated (according to the Pareto improvement criterion). A demonstration of this point will be provided in section 4.2 below. [It should be pointed out that this observation is not completely original for it has its antecedents in the literature, surveyed by Bhagwati [1971] and Corden [1984], concerned with the welfare-ranking of policy tools in open economies. This point will be explained a little more fully in section 4.2 below.]

Attention is also drawn to the fact that, because of the sheer relative and absolute size of the level of Pareto-improving compensation that may need to be paid (as a result of some relevant economic reform), politico-economic considerations may discourage the authorities from implementing complete compensated economic reform. This political behaviour may take the form of governments placing limits on the size of the budgets available to finance income compensation. Certainly, casual observation tends to support this assertion for governments rarely seem to provide complete compensation during periods of economic reform. (This political behaviour may also be a partial reflection of the incentive-compatible problems, mentioned above, associated with gathering the personal information required to calculate the appropriate level of individual compensating income transfers.)

Despite these weaknesses with the actual, practical, implementation of economic reform policies associated with the compensated Pareto improvement criterion, application of this criterion does provide a number of general insights into how economic reform, of a distorted economic system, might be implemented. For this reason the matter of Pareto-improving economic reforms is considered in some detail below - mainly within the realistic context of an open economy which is distorted by the imposition of non-lump taxes and the presence of markets that are not complete and competitive. These market failures appear on both the consumption and production sides of the economy. Out of that discussion emerge relatively general results indicating under what circumstances a community will experience a Pareto-improvement in social states as a result of: (i) reforming a consumption taxation system in a closed economy; (ii) reforming a tariff system in a highly distorted open economy; (iii) real economic growth taking place and (iv) reforming the tax-price system in the attempt to mitigate some of the adverse economic-social consequences resulting from the presence of markets that are not complete and competitive.

These matters are discussed in section 4 below. Most of the results, or insights, presented there tend to be more general than those to be found in the relevant literature. What is more, the bulk of these results are based on necessary and sufficient conditions. This observation implies that the second weakness present in the economic-reform literature, and which was mentioned above (namely, that much of this literature is concerned with special cases and that only sufficiency results are derived), does not apply to most of the relevant results presented in section 4 below.

1.2 Non-Pareto Improvement in Social States.

The next step in the argument is to confront the weaknesses, mentioned above, associated with the application of the compensated Pareto-improvement criterion, by abandoning the application of this criterion in the attempt to rank social states. Some alternative criterion is (or criteria are) required. In attempting to devise such an alternative, two considerations need to be allowed for: (i) The welfare ranking of non-Pareto-improving changes in social states should be possible without the need to possess detailed information concerning the form of the swf. (ii) The payment of compensating income transfers, if required, should be relatively well targeted and not suffer from severe incentive-compatibility problems.

These would seem to be relatively demanding requirements to satisfy. It is argued in sections 2 and 5.1 below, however, that these ends can be achieved by essentially applying marginal welfare dominance criteria (MWDC) to determine the rank ordering of differing social states. This approach, to the general problem of ranking social states, does not require any detailed information on the form of the swf. It is also argued, in section 5.1 below, that the application of MWDC assists with ensuring that compensating payments (if any are required at all) are comparatively well targeted and should not, if provided to certain clearly-identified groups within the community, raise serious incentive-compatibility problems.

The first to apply MWDC (at least as far as the author is aware), in the context of the general topic of economic reform, were Yitzhaki and Slemrod [1991] in a most interesting paper. [20] The general theory underlying their approach is generalised in section 2 below and applied to a range of general problems in economic reform in section 5.

As far as the discussion provided in section 2 below is concerned, for the present it is simply noted that the social ranking criteria devised there are essentially generalisations of MWDC which have been implicitly employed in the literature concerned with the social ranking of Lorenz curves.[21] In contrast to much of that literature, however, the criteria devised in the next section allow for: (a) individuals possessing non-identical utility functions based upon price, as well as income, information, (b) price changes taking place, and (c) the existence of third, as well

---

20 In an article by Turunen [1987] techniques of analysis, of a particular issue in taxation reform, were employed which are related to the dominance criteria referred to in the main text.

21 See, for example, Atkinson [1970] and Shorrocks [1983]. Much of this literature is surveyed by Lambert [1989, Ch. 5].

as second, degree marginal welfare dominance criterion.[22] Thus, amongst other things, the general theory of MWD criteria devised below are price, as well as income, dependent. This last observation is of some importance for, as Roberts [1980] has emphasised,[23] the social welfare ranking of individual income information alone, independent of information on price levels, is always valid if, and only if, individual and social preferences take rather restrictive forms.

It also noted that the MWD criteria developed in the next section are derived from forms of the swf which could be representing comparatively mild views concerning matters of economic and distributive justice. This and other matters are discussed in section 2 below.

As one might expect, there are, as with the application of the Pareto-improvement criterion, practical information problems associated with applying MWDC. These matters are discussed in section 5.1 below where it is argued that approximate (not accurate) relevant information may suffice in many pertinent situations to allow an acceptable ranking of social states. There the point is also made that even if this particular argument is not accepted (because it is thought that these information problems are insurmountable), this does not mean that the application of

---

[22] The bulk of the relevant literature is based upon the assumptions that individuals possess identical utility functions based only on income information. Also most of this literature has nothing to say about the third degree dominance criterion discussed in section 2 below in the main text.

[23] Also see Slivinski [1983].

MWDC should be abandoned. On the contrary, in a community where matters of distributive justice clearly are of concern, the application of MWD criteria serve to indicate that the Pareto-improving criterion is not the only criterion that can be, or should be, applied to the task of ranking social states.[24]

With these theoretical ideas established, it is now possible to combine the MWDC with a general system of economic distortions which makes it possible to socially rank situations where non-Pareto economic reforms take place. This part of the analysis, presented in section 5 below, is essentially an extension of the most general results, based on the Pareto improvement criterion, set out in section 4 below. And, as in that discussion, the main results presented in section 5 below are necessary and sufficient results. The main propositions presented in section 5 below state under what circumstances a community experiences non-Pareto improvements in social states when: (i) reforming a consumption taxation system in a closed economy; (ii) reforming a tariff system in a highly distorted open economy and (iii) experiencing real economic growth.

The results presented in section 5 below are not, as far as the author is aware, to be found elsewhere in the relevant literature. This is not surprising since, as indicated above, there has been virtually no published applications of MWDC within the general context of the theory of economic reform.

---

[24] This general point, in the context where obviously the community is concerned about matters of distributive justice, has also been made by Turunen [1987].

Finally, on a slightly different, but still related, matter, the analysis presented below always has to be disaggregated down to the level of individual members of the community. This fact implies that changes in the levels of individual real income need to be taken into account at all times. To make this possible, it so turns out, some care has to be taken in constructing the equations representing the production side of the economy. This point, it is hoped, will become clear from the discussion set out in section 3 below and elsewhere.

1.3 Outline of the Discussion.

In the next section the social welfare ranking criteria, which imply the use of marginal welfare dominance tests, are developed in general terms. In section 3 additional components of the model are devised which allow for a wide range of economic distortions (or information problems) to be introduced into the analysis. The basic reduced-form equations devised in this section have numerous applications. Some of these applications are provided in sections 4 and 5 below. [25] It is hoped that the discussion in these two sections demonstrates, by implication at least, that there is a close relationship between the numerous results to be found in the relevant literature. Above all it is shown there that there is a wide range of special cases, dealt with in the relevant literature, which, in fact, can be analysed by apply-

---

[25] Other applications are provided in the next set of lectures. There the discussion concentrates on the topic of determining the socially optimal provision of piecemeal economic policy.

ing this general economic model. It is just a matter of altering the particular, additional, assumptions applied to this general framework.

Section 4 is devoted to considering the matter of compensated Pareto improvements in social states. In the initial part of this section, the incentive-compatible and targeting problems, referred to above, are discussed in a little detail. The rest of the discussion in this section covers a range of relevant topics in some detail. The main reason for providing this discussion is that the relevant literature deals with many special cases which need to be considered - cases which, in their own right, raise matters of no little importance. These various special (but comparatively general) cases discussed in section 4 come to provide one of the points of departure for the discussion in section 5 where the marginal welfare dominance criteria are applied. Concluding remarks are made in section 6.

At this point it should be mentioned that all the special cases of economic reform, discussed in the following sections, are based on small changes in social states. It could be argued, however, that worthwhile economic policy changes are unlikely to be small. The point is well taken. There are, however, two reasons why large changes in social states are not considered in any detail below. The first is that the analysis, of the small changes considered below, are all based on differential equations which could be integrated, if required, over larger changes in relevant variables. To represent this integration in the discussion below would only complicate the mathematical notation without clarifying any of the central economic issues at stake. (In fact, on occasions, reference is made below to large changes in economic states.) Secondly, and as will become apparent below, on occasions it is difficult enough to determine in what direction small - let alone large - changes in socially-improving economic policy might go. Thus, before rushing on to introduce major economic reform, it may be best first to check that initial, small changes in economic states are moving the economy in the desired direction.[26] Hence, on both counts, only small changes in social states are considered in detail in the subsequent discussion.

1.4 The Main Conclusions.

As far as those conclusions are concerned, it is suggested that the overall implication that may be drawn from the discussion presented below is that for economic reform, in a highly distorted economy, to be successful (as judged by the criteria applied below), almost certainly a range of policy instruments (not just one or two) will need to be altered in a coordinated manner. This conclusion, in turn, implies that successful economic reform places considerable demands on relevant information. However, it is likely that these demands for information will tend to decline as the community adopts social values which indicate a growing concern for the matter of distributive justice.

---

[26] The caution, being recommended in the main text when implementing economic reform, reflects the influence of the careful remarks relating to these matters made by Sidgwick [1887, p. 525] - and which were quoted in the General Introduction in section 0 above.

Finally, the following discussion indicates, on various occasions, that the analysis required, when many non-identical individuals are present in the community, is quite different from that required when the community is assumed to be composed of only a single individual (or many identical individuals). The reason for this major difference in the way the analysis of economic reform may proceed is that in the former case distributional issues need to be an integral part of the analysis. This matter just does not arise when there is only a single individual in the community.

2. A General Equity-Regarding Approach for the Ranking of Social States

In this section the objective is to set out comparatively general criteria which will, given certain assumptions, allow a ranking of social states in a many-person community where non-Pareto changes in individual utility levels have taken place. Above all, these criteria do not depend on possessing detailed information concerning the form of the swf, or individual utility, functions. The argument presented in this section builds on, and generalises in a number of directions, some of the ideas to be found in Yitzhaki and Slemrod.

2.1 Rank Ordering the Social Value of Individual Utility Levels

An important element, in the criteria presented below for ranking social states, is the assumption that it is possible to rank order the social value of individual utility levels from smallest to largest. Exactly how this might be done, given that the social value of individual utility levels is not observable, is dependent on the assumptions made. The assumptions employed by Yitzhaki and Slemrod will be considered first before turning to consider the implications of generalising their assumptions.

Method A: The swf is assumed to take the additive separable form:

$$W = \sum_{h=1}^{H} \omega^h [v^h]. \qquad (2.1)$$

The values of ω^h $[v^h]$ represent the social value of the indirect utility, v^h, received by individual h, while $\omega^h[\ .\ ]$ is a function for socially weighting the indirect utility for this individual. There are H individuals in the community and the indirect utility function for any individual in the community takes the form:

$$v^h = v^h(q, y^h), \qquad (2.2)$$

where q denotes a vector of n+1 prices, all of which are positive, and y^h denotes the positive nominal income received by individual h. This function is homogeneous of degree zero in prices and income, increasing in y^h, non-increasing and quasi-convex in p, and at least continuously twice differentiable in all arguments. The indirect utility function defined in (2.2) above also implies that individuals have non-identical utility functions.

Given that the swf is continuously differentiable in all arguments, it is now assumed that

$$\frac{\partial \omega^h}{\partial v^h} \frac{\partial v^h}{\partial y^h} > 0, \qquad \text{for all h individuals,} \qquad (2.3)$$

and that, for any two individuals, k, m, if

$$y^k = y^m \quad \text{then} \quad \omega^k[\, v^k(q, y^k)] = \omega^m[\, v^m(q, y^m)] \qquad (2.4)$$

for any set of prices.

The first assumption requires that the level of social welfare is increasing in individual income. The second assumption requires that the social value of the income distributed to any individual, k, is the same as that distributed to any other individual m, if these two individuals receive the same level of income and face the same (but any) set of prices, q.

These two assumptions, taken together, imply that it is possible to rank order the social value of individual utility levels even though these levels are not observable. Specifically, the statements in (2.3) and (2.4) above imply that for any set of prices:

$$\text{if } y^k > y^m \text{ then } \omega^k[v^k(q,y^k)] > \omega^m[v^m(q,y^m)], \text{ for any } k, m. \tag{2.5}$$

Thus the social value of individual utility levels can be ranked in the same order as that for individual income levels.

It should be emphasised that the implication stated in (2.5) above applies even if, for the sake of argument :

$$v^k(q,y^k) \leq v^m(q,y^m) \text{ when } y^k > y^m \text{ for any } k, m; \tag{2.6}$$

i.e. the rank order of individual utility levels is not the same as that for individual income levels. The contradictory case represented in (2.6) above arises from assuming that individual indirect utility functions [defined in (2.2) above] are non-identical. Nevertheless, the rather special assumptions imposed on the form of the swf - namely, the assumptions stated in (2.1) and (2.4) above - ensures the rank ordering condition stated in (2.5) above always applies.

Method B: The alternative approach considered here is based upon a much more general form of the swf; namely,

$$W = W(v^1, v^2, \dots, v^H); \tag{2.7}$$

a swf which is assumed to be continuously differentiable in all arguments. It is also assumed that

$$\frac{\partial W}{\partial v^h}\frac{\partial v^h}{\partial y^h} > 0, \qquad \text{for all h individuals.} \tag{2.8}$$

The indirect utility function for any individual, h, takes the same, non-identical, form stated in (2.2) above.

The implications of these assumptions, and given the remarks made above in the context of (2.6), the rank order of the social value of individual utility levels need not be the same as the rank order of individual income levels. So, for example, it is quite possible that

$$\frac{\partial W}{\partial v^k}\frac{\partial v^k}{\partial y^k} \neq \frac{\partial W}{\partial v^m}\frac{\partial v^m}{\partial y^m}, \qquad \text{for any } k, m,$$

even though $y^k = y^m$ and $dy^k = dy^m$. This possibility implies that the income rank order for these two individuals (which is the same) need not be the same as the rank order for the social value placed upon their respective utility levels.

These rank orderings will be the same, however, if individual income levels are replaced with individual equivalent income levels - and given the form of the swf specified in (2.7) above. To explain this assertion let the non-identical indirect utility function for any individual h be re-written as follows:

$$v^h = v^h(q, y^h) = v(q, y^h, a^h), \qquad (2.9)$$

where a^h denotes a vector of characteristics associated with household h. [The indirect utility function set out in (2.9) may be that for a household, as distinct from an individual, where a^h denotes family size, geographic location and composition.] Next it is assumed that an equivalent income level, y_e^h, can be found such that for this individual h:

$$v^h = v[(q, y^h, a^h] = v(q, y_e^h, a^o), \qquad (2.10)$$

where a^o represents the reference vector of characteristics which is common across all individuals. Thus the equivalent real income for individual h, y_e^h, denotes the minimum income required by this individual, when faced with a given set of prices and characteristics which are common across all individuals, to reach the actual level of utility attained, v^h (given the common set of prices and the actual income and characteristics which apply for this individual).

The statement on the right-hand side of (2.10), along with the swf defined in (2.7), above implies that at a given set of prices, q,

$$\text{if } y_e^k = y_e^m \quad \text{then } v^k = v^m \qquad \text{for any } k,m, \tag{2.11}$$

and, therefore, that the social value of utility for these two individuals is identical.

Next, on substituting the right hand side of (2.10) into (2.7) above, it is assumed that

$$\frac{\partial W}{\partial v}\frac{\partial v}{\partial y_e^h} > 0, \qquad \text{for all } h. \tag{2.12}$$

This assumption implies that if $y_e^k > y_e^m$ then the utility *level* for individual k has a higher social value than the utility level for individual m. This observation, along with that stated in (2.11) above, implies that the rank ordering of the social value of individual utility levels is the same as that for individual equivalent income levels. Hence equivalent income levels may be employed, in place of individual utility levels, to provide a rank ordering of the social value of individual utility levels at a given set of prices.

This outcome was made possible not only by employing individual equivalent income levels, but also because the swf satisfies the assumption of anonymity (or symmetry) - i.e. the names of individuals do not matter when ranking social states. This assumption is implied by the statement of the swf in (2.7) above.

2.1.1 Assessment of the Two Methods

As the previous discussion indicates, method A is based upon a relatively strong set of assumptions. Above all (2.3) and (2.4) imply that the rank ordering of the social value of individual utility levels - which are based on the rank ordering of individual nominal income levels - is independent of the prices ruling in the economy. Thus this rank ordering will be the same for any set of market prices. To ensure that this is the case, and given that the swf is additively separable, the social and individual preferences need to take an extremely restrictive form - as a slight extension of the argument to be found in Roberts [1980] indicates.[27] Specifically, it must be that

$$W = \sum_h k \frac{[y^h]^{1-\varepsilon}}{1-\varepsilon}, \text{ where } \frac{[y^h]^{1-\varepsilon}}{1-\varepsilon} = \delta(q) + \beta(q) \frac{[y^h]^{1-\varepsilon}}{1-\varepsilon}$$

and $k \geq 0$. Should $\varepsilon = 1$ then these equations take a logarithmic form.

In contrast, the more general method B, outlined above, implies that the rank ordering of the social value of individual utility levels is dependent on the prices ruling in the economy. To demonstrate this point it is noted that method B requires that

[27] In particular see Roberts [1980, pp. 284 - 286].

individual measures of equivalent income need to be calculated. To provide such a calculation for some individual h first it is noted that

$$y_e^h = e(q, u^h, a^o),$$

where the term e(.) refers to the minimum expenditure required to attain the utility level u^h, given q and a^o. The relationship between y_e^h and the actual income level y^h can now be expressed as follows:

$$y_e^h = \frac{e(q,u^h,a^o)}{e(q,u^h,a^h)}\ e(q,u^h,a^h\ ) = \frac{y^h}{m^h}, \qquad (2.13)$$

where $m^h = m(q, u^h, a^o, a^h)$ is the equivalence scale for individual h for a given set of reference prices.[28] Thus given y^h, to determine the value of y_e^h the value of m^h must be known - an endogenous variable whose value is dependent on the prices ruling in the community. If the prices to be found in the vector, q, alter, so does the value of m^h, and hence the value of y_e^h.

It follows that method B is more general than method A for the rank ordering of the social value of individual utility levels. For this reason method B outlined above will be exploited in the following discussion - a method based upon the assumptions set out in (2.7), (2.10) and (2.12) above. Having said that, this in-

[28] These matters are discussed in detail in Deaton and Muellbauer [1980].

creased level of generality is achieved at the cost of placing added demands on information.

This matter is discussed in sub-section 5.1 below. For the present, however, the observation is made that if it is believed that it is not possible to measure individual equivalent incomes with the accuracy required, then the analysis is forced back into applying the assumptions employed by Yitzhaki and Slemrod - or some compromise set of assumptions. Such a compromise may be that it is assumed that, for any individual h,

$$v^h = v[q, y^h, a_1^h, a_2^h] = v[q, y_a^h, a_1^o, a_2^h], \tag{2.14}$$

where a_1^h refers to the vector of individual characteristics the community may regard as being of importance, and a_2^h denotes a vector of characteristics (such as tastes peculiar to an individual) which the community ignores when comparing social states. The term y_a^h may be thought of as being truncated equivalent income which only allows for the a_1^h characteristics. The statement in (2.14), along with the Yitzhaki-Slemrod assumptions stated in (2.1), (2.3) and (2.4) above, may then be employed to form the foundations of the analysis. Such a suggested compromise set of assumptions, which are more general than those employed by Yitzhaki and Slemrod (for it implies a limited degree of price dependence when ranking the social value of individual utility levels), will not be employed here, however. The reason is that it is thought that there are better ways of answering the question posed by this information problem - answers which are provided in section 5.1 below.

To conclude this sub-section it is noted that the literature most concerned with the central matter of interest here - namely, the ranking of social states based on information relating to the distribution of individual income levels - invariably employs the assumption that individuals possess identical utility functions. (See Atkinson [1970], Dasgupta, Sen and Starrett [1973], Shorrocks [1983] and Foster, Majumdar and Mitra [1990].[29]) This assumption, in turn, implies that the relevant ranking of social states is independent of the price levels ruling in the community. In contrast, the argument developed in the rest of this section is based upon measures of equivalent income. Thus price information is taken into account when determining how to rank social states based on the distribution of individual equivalent income.

2.2 Results Based on a Second Degree Welfare Dominance Test

Substituting (2.10) into the general form of the swf set out in (2.7) above, the resulting equation is totally differentiated with respect to all n prices and all h individual equivalent incomes. Since it is relative prices (not absolute price levels) that

---

[29] The exception to the rule, where allowance is made for households possessing different utility functions, is Atkinson and Bourguignon [1982, 1987]. The techniques of analysis employed in these papers are, however, quite different from those employed in the main text.

influence economic behaviour, the price of the numeraire (good 0) is held constant. The result is that

$$dW = \sum_{h=1}^{H} \beta^h [dv^h / v^h_{y_e}] = \sum_{h=1}^{H} \beta^h \, dv^{h*}, \tag{2.15}$$

$$= \sum_{h=1}^{H} \beta^h \left[\sum_{i=1}^{n} - c^h_{ei} \, dq_i + dy^h_e \right], \tag{2.16}$$

where $$\beta^h := \frac{\partial W}{\partial v} \frac{\partial v}{\partial y^h_e}, \tag{2.17}$$

$$v^h_{y_e} := \frac{\partial v}{\partial y^h_e}, \tag{2.18}$$

$$dv^{h*} := [dv^h / v^h_{y_e}] := \sum_{i=1}^{n} - c^h_{ei} \, dq_i + dy^h_e . \tag{2.19}$$

In deriving (2.16) above use has been made of Roy's identity. The term c^h_{ei} denotes the uncompensated equivalent level of demand, $c^h_{ei}(q, y^h_e)$, for good i by individual h. [30]

Before deriving any results from (2.15) above the following definition is employed to define a set of relevant swfs -

---

[30] To save on notation reference to the characteristic common to all individuals, a_0, is omitted.

Definition of Ω: Ω only includes any continuously differentiable swf which takes the general form represented by combining (2.7) and (2.10) above and for which $\beta^h > 0$ if h =1, $\beta^h \geq 0$ for all other h (=2 to H) and $\beta^h_{y_e} < 0$ if $\beta^h > 0$ for any h individual.

The following can now be stated:

Proposition 2.1:

$$dW > 0 \text{ for all } W[\, v(q, y_e)\,] \in \Omega \text{ iff } \sum_{h=1}^{k} dv^{h*} > 0 \text{ for all } k = 1,$$

2, ... , H, where, at the initial set of prices, $y_e^1 \leq y_e^2 \leq y_e^3 \leq \ldots \leq y_e^H$, and where a strict inequality lies between at least two individuals.

Proof: (Sufficient) Assume, to begin with, that only the utility levels for the poorest individuals [those receiving the smallest v^h - or smallest y_e^h] in the community are to count when measuring changes in social welfare. There are P such individuals in the community - individuals who all receive an equivalent income equal to y_e^1 at the initial set of prices. These assumptions, along with the requirement that $W \in \Omega$, imply that $\beta^i > 0$ for all $i \in P$ and $\beta^j = 0$ for all $j \notin P$. Applying this observation to (2.15) above implies that $dW > 0$ when $\sum_{h=1}^{P} dv^{h*} > 0$.

Next let $\beta^1 > 0$ and $\beta^h > 0$ for all h = 2 to h. Also the extreme boundary assumption is adopted that $y_e^1 < y_e^2 = y_e^3 = \ldots = y_e^H$ at the initial set of prices. Thus, since $W \in \Omega$, it follows that

$$\beta^h = \beta^2 \qquad \text{for all } h = 2 \text{ to } H. \tag{2.20}$$

It is also assumed that

$$\sum_{h=2}^{k} dv^{k*} < 0, \text{ for all } k = 2 \text{ to } H, \tag{2.21}$$

Without any loss of generality, it is also assumed that there is a set of values for some parameter, α_k (> 0), such that

$$dv^{1*} = -(1 + \alpha_k) \sum_{h=2}^{k} dv^{k*} > 0, \text{ where } \alpha_k > 0, \quad \text{for all } k = 2 \text{ to } H. \tag{2.22}$$

Combining (2.21) and (2.22) implies that

$$\sum_{h=1}^{k} dv^{k*} = -\alpha_k \sum_{h=2}^{k} dv^{k*} > 0, \quad \text{for all } k = 2 \text{ to } H. \tag{2.23}$$

Finally, applying the assumptions set out in (2.20) and (2.22) to (2.15) above results in

$$dW = [\beta^2 - \beta^1] \sum_{h=2}^{k} dv^{k}* - \beta^1 \alpha_k \sum_{h=2}^{k} dv^{k}*, \quad \text{for all } k = 2 \text{ to } H. \tag{2.24}$$

Now since since $W \in \Omega$ it follows that $\beta^1 > 0$ and that $\beta^2 < \beta^1$ - as $y_e^1 < y_e^2$. Thus sufficient to ensure that (2.24) takes a positive value is that the assumption set out in (2.21) above is satisfied and that $\alpha_k > 0$ for all k. But this implies that the statement in (2.23) above is sufficient to ensure that (2.24) takes a positive value for all k.

Relaxing the assumption set out in (2.20) above with the weaker assumption that $\beta^2 > \beta^3 \geq \beta^4 \geq \ldots \geq \beta^H$ would only strengthen the result just derived.

<u>Necessary</u>: Let $dv^{1*} < 0$ and $\sum_{h=2}^{k} dv^{h*} > 0$ for all k=2 to H. In this case it is possible that

$$dW = \beta_1 dv^{1*} + \sum_{h=2}^{k} \beta_i \, dv^{h*} < 0, \text{ for at least one } k = 2 \text{ to } H,$$

even though $W(.) \in \Omega$. In this case it is necessary that $\sum_{k=1}^{h} dv^{h*} > 0$ for all k=1 to H if dW is to take a positive value when $W(.) \in \Omega$.||

The result presented in proposition 2.1 above is a general statement of the principle which underlies the particular (but central) result to be found in Yitzhaki and Slemrod (namely, their theorem 1). This result will be exploited in section 5 below to analyse economic reform where non-Pareto changes in social states take place.

2.2.1 Alternative Interpretations of Proposition 2.1

There are a number of possible interpretations of proposition 2.1 above. One such interpretation in that the requirement that $\sum_{h=1}^{k} dv^{k*} > 0$ for all k implies that one set of individual utility levels $\left\{ v(q, y_e^h) \right\}$ dominates another set of utility levels $\left\{ v(q', y_e^{h'}) \right\}$. Given this interpretation, and if, and only if, $W[v(q, y_e)] \in \Omega$, then $W[v(q, y_e)] > W[v(q', y_e')]$. But since it is the property of the second derivative of the swf which is of particular importance when establishing this result, proposition 2.1 may be thought of as reflecting the application of a marginal second degree welfare dominance test.[31]

The statement in proposition 2.1 above can also be expressed in an alternative form by first noting that a bistochastic matrix B is defined as a square H X H matrix in which the non-negative entries in each column and row sum to one. If all these entries, except one in each column and row, take a value of zero, then the B matrix is a permutation matrix. Next it is noted that on pre-multiplying a vector of individual income levels $y \in R^H$ by B, which is not a permutation matrix, so that $By = y'$, the conse-

---

31 For a discussion of this dominance test in the theory of uncertainty see, for example, Hadar and Russell [1974].

quence is that the variance for the set of entries to be found in the new vector, y', is less than that for the set of entries to be found in vector y - although the mean value for both sets of entries is the same. Finally, the following definition is required: W is strictly S-concave in y when W(By) > W(y) where B is not a permutation matrix.[32]

Based on these definitions, and their implications, it is not difficult to show that any swf, W, based on (2.7) and (2.10) above, which is continuously differentiable in all arguments and which is also strictly S-concave must have the following properties: $\beta^h > 0$ and $\beta^h_{y_e} < 0$ for all h individuals. Thus a revised definition of Ω can be stated as follows -

<u>Definition of **Ω***:</u> Ω* only includes any continuously differentiable swf which takes the general form represented by combining (2.7) and (2.10) above and which is strictly S-concave in y_e.

Proposition 2.1 above can now be restated as follows:

<u>Proposition 2.1*</u>: The same as proposition 2.1 above except that now $W[(v(q,y_e)] \in \Omega^*$.

Yet another alternative interpretation of proposition 2.1 is provided by noting that a generalised Lorenz (GL) curve, based on

32 See Dasgupta *et al.* [1973, p.183n].

information for individual utility levels in the community, can be defined as the plot of

$$\sum_{h=1}^{k} v^h \text{ against } k \text{ for all } k = 1 \text{ to } H,$$

where individuals are rank ordered in terms of equivalent incomes such that $y_e^1 \leq y_e^2 \leq ... \leq y_e^H$. (In this case the upper boundary on the generalised Lorenz curve represents the total utility in, and the total population for, the community.) Thus in proposition 2.1 (or 2.1*) above the requirement that $\sum_{h=1}^{k} dv^{k*} > 0$ for all k, where individual utility levels are rank ordered, can be interpreted as stating that one distribution, v, generalised Lorenz dominates another distribution, v', by a small amount. This observation can be generalised by taking account of large changes in individual utility levels. Thus proposition 2.1 (or 2.1*) can be re-stated in the following form:

<u>Proposition 2.1**</u>

$$W[v(q,y_e)] > W[v(q', y_e')] \text{ for all } W[v(q_1 y_e)] \in \Omega \text{ (or } \Omega^*)$$

$$\text{iff } GL[v(q, y_e),k] > GL[v(q', y_e'), k] \text{ for all } k.$$

This result is a generalisation of the central result to be found in Shorrocks [1983, p.6] who was the first to discuss the concept of generalised Lorenz curves - albeit only in the context of the distribution of total community income where all individuals possess identical utility functions. The main result in Shorrocks, in turn, was a generalisation of the central result stated in Dasgupta *et al.* [1973] - a result derived for ordinary Lorenz curves based on individual income information.

To conclude this sub-section it is emphasised that application of proposition 2.1 above (or propositions 2.1* and 2.1**) will only provide an accurate ranking of social states if, and only if, pertinent utility information is available, and this information is measured with enough accuracy. So, for example, (2.15) above indicates that the extent of changes in individual utility levels need to be measures which are dependent not only on changes in individual equivalent income levels, but also on all changes in the prices facing households. [See (2.19) above.] Not to take account of this latter set of changes, for example, when applying the marginal welfare dominance criteria stated in proposition 2.1 above, may well result in an erroneous ranking of social states. A similar point has also been made Foster *et al.* [1990, pp. 359-360] - although in their discussion prices are made dependent on the distribution of total community income. In contrast, in the present discussion relative prices can alter independently of the distribution of individual equivalent incomes.[33]

Not so obvious is the fact that the application of the marginal welfare dominance criterion set out in proposition 2.1

---

33 Forster *et al* .[1990] also based their analysis on the assumption that individual utility functions are identical.

above will provide an acceptable ranking of social states only if individual utility levels can be accurately rank ordered. (This rank ordering is required to determine the relative size of the social weights to attach to changes in individual utility levels.) As explained in sub-section 2.1 above, when individuals possess non-identical utility functions, this rank-order requirement will be satisfied only when accurate measures of individual equivalent income are available. This observation alludes to the empirical problem that pertinent and accurate utility information needs to be available before the marginal welfare dominance criteria can be utilised to rank social states. This problem is returned to, and discussed in a little detail, in section 5.1 below.

2.3 Results Based on a Third Degree Welfare Dominance Tests

One limitation of the result presented in proposition 2.1 above is that it has nothing to say about cases where the summation, $\sum_{h=1}^{k} dv^{h*}$, takes negative values for some values of k. [This case implies that the pertinent generalised Lorenz curves intersect at least once.] Nevertheless that proposition does indicate how this limitation can be overcome to some degree if more information is provided concerning the form of the swf - information relating to the third derivative of the swf. This additional information, which represents the degree of curvature of the swf, essentially is providing more information relating to how the community views matters of distributive justice. This point is explained by first stating the following definition:

<u>Definition of Ω^T</u>: Ω^T only includes swfs which are to be found in Ω and which also possess the additional property that $[\partial\beta^h_{y_e} / \partial y^h_e]$ > 0 for any individual h for which $\beta^h_{y_e} < 0$.

The requirement that $[\partial\beta^h_{y_e} / \partial y^h_e] > 0$ (if $\beta^h_{y_e} < 0$) implies that the swf satisfies certain curvature requirements. This fact in turn implies that if the community adopts a swf which satisfies Ω^T, then this community is more averse to increases in utility inequality amongst the relatively poor in the community, compared to increases in utility inequality amongst the better off in the community. Thus if the community adopts the social values reflected in Ω^T, then this fact may be thought of representing the concept that the community is averse to downside utility inequality.[34]

<u>Proposition 2.2:</u>

$$dW > 0 \text{ for all } W[v(q, y_e] \in \Omega^T \text{ iff}$$

---

[34] The term "aversion to downside inequality" was first coined by Davies and Hoy [1991]. Alternative terms that have been employed to describe this concept are "principle of diminishing transfer" (Kolm [1976]) and "transfer sensitivity" (Shorrocks and Foster [1987]).

$$dv^{1*} > 0, \sum_{h=1}^{k} dv^{h*} \geq 0 \text{ for all } k=1 \text{ to } P, \text{ and } \sum_{h=P+1}^{m} dv^{h*} \leq 0 \text{ for all}$$

$m=P+1$ to H,

and (2.25)

$$| \sum_{h=1}^{k} dv^{h*} | \geq | \sum_{h=P+1}^{m} dv^{h*} | \quad \text{for all } k, m,$$

where $k=1, 2, \ldots, P$ and $m = P+1, \ldots, H$, where $P \geq [H - (P+1)]$, and where $y_e^1 < y_e^2 < \ldots < y_e^H$ at the initial set of prices.

<u>Proof</u>: Suppose, to begin with, that there are just four individuals in the community. Also, it is assumed initially that the following boundary conditions apply to represent the assumptions stated in (2.25) above:

$$dv^{1*} > 0, \sum_{h=1}^{2} dv^{h*} = 0, dv^{3*} < 0 \text{ and } \sum_{h=3}^{4} dv^{h*} = 0$$

and $| dv^{1*} | = | dv^{3*} |$. (2.26)

Applying these assumptions to (2.15) above results in the following:

$$dW = (\beta^1 - \beta^2)\, dv^{1*} - (\beta^3 - \beta^4)\, dv^{3*}, \tag{2.27}$$

where $| dv^{1*} | = | dv^{3*} |$

Case 1: Since $W \in \Omega^T$, let $\beta^1 > 0$, $\beta^3 > 0$, $\beta^2 = \beta^4 = 0$ and $\beta^1_{y_e} < 0$ and $\beta^3_{y_e} < 0$. Applying these assumptions to (2.27) above implies that

$$dW = \beta^1 dv^{1*} - \beta^3 dv^{3*}.$$

But $y_e^1 < y_e^3$ so $\beta^1 > \beta^3$. Also $|dv^{1*}| = |dv^{3*}|$, by assumption. Thus $dW > 0$.

If $|dv^{1*}| < |dv^{3*}|$ then it is possible that $dW < 0$, even though $\beta^1 > \beta^3$.

It follows that $dW > 0$ for all $W \in \Omega^T$ iff $dv^{1*} > 0$ and $|dv^{1*}| \geq |dv^{3*}|$ where $y_e^1 < y_e^3$.

Case 2

Since $W \in \Omega^T$ let $\beta^h > 0$ for all h. This in turn implies that

$$(\beta^1 - \beta^2) > (\beta^3 - \beta^4) > 0 \qquad (2.28)$$

given that $y_e^1 < y_e^2 < y_e^3 < y_e^4$. Applying this observation to (2.27) implies that $dW > 0$.

Next suppose that

$$\left|\sum_{h=1}^{2} dv^{h*}\right| < \left|\sum_{h=3}^{4} dv^{h*}\right|$$

where $\left|\sum_{1=1}^{2} dv^{h*}\right| = 0$, $dv^{1*} > 0$, $dv^{3*} < 0$, $dv^{4*} > 0$ and

$$\left|dv^{1*}\right| < \left|dv^{3*}\right| = \alpha\left|dv^{4*}\right| \text{ where } \alpha > 1.$$

Applying these assumptions to (2.15) above results in

$$dW = (\beta^1 - \beta^2)\, dv^{1*} \quad - \left[\beta^3 - \frac{\beta^4}{\alpha}\right] dv^{3*}. \qquad (2.29)$$

Since $W \in \Omega^T$, the inequalities in (2.28) above still applies.

Now even though $|dv^{3*}| > |dv^{1*}|$ it is still possible that $dW > 0$. However, a value for α (>1) can always be found to ensure that $dW < 0$.

It follows that $dW > 0$, for all $W \in \Omega^T$ iff

$$\left|\sum_{h=1}^{2} dv^{h*}\right| \geq \left|\sum_{h=3}^{4} dv^{h*}\right| \text{ and where } y_e^1 < y_e^2 < y_e^3 < y_e^4.$$

The argument in cases 1 and 2 can be combined and employed to analyse all cases k = 3 to P and m = P+1 to H, and where $P \geq [H-(P+1)]$.

If $P > [H-(P+1)]$, and given the assumptions employed in cases 1 and 2, then *a fortiori* $dW > 0$.

If, however, $P < [H - (P + 1)]$ then the sign of dW becomes indeterminate. The reason is that now it is possible that

$$| \sum_{h=1}^{k} dv^{h*} | \leq | \sum_{h=P+1}^{m} dv^{h*} |$$

where $k = P$, $m = H$ and $P < [H - (P + 1)]$. In these circumstances, and even though $\beta^h_{y_e} < 0$, and $\beta^h_{y_e y_e} > 0$, there is no knowing what the sign of dW will be - without more information being available. ||

The result presented in proposition 2.2 above can be interpreted as indicating a relatively simple procedure that needs to be followed when applying a third degree marginal welfare dominance test. This proposition could be generalised to allow for the case where generalised Lorenz curves (based on utility information) intersect any number of times.[35] This matter will not be considered here mainly because, as the argument developed in sub-section 5.1 below indicates, this generalisation (of proposition 2.2 above) will not really be required if appropriate compensating income transfers can be applied when reforming the economic system.

---

[35] Actually proposition 2 also covers that case where generalised Lorenz curves intersect twice, with the first intersection being from above.

2.4 The Extent of the Community's Preferences for Distributive Justice.

At this point in this discussion it seems appropriate to emphasise that, because it was assumed in proposition 2.2 above that the swf, W(v), is to be found in the set Ω^T, this does not necessarily mean that the community has adopted a particularly radical set of social values with respect to the matter of distributive justice. On the contrary, swfs, which reflect comparatively mild social views of distributive justice, are also to be found in the set represented by Ω^T. To demonstrate this point consider the additive separable iso-elastic form of the swf:

$$W = \sum_{h=1}^{H} \frac{1}{1-\varepsilon} [v^h(p, y_e^h)]^{1-\varepsilon}, \qquad \infty \geq \varepsilon \geq -\infty, \qquad (2.30)$$

$$= \sum_{h=1}^{H} \log v^h(p, y_e^h), \qquad \varepsilon = 1, \qquad (2.31)$$

where individual income is expressed in terms of equivalent income and where individual utility functions possess a standard set of properties; namely,

$$[\partial v^h/\partial y_e^h] > 0, \ \{\partial^2 v^h/[\partial y_e^h]^2\} < 0 \text{ and } \{\partial^3 v_h/[\partial y_e^h]^3\} > 0 \text{ for all h.}$$

This reasonably general form of the swf satisfies the requirements stated in Ω^T, for all values of $\infty \geq \varepsilon \geq 0$. So, for example, if $\varepsilon = 1$, then this swf is to be found in Ω^T for any individual utility function satisfying the standard set of properties stated above. Thus, so for any individual h, in this particular case:

$$\beta^{h} = v^{-1} [\partial v^{h}/\partial y_{e}^{h}] > 0,$$

$$\beta_{y_e}^{h} = - v^{-2} [\partial v^{h}/\partial y_{e}^{h}] + v^{-1} \{ \partial^{2} v^{h}/[\partial y_{e}^{h}]^{2} \} < 0,$$

and ignoring the details,

$\beta_{y_e y_e}^{h} > 0$, given the properties of individual utility functions, and the assumed form of the swf, set out above. This is as required.

Naturally a swf of the logarithmic form stated in (2.31) above does not reflect a particularly radical view of distributive justice - certainly it is a long way from the maximim case where $\varepsilon = \infty$.[36]

This set of observations implies that any applications of the third degree marginal welfare dominance criterion - as, for

---

36 This case is often called the "Rawlsian" case since, when $\varepsilon = \infty$, only the preferences of the least well off in the community are to count when determining the direction of change of social welfare. (See, for example, Atkinson and Stiglitz [1980, p. 339 -340].) This particular situation, however, only reflects Rawls' [1971] second principle of social justice. The first principle of social justice, on the other hand, requires that certain basic principles of individual liberty be satisfied. What is more, this first principle must be satisfied prior to the second principle of social justice coming into operation. This rank-ordering requirement would seem to limit the potential for radical egalitarian reform that might be based upon the second principle of economic justice.

example, those found in section 5 below - do not support the inference that particularly radical views of distributive justice have had to be adopted by the community.

3. Introducing Various Constraints.[37]

The discussion in the previous section was based upon the implicit assumption that each individual consumes in an economy free of any distortions which may constrain individual behaviour. The central objective in this section is to introduce a wide range of distortions into the economic system facing individuals - distortions which appear in various sectors of the economy (specifically in the production and consumption, and the traded-goods and non-traded-goods, sectors of the economy). The reason for introducing this level of generality into the basic model is that it will allow the analysis of a wide range of cases concerned with the reform of economic distortions. [The context in which these cases arise in practice will be explained in more detail at various points in the discussion to be found in subsequent sections.] What is more, it will become apparent below that the precise form of the distortion present in the economy has a marked influence of the general (let alone the specific) form of the results that can be derived in the later sections 4 and 5.

---

[37] If the reader is just interested in learning about specific results, without being concerned about the details as to how these results are derived, this section can be omitted - although one should be aware of the results set out in (3.24), (3.25) and (3.26) below in the main text. These results are fundamental.

One implication of taking these various distortions into account is that the $dv^{h}*$ terms, initially defined in (2.19) above, turn out to take a much more complicated form than indicated earlier.

3.1. <u>The Consumption Side</u>.

The consumption side of the model is essentially that reflected in the individual indirect utility function specified in (2.10) above except that now individuals are also assumed to consume a public good (bad), g, which creates a global consumption externality.[38]

In place of (2.10) above the following now applies, for any individual h:

$$v^h = v^h(q, g, y^h) = v(q, g, y^h, a^h) = v(q, g, y_e^h, a^o). \qquad (3.1)$$

The equivalent income for individual h, y_e^h, must now also take account of the fact that, since individuals possess different tastes, the personal marginal value (shadow price) placed upon the public good will tend vary from individual to individual in the community. In this case the equivalence scale for individual h will be $m^h = m(q, g, v^h, a^o, a^h)$.[39]

---

[38] The term, g, may, if required, be taken to represent a vector of public goods (bads).

[39]This point is discussed in King [1983].

[That the shadow price for the public good does vary across individuals is demonstrated by totally differentiating the left-hand side of (3.1) above to give (after applying Roy's identity):

$$\frac{dv^h}{v_y^h} = -\sum_i c_i^h \, dq_i + \lambda^h \, dg + dy^h, \qquad (3.2)$$

where $\lambda^h := \left[\frac{\partial v^h}{\partial g} \Big/ \frac{\partial v^h}{\partial y^h}\right]$.

Since individuals are assumed to possess heterogeneous utility functions, the shadow price of the public good for individual h, λ^h, will vary across individuals. Hence the measure of equivalent income will need to take account of this fact.]

In those circumstances where equivalent income is required to measure changes in utility levels, the relevant, adjusted, version of (3.2) above, is the following:

$$\frac{dv^h}{v_{ye}^h} = -\sum_i c_{ie}^h \, dq_i + \lambda^r \, dg + dy_e^h, \qquad (3.3)$$

where $\lambda^r := \left[\frac{\partial v}{\partial g} \Big/ \frac{\partial v}{\partial y_e^h}\right]$,

where λ^r denotes the shadow price for the public good for some reference individual - a shadow price which is common to all individuals in the community.[40]

---

40 This point is discussed in more detail in King [1983].

As for the term, c^h_{ie}, in (3.3) above, it refers to the uncompensated level of demand for good i by individual h - a level of demand which is dependent on the vector of consumer prices, q, the supply of the public good and the equivalent income for this individual; i.e. $c^h_{ie} = c_i(q, g, y^h_e)$.

Various versions of (3.2) and (3.3) above will be applied in the discussion provided in the following sections.

3.2 <u>The Production Side.</u>

To determine how changes in social states influence the utility of a single individual in the community, allowance must also be made for changes on the production side of the economy which flow through, eventually, to influence individual utility levels. To allow for this consideration, the production sector of the economy is decomposed by considering the supply of any good i (= 0 to n) to any individual h. Thus the term x^h_i refers to the supply of good i to individual h at some given market price. This individual level of supply is produced by applying the following fixed technology in the production of any good i supplied to individual h:

$$x^h_i = X^h_i [F^h_{i1}, F^h_{2i}, \dots, F^h_{Ni}, x_i], \text{ for all i and all h, (3.4)}$$

where F^h_{fi} refers to factor f (=1 to N) required in the production of good i supplied to individual h. If the term x_i is held constant then the production function, $X_i^h [\ .\ ]$, is assumed to be differentiable, increasing, linear homogeneous and strictly quasi-concave in factor inputs. The presence of the term x_i allows for the possibility that the level of production of good i is dependent on the total level of production in the industry producing this good. In other words there are inter-firm production externalities which result in firms experiencing variable returns to scale even though markets are perfectly competitive.[41]

This latter point can be demonstrated by first totally differentiating (3.4) above to give:

$$dx_i^h = \sum_{f=1}^{N} \frac{\partial X_i^h}{\partial F_{fi}^h} dF_{fi}^h + \varpi_i dx_i^h, \text{ for all i, h,} \qquad (3.5)$$

where the term, ϖ_i $\{ := [\partial X_i^h / \partial x_i] \}$, is assumed to take, for the sake of simplicity, the same value over all h individuals. If there are increasing returns to scale (IRS) [decreasing returns to scale (DRS)] in the production of good i, supplied to individual h, then $\varpi_i > 0$ ($\varpi_i < 0$). Should constant returns to scale apply then $\varpi = 0$.

Next private factor and product markets are assumed to be perfectly competitive so that any factor of production employed in a profit-maximizing firm is demanded up to the point

---

41 This class of assumption is employed, for example, in Kemp and Schweinberger [1991].

where the value of the marginal product of this factor is equal to the equilibrium market wage rate paid to this factor - this wage rate being the same across all firms in which this factor is employed.[42] Thus

$$w_f = p_i \, [\, \partial x_i^h \,/\, \partial F_{fi}^h \,], \quad \text{for all } f, i, h, \tag{3.6}$$

where p_i is the current price of good i facing producers of this good.

On multiplying (3.5) above through by p_i, substituting (3.6) into the resulting equation and summing over all i goods, the result is that

$$\sum_{i=o}^{n} p_i \, dx_i^h = dY^h + dS^h, \quad \text{for all } h,$$

or that

$$dY^h + dS^h - \sum_{i=o}^{n} p_i \, dx_i^h = 0, \qquad \text{for all } h, \tag{3.7}$$

where

$$dY^h := \sum_{f=1}^{N} w_f \sum_{i=0}^{n} dF_{fi}^h, \qquad \text{for all } h, \tag{3.8}$$

and

---

42 This assumption could be relaxed if required. This point is returned to below in sub-section 4.4 B the main text in the context of proposition 4.7*.

$$dS^h := \sum_{i=0}^{n} p_i \ \varpi_i \ dx_i^h, \qquad \text{for all } h. \qquad (3.9)$$

The result in (3.7) above was derived, as indicated earlier, by the application of the assumption that all private factor and product markets are perfectly competitive. Nevertheless, the economies of scale may vary as the level of production varies in the community. This fact, which is due to the presence of production externalities, would be representing by the term dS^h varying over changes in economic states.

At this point in the present discussion it is also useful to note that if all aggregate supplies are fixed, and the technology is constant, then

$$\sum_{i=0}^{n} \sum_{h=1}^{H} dF_{fi}^h = \sum_{i=0}^{n} dF_{fi} = 0, \quad \text{for all n goods,}$$

which implies that

$$dY := \sum_{h=1}^{H} dY^h := \sum_{f=1}^{N} w_f \sum_{i=0}^{n} \sum_{h=1}^{H} dF_{fi}^h = 0. \qquad (3.10)$$

This will be so even though for any individual, h, the term representing changes in individual real income, dY^h, may take non-zero values. This latter change would occur if the distribution of total income in the community altered over changes in social states. This point is returned to at the end of this section.

If there are factors of production which are under-employed, and the level of under-employment rises over the change in economic states, then dY will take a negative value. In contrast, if there are falling levels of under-employment, or more resources are made available to the community (due, say, to improvements in the production technology), then dY will take a positive value. Finally, if there are only constant returns to scale present in the economy (i.e. $\varpi_i = 0$ for all i goods), then (3.7) above becomes, after simply aggregating over all h individuals,

$$dY := \sum_{h=1}^{H} dY^h = \sum_{i=o}^{n} p_i \; dx_i^h . \qquad (3.11)$$

And since the producer prices, the p_i s, refer to current, or final, producer prices, the term dY refers to the Paasche measure of changes in real national product. This observation will be exploited in the next section.

3.3 The Market Clearing and Government Budget Constraint

In the process of maximizing individual utility, any individual h is assumed to consume goods at a level just equal to the value of the goods supplied (to this individual) at the relevant set of market prices. In the case of goods traded only in the domestic market [i.e non-traded (NT) goods] the market clearing set of prices are those facing domestic producers. In the instance of goods traded in international markets [i.e. traded goods (T)] the market clearing prices are those facing foreign producers. Thus, for any individual, h, the market clearing conditions are the following:

at the equilibrium domestic producer prices, p_i, for good i

$$(c_i^h - x_i^h) = 0, \quad \text{for all } i \in NT, \tag{3.12}$$

and at the international (or world) price (terms-of-trade) p_j^* for good j

$$\sum_j p_j^* (c_j^h - x_j^h) = 0, \quad \text{for all } j \in T.$$

The number of goods referred to in this market-clearing condition only number n (not n+1). That being the case, by Walras' Law, it must be that

$$(c_o^h - x_o^h) = 0, \quad o \in NT. \tag{3.13}$$

It is next assumed that taxes are imposed on the consumption of goods. In the instance of non-traded goods

$$q_i = p_i + t_i \quad \text{for all } i \in NT \text{ (except the numeraire)} \tag{3.14}$$

where t_i is the consumption tax imposed on good $i \in NT$. As for the traded goods, it is only assumed that a tariff is imposed on the level of trade in these goods [i.e. $(c_j - x_j)$ in the case of good $j \in T$] so that

$$q_j = p_j^* + \tau_j \quad \text{and} \quad p_j = p_j^* + \tau_j ,$$

or that

$$\tau_j = q_j - p_j^* \quad \text{and} = - \tau_j = p_j^* - p_j \quad \text{for all } j \in T, \qquad (3.15)$$

where τ_j is the tariff rate applied to good $j \in T$.[43] [The term $-\tau_j$ implies that a production subsidy is being applied as a result of imposing a tariff on good j.]

On occasions in the discussion below, consumption taxes will also be imposed on traded goods as well. This particular detail will be ignored for the present, however.

Since it is relative prices, and not the absolute level of prices, which influence economic behaviour, at least one good needs to remain untaxed to ensure that relative prices vary as non-lump-sum taxes are altered in size. In the present discussion the untaxed good is assumed to be the numeraire.

---

[43] In the case of traded goods distinct and separate consumption and production taxes could also be applied. On occasions below, in the main text, this detail needs to be taken into account.

The budget, and pricing, constraints set out above also imply the government budget constraint. To indicate that this is so, (3.12) and (3.13) are aggregated over all h individuals to give:

$$p_0 c_0 + \sum_i p_i c_i + \sum_j p_j^* c_j$$

$$= p_0 x_0 + \sum_i p_i x_i + \sum_j p_j^* x_j, \; i \in T, j \in NT. \qquad (3.16)$$

Next the constraints on prices facing consumers (in the case of T and NT goods), and prices facing producers (in the case of T goods), which are set out in (3.14) and (3.15) above, are substituted into (3.16) above to give the following:

$$\sum_i t_i c_i + \sum_j \tau_j [c_j - x_j]$$

$$= \sum_i [q_i c_i - p_i x_i] + \sum_j [q_j x_j - p_j x_j], \qquad i \in T, j \in NT.$$

On applying the price constraints again to the right-hand side of this last equation, and applying the market clearing condition set out in (3.16) above, the result emerges that

$$R := \sum_{i \in NT} t_i c_i + \sum_{j \in T} \tau_j [c_j - x_j], \qquad (3.17)$$

where R refers to the net revenue raised by the government from applying consumption taxes on NT-goods and tariffs on T-goods.

Finally, assuming that the revenue raised is only applied to financing general government expenditures, G, and lump-sum income transfers, b, to all individuals in the community, then (3.17) above equally can be written as follows:

$$R = \sum_{i \in NT} t_i \, c_i + \sum_{j \in T} \tau_j \, [c_j - x_j] = \sum_h b^h + G, \qquad (3.18)$$

where b^h is the personal lump-sum income transfer paid to individual h.

The government budget condition presented in (3.18), takes on some importance in the argument developed at the beginning of the next section and elsewhere.

3.4. Combining the Various Constraints.

Exactly how the various constraints set out above are combined, to form some pertinent reduced-form equations to represent distorted economic systems, depends on what question is being posed. The broad question considered in the next section, for example, is only concerned with compensated Pareto changes in economic states. Hence in this case there is no need to make use of measures of individual equivalent income - measures of individual nominal income will do. As a result (3.2) above can be combined, as it stands, with the production constraint stated in (3.7) by applying the budget constraint set out in (3.12) and (3.13) above. Finally the price distortions, represented in (3.14) and (3.15) can be applied to the resulting equation.

Exactly how this might be done is demonstrated by first noting that in (3.2) above the following identity applies:

$$dy^h := dc_o^h + \sum_{i=1}^{n} [\, q_i \;\; dc_i^h + c_i^h \; dq_i^h \,], \qquad \text{for all h,} \quad (3.19)$$

where the price of the numeraire has been normalised by setting it equal to one. [44] The production constraint, set out in (3.7) above, is added to the right-hand side of (3.19). The result is:

$$dy^h = \sum_{i=1}^{n} [\, q_i \;\; dc_i^h + c_i^h \; dq_i^h \; - p_i \;\; dx_i^h \,] + [\, dc_o^h - dx_o^h \,] + dY^h + dS^h,$$

$$\text{for all h.}$$

As before, the producer and consumer price for the numeraire has been set equal to one. On making use of Walras' Law [as reflected in the total differential of the budget condition stated in (3.13) above], the previous equation becomes:

$$dy^h = \sum_{i=1}^{n} [\, q_i \;\; dc_i^h + c_i^h \; dq_i^h \; - p_i \;\; dx_i^h \,] + dY^h + dS^h, \quad (3.20)$$

$$\text{for all h.}$$

44 As noted above, in the main text, since it is relative prices of goods (not their absolute level) which influence economic behaviour, the price of one good - say good zero - needs to remain fixed.

The constraints on (or distortions in) prices, represented in (3.14) and (315) above, can now be applied to (3.20) above to give:

$$dy^h = \sum_{i\in NT} t_i \; dc_i^h + \sum_{i\in T} \tau_j \; (dc_i^h - dx_i^h) + \sum_{i\in T+NT} c_i^h \, dq_i$$

$$+ \; dY^h + dS^h + \sum_{i\in NT} \dot{p}_i \; [\, dc_i^h - dx_i^h \,]$$

$$+ \sum_{j\in T} p_j^* \; [\, dc_j^h - dx_j^h \,], \text{ for all h.} \qquad (3.21)$$

Finally the total differential of the budget constraint, set out in (3.12) above, is applied to (3.21). In the present case, and for the sake of simplicity, it is also assumed that the domestic economy is small in size, relative to the world economy, so that the international terms-of-trade are fixed.[45] These assumptions imply that (3.21) above can be simplified to the reduced-form equation:

$$dy^h = dR^h + \sum_{i\in NT} c_i^h \, dp_i \; + dY^h \; + dS^h, \quad \text{for all h,} \qquad (3.22)$$

where

[45] The discussion presented in the next two sections, in the main text below, could easily be extended to allow for variations in the international terms-of-trade. This complication is omitted here, however.

$$dR^h := \sum_{i \in NT} t_i \, dc_i^h + \sum_{i \in T} \tau_j \, (dc_j^h - dx_j^h)$$

$$+ \sum_{i \in NT} c_i^h \, dt_i + \sum_{j \in T} c_j^h \, d\tau_j \, , \qquad (3.23)$$

and use was made of the relationship: $dq_i = dp_i + dt_i$ for all $i \in NT$ (except the numeraire) and $dq_j = d\tau_j$ for all $j \in T$. This last observation also implies that producer prices are allowed to vary in the present model.

The reduced-form equation in (3.23) above can now be substituted back into (3.2) above, and making use of the price constraints and the assumption that the terms-of-trade are fixed, the latter equation becomes:[46]

$$\frac{dv^h}{v_y^h} = - \sum_{i \in NT} c_i^h \, dt_i - \sum_{j \in T} c_j^h \, d\tau_j + dR^h + \lambda^h dg$$

$$+ dY^h + dS^h, \qquad \text{for all } h, \qquad (3.24)$$

where the various relevant terms have been defined above.

---

46 Again it is noted that $dp_i = dq_i + dt_i$ for all $i \in NT$ (except the numeraire) and $dp_j = d\tau_j$ for all $j \in T$.

On substituting (3.23) above into (3.24), and cancelling terms, the alternative reduced-form equation emerges:[47]

$$\frac{dv^h}{v^h_y} = \sum_{i \in NT} t_i \, dc^h_i + \sum_{j \in T} \tau_j \, dE^h_j + \lambda^h dg$$

$$+ \, dY^h + dS^h, \qquad \text{for all } h, \qquad (3.25)$$

where $dE^h_j := [\, dc^h_j - dx^h_j \,]$, for $j \in T$.

It is noted in passing that the sum of the traded goods (T) and non-traded goods (NT) aggregate to n goods - the numeraire not having a tax imposed upon it.

Of the two reduced-form equations just derived, the result stated in (3.24) above is employed far more frequently in the discussion which follows.[48] [On the other hand, in the subsequent second set of lectures, it tends to be the other way around - the reduced-form equation presented in (3.25) is (implicitly) employed far more often than, or in combination with, (3.24).]

It remains to derive the relevant reduced-form equations for the case where the central question posed requires the ranking of individual utility levels and, hence, requires the use of measures of individual equivalent income. The relevant argument

47 It can also be shown that (3.25) can be derived by employing the direct, instead of the indirect, utility function, along with applying the various constraints discussed above in the main text.

48 A less general, and aggregated, version of (3.25) in the main text is to be found in Lloyd [1974].

begins with (3.3) above. Next the production and budget constraints need to be expressed in terms of equivalent levels of consumption and production of all goods for any individual h.[49] The rest of the argument is as before.

The result, to replace (3.3) above, for any individual h, is the following for all h individuals:

$$[\, dv^h / v^h_{Y_e} \,] = - \sum_{i \in NT} c^h_{ei}\, dt_i - \sum_{j \in T} c^h_{ej}\, d\tau_j + dR^h_e$$

$$+ \lambda^r dg + dY^h_e + dS^h_e, \qquad (3.26)$$

where, drawing on (3.23), (3.7) and (3.9) above:

$$dR^h_e := \sum_{i \in NT} t_i\, dc^h_{ei} + \sum_{i \in T} \tau_j\, (dc^h_{ej} - dx^h_{ej}) + \sum_{i \in T} c^h_{ei}\, dt_i$$

$$+ \sum_{j \in NT} c^h_{ej}\, d\tau_j\,, \qquad (3.27)$$

---

[49] This requires that, on the consumption side of the economy, for all i goods, and all h individuals, the c^h_i [$= c^h_i(q, g, y^h)$] terms are replaced with c^h_{ie} [$= c_i(q, g, y^h_e)$] terms. Corresponding adjustments are made to the production side of the economy. Thus, for example, x^h_{ei} (p) represents the equivalent level of supply of good i required to satisfy the equivalent level of demand for good i by individual h at the equilibrium set of market prices.

$$dY_e^h = \sum_{i=o}^{n} p_i \; dx_{ei}^h - dS_e^h, \tag{3.28}$$

and

$$dS_e^h := \sum_{i=0}^{n} p_i \; \varpi_i \; dx_{ei}^h. \tag{3.29}$$

The alternative reduced-form equation, corresponding to (3.25) above, is omitted.

It is variations of (3.26) above which are employed throughout much of the discussion in section 5 below. For the present it is noted that that equation confirms a point made in the introduction of this section; namely, that in a distorted economic system, the dv^{h*} terms will take a much more complicated form than that indicated in (2.19) above. And matters could be made even more complicated by relaxing, for example, the assumptions that the international terms-of-trade are fixed and that there are no distortions in factor markets.

Another point that needs to be emphasised, concerning the results presented in the reduced-form equation presented in (3.24), (3.25) and (3.26) above, is that changes in individual utility levels are dependent on changes in individual real income - as represented by the term dY^h [or dY_e^h] for individual h. Thus, even if the level of aggregate total income in the community remains constant - i.e. $\sum_h dY^h = dY = 0$ - the individual dY^h terms may alter in size over some change in social states. Thus the reduced-form equations set out above capture, amongst other things, small changes in the distribution of total community income as this community moves from one social state to another. This particular property, of those equations, takes on some importance in the discussion presented below.

It is also worth pointing out, in passing, that in the process of deriving the reduced-form equations set out above, producer prices (but not the international terms-of-trade) were allowed to vary within perfectly competitive markets for private goods. This fact contrasts with the assumption, often employed in the relevant literature, that producer prices are fixed.[50]

It is helpful to summarise the central argument developed in this section. This is done by noting that the reduced-form equations above are derived from a basic set of assumptions which are stated as follows:

<u>Basic Assumptions (BA)</u>:

(i) There are many non-identical, utility maximizing individuals in the community; (ii) the indirect utility function for any individual is at least continuously twice differentiable in all arguments, increasing in individual income and non-increasing and quasi-convex in prices and homogeneous of degree zero in prices

---

50 See, for example, Auerbach [1985, pp.118 - 124] for a survey of this literature.

and income; (iii) firms maximize profit and produce private goods in perfectly competitive markets employing production functions which are increasing and once differentiable in the factors of production employed; (iii) all private markets are in equilibrium at the relevant set of equilibrium prices and (iv) there are various price and market distortions present in the economy.

4. Compensated Pareto Improvements in Social States.

Before turning to combining the results presented in the previous section with those presented in section 2 above, there is an alternative approach that can be employed to determine a welfare ranking of social states; namely, the reduced-form equation presented in (3.24) above can be exploited to determine under what circumstances Pareto-improving changes in social states take place when compensation is actually paid to any individual in the community who has suffered an economic loss as a result of this change in social states. As indicated in the introduction, while application of this compensated Pareto criterion for ranking social states possesses the advantage of not requiring any information concerning the form of the social welfare function (except that the swf be increasing in individual utility levels), it suffers from at least two weaknesses when it comes to the matter of implementation. The discussion in the next two subsections attempts to demonstrate the nature of these weaknesses by considering a particular, but fairly general, application of the compensated Pareto-improving criterion.

The discussion then goes on to consider a range of topics, in the subsequent sub-sections, where the compensated Pareto-improving criterion is applied. The most general of the results presented in these sub-sections provide one of the points of departure for the discussion in the subsequent section 5 - where the marginal welfare dominance criteria are applied.

4.1 Consumption Tax Reform and the Incentive-Compatibility Problem.

The following definition is required in the discussion below:

Compensated Pareto Improvement Criterion (CPIC): If, as a result of some change in social states and the provision of compensating income transfers, all individuals in situation A are no worse off, and at least one individual is better off, compared to the actual individual utility levels attained in situation a, then situation A satisfies CPIC.

Amongst other things, this definition may be interpreted as embodying the assumption that the swf is increasing in individual utility levels.

The discussion in this, and the next, sub-section, is based upon the simplest relevant case that can be considered; namely, it is assumed that the economy is closed to international trade, all factors of production are in fixed aggregate supply, the technology is fixed, and all distortions are absent from the economy except for the presence of a set of consumption taxes. Based on these assumptions, (3.24) above reduces to the following:[51]

---

[51] In this case $R^h := \sum_i t_i c_i^h$.

$$\frac{dv^h}{v^h} = - \sum_i c_i^h \, dt_i + dR^h + dY^h, \qquad \text{for all h,} \qquad (4.1)$$

where $$\sum_h dY^h = 0. \qquad (4.2)$$

Since, as is well known, lump-sum taxes are not feasible (because they are not incentive compatible with individual behaviour)[52], the reformed taxation system is also called upon to raise the revenue required to finance the actual income transfers made to compensate any individuals who have suffered a reduction in utility as a result of the assumed change in economic states. It is also assumed, for the present, that these income transfers take the form of personal lump-sum transfers - where b^h is the lump-sum transfer made to individual h.

Proposition 4.1: Suppose that the Basic Assumptions (BA) are satisfied, the economy is closed, aggregate factor supplies and the technology are fixed, and there are no distortions present except for the presence of consumption taxes. Personal lump-sum income transfers can be financed from these taxes to provide personal income compensation. Then a small reform of the consumption taxation system will always satisfy CPIC iff $[- \sum_i c_i \, dt_i + dR] > 0$.

52 This point is discussed, for example, in Hammond [1990, p.11] and Roberts [1984] and the references cited there.

Proof: On summing the statement in (4.1) above over all h individuals, and applying the assumption that factors are in aggregate fixed supply (i.e. the assumption in (4.2) above applies), the resulting equation is the following:

$$\sum_h \frac{dv^h}{v^h} = \sum_h \left[-\sum_i c_i^h \, dt_i + dR^h + dY^h \right]$$

$$= -\sum_i c_i \, dt_i + dR, \qquad (4.3)$$

where $dR^h = \sum_i \frac{\partial R^h}{\partial t_i} dt_i + \frac{\partial R^h}{\partial b^h} db^h$, and

$$dY^h = \sum_i \frac{\partial Y^h}{\partial t_i} dt_i + \frac{\partial Y^h}{\partial b^h} db^h.$$

In deriving this result use has been made of the assumption that, since markets clear at equilibrium prices, the government's budget must be in balance. Hence any change in the level of government revenue can be balanced by a change in the level of personal lump-sum income transfers. [See the discussion leading up to (3.18) above.]

(Necessary) CPIC requires that, in (4.3) above, $[-\sum_i c_i \, dt_i + dR] > 0$.

(Sufficient) Since, by assumption, personal lump-sum income transfers are available to distribute income compensation, these transfers can be arranged across individuals such that, for any h individual:

$$\left[-\sum_i c_i^h \, dt_i + \sum_i \frac{\partial R^h}{\partial t_i} dt_i + \sum_i \frac{\partial Y^h}{\partial t_i} dt_i + \frac{\partial R^h}{\partial b^h} db^h + \frac{\partial Y^h}{\partial b^h} db^h \right] \geq 0, \qquad (4.4)$$

and that (4.4) takes a positive sign for at least one individual in the community. If this is so then (4.3) above indicates that the statement in (4.4) is sufficient for CPIC to be satisfied. ||

Proposition 4.1 above provides a comparatively general statement of the conditions which are necessary and sufficient to ensure that a small reform of the consumption taxation system satisfies CPIC.[53] Nevertheless, that proposition is based upon the assumption (amongst others) that the compensating lump-sum income transfers can be provided in exactly the right marginal amounts precisely to the individuals who need to be compensated. But determining the appropriate size of these personal income transfers is almost certainly dependent on each individual providing relevant and accurate private information relating to the losses, or gains, each may have experienced as a result of the small reform of the consumption taxation system. This implies

---

[53] A more general version of proposition 4.1 in the main text is to be found in Dixit [1987, p. 145].

that each individual has the incentive to misrepresent the size of the losses (gains) incurred as a result of the reform of the taxation system. [This is so for, by overstating marginal losses, or understating marginal gains, each individual stands to benefit by being paid a greater level of compensating income transfer than the compensation principle actually suggests.] If individuals indeed behave in this strategic manner, then redistributing income, by employing a personal lump-sum income transfer system, is inconsistent, or incentive incompatible, with the need to obtain relevant accurate personal information.[54]

The main implication of this strategic behaviour is that, even if the necessary and sufficient condition in proposition 4.1 above is satisfied, the community may still believe that the reformed consumption taxation system does not satisfy CPIC. The reason is that, as a result of the misrepresentation of individual losses and gains, the *measured* amount of change in aggregate real income, dY_m, will now take a negative value - even though the *actual*, or true, value for this variable, dY, is zero (by assumption). As a result, instead of the community observing (4.3) above, they will actually observe the following:

$$\sum_h \frac{dv^h}{v^h} = -\sum_i c_i\, dt_i + dR + dY_m,$$

54 This point is also made in a slightly more general context by Dixit [1987, p.145]. Also see Dixit and Norman [1986, p. 121].

where $dY_m < 0$.

Thus, even if the term, $[-\sum_i c_i \, dt_i + dR]$, does take a positive value, the community may believe that this is not sufficient for the reformed taxation system to satisfy CPIC.

While this argument is based upon a particularly simple case, clearly it also applies to any of the numerous alternative analyses, of personal compensated economic reform, that can be based on variations of (3.24) above. The conclusion, therefore, that can be drawn from this particular argument is the following:

Proposition 4.2: It will be impossible to determine if all potential reforms of the economic system have actually satisfied CPIC, or not, if, as a consequence of employing personal lump-sum income transfers to provide compensation, strategic individual behaviour is prevalent in the community.

This incentive-compatibility problem, alluded to in this proposition, can be avoided, however, if the following assumption is satisfied:

Assumption W : In the initial situation there is at least one good, w, such that

$$\frac{dv^h}{v^h_y} = -c^h_w \, dt_w + \left[\frac{\partial R^h}{\partial t_w} + \frac{\partial Y^h}{\partial t_w}\right] dt_w > 0 \ (< 0), \quad \text{for all } h$$

individuals.

In this case all individuals in the community can be provided with an implicit income subsidy by the price of the w-good(s) being manipulated as required.[55] So, for example, if all goods are taxed in the initial situation, then the consumption taxes will need to be altered in a particular, differential manner when reforming the taxation system. In this way implicit income compensation will be provided to each individual, simultaneously with reforming the taxation system. What is more, since the size of the compensating implicit income subsidy provided is not dependent on the use of private individual information, the incentive-incompatible problem does not arise.

As for Assumption W itself, it would be met if the Weymark [1979] condition is satisfied; namely, there are pure, or Hicksian, goods which, in the initial situation, all consumers are net buyers (sellers) and these goods are not free goods (the only valuable good).[56]

<u>Proposition 4.3:</u> Suppose that the Basic Assumptions (BA) are satisfied, the economy is closed, aggregate factor supplies and the technology are fixed, and there are no distortions present except for the presence of consumption taxes. Assumption W is also satisfied. The consumption taxes are capable of financing subsidies applied to goods satisfying Assumption W. Then a

---

[55] The Assumption W in the main text is similar to Assumption 2 in Diewert *et al.* [1989, p. 207].

[56] The Weymark condition is discussed in Dixit and Norman [1986, p. 17] and Diewert <u>et al</u> [1989].

small reform of the consumption taxation system will always satisfy CPIC iff $[- \sum_i c_i \; dt_i + dR] > 0$.

The proof for this proposition follows that for proposition 4.1 above, except that now, instead of providing personal lump-sum income transfers, compensation takes the form of providing the general implicit income subsidy (to all individuals in the community) by manipulating the price of the w-good(s). In this regard it should be emphasised that, as Diewert *et al.* [1989, p. 208] note,[57] this general implicit subsidy must be paid to every individual in the community. In contrast, Dixit and Norman [1986] and Dixit [1987] seem to imply that this subsidy is only provided randomly to some individuals in the community. (The assumption 3 in Dixit [1987], for example, implies that only some individuals will receive the implicit subsidy.) But in this case there is no certainty that CPIC would be satisfied by the consumption tax reform - it is possible that some individuals, who need be compensated if CPIC is to be satisfied, receive no compensation.

4.2 The Targeting-of-Compensation Problem.

But providing implicit income compensation to all individuals in the community in the form just suggested implies that there are individuals in the community who are receiving compensation in excess of what is required, to ensure that CPIC is sat-

---

[57] Also see Turunen [1987, p. 417].

isfied when the consumption taxation system is reformed. In other words, this form of compensation is not targeted precisely at the individuals, and only these individuals, in the community who actually need to be compensated to ensure that CPIC is satisfied (as a result of some economic reform).

An implication of this lack of precision, in the targeting of compensation, is that compensated Pareto-improving economic reform cannot be taken as far as could be attained had personal income transfers been available for use. In other words, by employing relatively imprecise methods to redistribute income, the community may soon find - that is compared to the situation where more precise policy tools are available to redistribute individual incomes - that there are no compensated Pareto-improving differential tax reforms available to implement.

To demonstrate this point first it is supposed that the following two alternative types of income transfers are available to redistribute individual incomes: (i) a personal lump-sum income transfer, b^h, for any individual h, and (ii) a uniform lump-sum income transfer, b, for each individual in the community. In the case of the first type of income transfer system, the incentive-compatibility problem is assumed (for the sake of the present argument) not to apply. As for the uniform lump-sum income transfer system, there does not seem to be any *a priori* reason why the use of this compensation system is any less, or more, successful in targeting assistance (only to those who require this assistance), than that attained by altering consumption taxes in an appropriately differential manner (assuming that assumption W is satisfied). Thus it seems reasonable to suggest that this latter system of income transfers can be represented by the uniform lump-sum income transfer system.

Next it is assumed that a given reform of the consumption taxation system takes place and a given amount of additional tax revenue is raised. This additional revenue is redistributed in either of the two forms assumed above such that (remembering that the government budget must be in balance)

$$R = \sum_h b^h = H b > 0. \tag{4.5}$$

This case is also taken to represent the marginal situation where no further reforms of the consumption taxation system, along with the provision of the general lump-sum transfer, are possible without violating CPIC.[58]

Attention now concentrates on the individual, m, whose utility level is assumed to remain unaltered after the tax reform and after being paid the additional general lump-sum transfer, db. In these circumstances the difference in the change in utility, for individual m, resulting from employing these alternative forms of income transfers, is the following:

---

58 Such a situation might arise where, even though $[-\sum_i c_i \, dt_i + dR] > 0$, dR takes a negative value and, as a result, the government budget is just large enough to finance the general income transfer required to ensure that CPIC is satisfied.

$$dv^m_{b^m} - dv^m_b = \left[\frac{\partial R^m}{\partial b^m} + \frac{\partial Y^m}{\partial b^m}\right] db^m - \left[\frac{\partial R^m}{\partial b} + \frac{\partial Y^m}{\partial b}\right] db,$$

(4.6)

where

$$dv^m_b = - \sum_i c^h_i \, dt_i + \left[\sum_i \frac{\partial R^h}{\partial t_i} + \sum_i \frac{\partial Y^h}{\partial t_i}\right] dt_i$$

$$+ \left[\frac{\partial R^m}{\partial b} + \frac{\partial Y^m}{\partial b}\right] db = 0.$$

Next it is assumed that the personal income transfers are carefully targeted. This would be so if any non-marginal individual, nm, receives a personal income transfer, db^{nm}, which is just enough to ensure that $du^{nm} > 0$. This level of additional income transfer must also satisfy the inequality

$$db^{nm} < db, \qquad \text{for all nm individuals.} \qquad (4.7)$$

This reasonable requirement, along with the balanced government budget condition set out in (4.5) above, implies that

$$db^m > db, \qquad \text{for individual m.} \qquad (4.8)$$

Given the additional, reasonable assumption, that

$$\left[\frac{\partial R^m}{\partial b^m} + \frac{\partial Y^m}{\partial b^m}\right] \geq \left[\frac{\partial R^m}{\partial b} + \frac{\partial Y^m}{\partial b}\right],$$

it follows that in (4.6) above $[\, du^m_{b^m} - du^m_b \,] > 0$.

The implication of this result is that a community may find that, as a result of employing relatively imprecise methods to redistribute income, there are no CPI differential tax reforms available for implementation even though, in this initial situation, CPI reforms could be implemented if more precise methods for redistributing income were available. And while this observation has been based upon the assumption that personal lump-sum income transfers are incentive compatible - an assumption which is questionable, as pointed out in the previous sub-section - the present argument does indicate that there are gains in social welfare to be derived from devising income transfer systems which can be targeted with greater precision than a uniform lump-sum income transfer system (as defined above). At the same time this more-precise income transfer system must not create severe incentive-compatible problems. This general matter is returned to sub-section 5.1 below.

[In passing it is noted that these observations are not completely new or original - a point that was made in the introduction. Specifically, in the literature dealing with the social ranking of economic policy tools, it has been demonstrated that the more precisely such a tool can be directed at correcting the particular economic distortion of concern, the higher the level of social welfare (given certain assumptions such as that matters of distributional justice do not arise and other distortions are absent from the economy).[59] The discussion provided in this sub-section has essentially applied this general principle to the matter of providing compensating income transfers.]

Finally, while the analysis, based on the statement in (4.6) above, applies a strictly economic argument, that argument also alludes to an issue in political economy which may also be of some relevance. Specifically, the payment of general compensating income transfers may have the consequence of creating relatively large demands for additional government revenue - indeed demands so large that it may become politically untenable for the government to continue to provide additional compensating general income transfers.[60] To curb this level of expenditure the government may place a binding upper limit on the size of the budget available to finance compensating income transfers. If this in fact occurs, then the imposition of this binding government budget constraint would provide further grounds for suggesting that the scope for economic reform will be increased if compensating income transfer systems could be devised such that they could be targeted relatively precisely - yet still not create severe incentive-compatibility problems. This is a matter which is returned to in sub-section 5.1 below.

---

59 This general principle is discussed in some detail by Bhagwati [1971] and assessed more critically by Corden [1984, pp. 86 - 96].

60 This political behaviour would seem to be particularly likely once it is realised that the general compensating income transfer is paid to, amongst others, individuals who have suffered no losses as a result of some relevant economic reform.

4.3 Compensated Pareto Distortion Reform - A Limited Case.

The present discussion is based upon the assumption that incentive-compatible income transfers can be made. [This assumption can be satisfied by assuming either that incentive compatible lump-sum income transfers are available for use, or that assumption W applies and that consumption taxes are altered in a differential manner as required.] The relatively general assumption,that the economy is open, is also adopted. In addition, since the terms-of-trade were assumed to be fixed when deriving (3.24) above, the economy for the community concerned can be taken to be small in size (relative to the size of the world economy).[61] Based on these assumptions, the first case to be considered is based upon the following additional assumption:

Assumption 1(A1): Taxed goods are normal in the sense that the amount of tax revenue raised, from the taxes imposed on consumption alone, does not fall if the level of real national income rises - and consumption tax rates remain unaltered.

Based upon this assumption it is possible to extend the argument employed to establish proposition 4.1 above.

Proposition 4.4: Initial Assumptions: Given (BA) [upon which (3.24) above is based] it is supposed, however, that there are no distortions present in the economy except for the presence of

---

[61] Within the context of the model developed above in the main text, it is not difficult to allow for variable terms-of-trade effects. This complication will not be considered here, however.

non-prohibitive tariffs and consumption taxes. Taxes on consumption are employed to finance compensating income transfers, and incentive-compatible income transfer systems are employed to distribute this compensation. Additional Assumptions: (A1) is satisfied. It follows that a small reform of the tariff system, offset exactly by changes in the consumption taxes in the consumption sector of the economy , will always satisfy CPIC iff there is a rise in the level of real national income valued at final international prices; i.e.[62]

$$p_0 dx_0 + \sum_{i \in NT} p_i\, dx_i + \sum_{j \in T} p_j^* dx_j > 0. \qquad (4.9)$$

Proof (Necessary): Drawing on (3.24) above, applying the initial assumptions in proposition 4.4, the resulting equation is aggregated over all h individuals. The consumption taxes are, however, in the present case also applied to the traded goods in such a way that the changes in the tariff rates are offset exactly by changes in these consumption taxes; i.e.

$$-\sum_{j \in T}[\, c_j\, d\tau_j + c_j\, d\, t_j\,] = 0.$$

It follows that the condition sufficient to ensure that CPIC is always satisfied is the following:[63]

[62] In the case of the non-traded goods, their domestic producer prices are taken to represent relevant international prices.

[63] See the definition of dR^h in (3.23) above in the main text.

$$- \sum_{j \in T} \tau_j \, dx_j + dR^* + dY > 0 \tag{4.10}$$

where R* refers to revenue raised from imposing consumption taxes on traded and non-traded goods alone; i.e.

$$R^* := \sum_{i \in NT} t_i \, c_i + \sum_{j \in T} \tau_j c_j + \sum_{j \in T} t_j c_j . \tag{4.11}$$

(4.10) can be re-written as follows - on making use of the definitions of dY and $-\tau_j$, for all j, respectively:[64]

$$dR^* + \sum_{j \in T} [p_j^* \, dx_j - p_i \, dx_i] + \sum_{j \in T} p_i \, dx_i$$

$$+ \sum_{i \in NT} p_i \, dx_i + p_o dx_o ,$$

$$= dR^* + [\sum_{j \in T} p_j^* \, dx_j + \sum_{i \in NT} p_i \, dx_i + p_o dx_o] > 0.$$

Also it is noted that $- \sum_{j \in T} c_j \, [\, d\tau_j + d\, t_j \,] = 0$ by assumption; i.e. the consumption taxes and tariff offset one another. Thus by (A1) above it must be that:

$$dR^* := \frac{\partial R^*}{\partial Y^*} dY^* \geq 0, \tag{4.12}$$

if

64 See (3.11) and (3.15) above in the main text.

$$dY^* := [\sum_{j \in T} p_j^* \ dx_j + \sum_{i \in NT} p_i \ dx_i + p_o dx_o] > 0.$$

It follows that, on applying (A1), the statement in (4.9) above is necessary for CPIC to be satisfied.

The rest of the proof, to establish sufficiency, essentially follows the latter part of the proof provided for proposition 4.1 above where lump-sum income transfers are provided. Alternatively, if assumption W is applied, then the prices of relevant consumption taxes are altered by an appropriate small amount. ||

The result stated in this last proposition is similar to that to be found in Wong [1991, pp. 58 -59],[65] although there no mention was made of the assumption that taxed goods are normal in the sense defined in (A1) above. However, as the proof of the previous proposition makes clear, (A1) has to be applied if the required result is to be established. {The need to impose this assumption was hinted at in Wong [1991, p. 57, fn 11] where reference is made to the fact that difficulties arise in the relevant proof (provided by Wong) when, essentially, the sign condition stated in (4.12) above is not satisfied.} Nevertheless proposition 4.4 above tends to confirm, as Wong pointed out, the view expressed by Little and Mirrlees [1969] and Bhagwati and Hansen [1973] that changes in national income valued at final international or world prices, instead of final domestic prices, allow a

---

65 A related result is also to be found in Diewert, *et al.* [1989, proposition 4].

more accurate indication of the direction of change of compensated social welfare in an economy distorted by taxes on consumption.

It is also worth pointing out that the result set out in proposition 4.4 above is reasonably general in that it does not assume that aggregated factor supplies are fixed. Thus that proposition (implicitly) allows for the possibility that the level of employment may rise (or fall) over the relevant change in social states.

Continuing the general theme to be found in the previous proposition, a special case implied by that proposition is the following:

Proposition 4.5: The initial assumptions are the same as those stated in proposition 4.4 above. In addition (A1) is applied. In this instance an exogenous change in real national income will always satisfy CPIC iff the statement in (4.9) above is satisfied.

Proof: The proof is the same as that for proposition 4.4 above except that in the present case consumption taxes remain unaltered.||

This result is similar to proposition 3 in Wong [1991, p.58], although here the terms-of-trade are assumed fixed[66] and both tariffs and consumption taxes are imposed to raise government revenue - Wong only assumed that consumption taxes are

---

66 Relaxing this assumption is easily allowed for within the present model.

applied but did allow the terms-of-trade to vary.[67] Having said that, proposition 4.5 above indicates, as before, that real national income should be valued at world trade prices when the economy is distorted only by consumption taxes and tariffs.

To provide a point of comparison it can also be shown that changes in real national production, valued at domestic prices and adjusted for changes in net tax revenue, can also provide a satisfactory measure of changes in compensated social welfare. This point is demonstrated in the following proposition.

Proposition 4.6: Given the initial assumptions stated in proposition 4.4 above it follows that a small reform of the tariff system, offset in the consumption sector of the economy by changes in the consumption taxes, will always satisfy CPIC iff

$$[\, dR + dY \,] > 0 \qquad (4.13)$$

where

$$R := \sum_{i \in NT} t_i c_i + \sum_{j \in T} \tau_j [\, c_j - x_j \,]. \qquad (4.14)$$

Proof: Drawing on (3.24) above, applying the initial assumptions in proposition 4.4, aggregating the resulting equation over all h individuals, and noting that $- \sum_{j \in T} [\, c_j \, d\tau_j + c_j \, dt_j \,] = 0$, it is clear that the condition, sufficient to ensure that CPIC is always satisfied, is (4.13) above. The term, R, is defined in (4.14) above.

[67] A similar result is also to be found in Diewert *et al.* [1989, proposition 6].

As for that the part of the proof required to establish sufficiency, the relevant remarks made at the end of the proof for 4.4 above apply here as well. ||

This result does not make use of (A1) above. The reason for omitting this assumption is explained below, but for the present it is simply noted that if the additional assumption is imposed that aggregate factor supplies and the technology are fixed, then the term dY must take a value of zero. In these circumstances proposition 4.6 extends certain results to be found in Kemp and Negishi [1970], Ohyama [1972] and Eaton and Panagariya [1979] who indicated that, in a single-person community, a sufficient condition to satisfy CPIC is that the total amount of net revenue raised by applying tariffs and consumption taxes[68] does not fall ($dR \geq 0$) as a result of an increased level of trade resulting from a reform of the tariff system.

If the term dY does not take a value of zero, then the statement in (4.13) above indicates that the condition that

$dR\ [\ =(\partial R/\partial Y)] \geq 0$ is not necessary, to ensure that CPIC is satisfied, if the level of real national production, valued at domestic producer prices, increases as a result of the small reform of the tariff system. The condition that $dR \geq 0$ is also not sufficient (to ensure that CPIC is satisfied) if this tariff reform results in a decline in the level of real national production, valued at domes-

---

68 The references just cited in the main text only referred to tariffs, or consumption taxes, but not their combined influence on government revenue.

tic prices. [Such changes in the level of real national production could arise if the aggregate supply of factors of production are not fixed, but rather respond to changes in tariff rates.[69]] Although not expressed in these terms, a similar set of observations have been made by Lloyd and Schweinberger [1988, pp. 294 - 5].

As for reconciling proposition 4.4 with proposition 4.6 above, clearly either one implies the other for these propositions are based upon exactly the same reduced-form equation. Nevertheless, the former proposition is expressed in a more compact form.[70] This is made possible by applying the reasonable assumption stated in (A1). In contrast, a similar assumption was not be employed in proposition 4.5 above. The reason is that it does not seem reasonable to suppose that $[\partial R/\partial Y]$ will take a positive value for R is defined in terms of taxes on both con-

---

[69] Remember that $dY := \sum_f w_f \sum_i dF_{fi}$. If factors are not in fixed supply then the term, $\sum_i dF_{fi}$, may take a non-zero value in response to reforms of the tariff system. Also see the discussion after (3.9) in sub-section 3.2 above in the main text.

[70] It is noted in passing that in proposition 4.4, changes in total national production, valued at world prices (not domestic prices), are possible even if aggregate factor supplies and the technology are fixed. This can be seen by noting (as was essentially done in the proof of proposition 4.4 above [see (4.10) above in the main text]), that

$$dY^* = dY + \sum_{j \in T} \tau_j \, dx_j.$$

Thus even if $dY = 0$, the value of national income, valued at world prices, will rise if $\sum_{j \in T} \tau_j \, dx_j > 0$. This last inequality implies that there is a rise in the real value of production of traded goods valued at the end tariff rates.

sumption and production levels. [See (4.14) above.] Thus it is possible, in certain situations, that $[\partial R/\partial Y] < 0$. Consequently it also is possible, in the case of (4.13) above, that $\{ [\partial R/\partial Y] + 1 \} dY < 0$, even though $dY > 0$. It is for this reason that proposition 4.6 above is expressed in the form it is.

Results of the class discussed in this sub-section, where the provision of personal income compensation is explicitly financed by imposing consumption taxes, were first derived by Dixit and Norman [1980, 1986]. A criticism of this class of result, made by Kemp and Wan [1986], is that if there is no substitution on both the production and consumption sides of the economy, then at the margin additional revenue cannot be raised to finance compensating income transfers.[71] This possibility is implicitly ruled out by the assumptions employed in the propositions stated in this sub-section. [Specifically in the basic assumptions (BA) it was assumed that all relevant functions are differentiable to an adequate degree.]

---

[71] This would be the case because in, say, the condition (required to establish proposition 4.4 above in the main text):

$$\sum_h dv_h{}^* = dR^* + dY^*,$$

the term $dY^* = 0$ and $dR^* = 0$ – remembering that, by assumption, $-\sum_{j\in T}[\, c_j\, d\tau_j + c_j\, dt_j \,] = 0$.

4.4 Compensated Pareto Distortion Reform Where Additional Distortions are Present.

On consulting (3.24) above, in conjunction with the results presented in the previous sub-section, it becomes apparent that if there are distortions in the economy (in addition to consumption taxes and tariffs) then possibly the propositions stated in the previous section require modification. This is not, in fact, the case in the instance of propositions 4.4 and 4.5 above if the only additional distortion present in the economy is that variable scale economies are present.

4.4A Variable Scale Economies and Other Production Distortions.

This point is demonstrated by way of stating the following proposition:

Proposition 4.7: The assumptions are exactly the same as in proposition 4.4 above except that now there is an additional distortion present, namely, production takes place under conditions of variable scale economies. In these circumstances a small reform of the tariff system, offset by changes in the consumption taxes in the consumption sector of the economy, will always satisfy CPIC iff there is a rise in the level of real national income valued at final international prices; i.e. (4.9) above applies:

$$p_0 dx_0 + \sum_{i \in NT} p_i\, dx_i + \sum_{j \in T} p_j^{*} dx_j > 0.$$

<u>Proof</u>: The same argument is employed as that required to derive (4.10) above, except that now allowance has to be made for the presence of variable scale economies. This additional consideration requires that, in place of that equation, the following needs to appear:

$$- \sum_{j \in T} \tau_j \, dx_j + dR^* + dY + dS > 0, \qquad (4.15)$$

where the term dS is defined in (3.9) above. The statement, representing the production side of the economy, set out in (3.7) above, implies that terms can be found to substitute for the [dY + dS] term in the previous equation. On making the required substitutions, (4.15) can be re-written as follows:

$$dR^* + \sum_{j \in T} [p_j^* \, dx_j - p_i \, dx_i] + \sum_{j \in T} p_i \, dx_i$$

$$+ \sum_{i \in NT} p_i \, dx_i + p_o dx_o,$$

$$= dR^* + [\sum_{j \in T} p_j^* \, dx_j + \sum_{i \in NT} p_i \, dx_i + p_o dx_o] > 0.$$

On applying the assumption (A1), the rest of the argument is the same as that to be found in the proof for proposition 4.4 above.‖

The following can also be stated:

Proposition 4.8: The assumptions are the same as those stated in proposition 4.4 above except that now there is an additional distortion present; namely, production takes place under conditions of variable scale economies. In this instance an exogenous change in real national income will always satisfy CPIC iff the statement in (4.9) above is satisfied.

The proof for this proposition is virtually the same as that just provided for proposition 4.7 above.

As far as can be determined, the result stated in proposition 4.8 above is not to be found elsewhere in the relevant literature. Nonetheless, the comments made earlier with respect to proposition 4.5 above still applies; namely, the direction of change of national production, valued at final international prices, tends to provide a clearer indication of the direction of change of compensated social welfare than do national production, valued at domestic prices.

The result stated in proposition 4.7 is not completely new for it is similar to the main result to be found in Kemp and Schweinberger [1991, pp. 810 -811]. Certainly, the interpretation Kemp and Schweinberger [1991, pp. 811 - 813] place upon their result can equally be applied to proposition 4.7 above. So, for example, if the level of trade is controlled by varying quantitative restrictions, instead of tariff rates [i.e. $d\tau_j = 0$ for all $j \in T$], the community may still gain from allowing increasing levels of international trade. The reason is that even if the market prices facing consumers and producers do not vary, there may well be changes in the shadow prices facing domestic producers. These changes, in turn, may induce changes in the composition of the goods produced, and this new set of goods, when valued at the world set of prices, may be more highly valued by the community than the original mix of goods produced.

This point can be explained further by returning to the equation and identities representing the production side of the economy - i.e. (3.7) to (3.9) above. Assuming that the aggregate supply of each factor is fixed, then (3.7) above can be re-written as follows [after aggregating over all individuals and employing (3.9)]:

$$p_0 (1 - \varpi_0) dx_0 = \sum_{i=1}^{n} p_i (\varpi_i - 1) dx_i . \qquad (4.16)$$

Now even if the market prices facing domestic producers are fixed, as assumed above, the shadow prices facing these producers may well vary as the level of trade varies - a possibility which can be represented by the $[p_i \varpi_i]$ terms varying in size.[72]

---

72 The shadow price in production of any good i is defined as the marginal change caused to the level of social welfare [where the distributional weights for all h individuals have been set equal to one] resulting from the availability of an extra unit of this good - other things remaining the same. (This definition is based on, but not identical to, that to be found in Drèze and Stern [1990, p. 5].) Applying this definition to (3.24) above in the main text, it can be shown that $(\partial W/\partial x_i) = p_i \varpi_i + (\partial R/\partial x_i)$ for any i good. Hence changes in the $[p_i \varpi_i]$ terms can be taken to represent changes of the shadow prices in production.

Assuming that they do vary, and producers respond to these new shadow-price signals by producing a different combination of goods, this new set of goods may be more highly valued by the community than the original set of goods - both sets of goods being valued at the constant set of foreign prices.

This last-mentioned outcome is not certain, however. The new mix of goods produced may be assigned a value lower than that applying at the initial production position.

These observations indicate that when variable scale economies are present in the economy, determining the direction in which a distorted economic system should be reformed, such as to satisfy CPIC, may be difficult to calculate in practice. This is so, essentially because, as Kemp and Schweinberger [1991] have emphasised, in such an economy a number of production equilibria may exist where compensated social welfare is maximized locally. And these different local equilibria may not refer to the same level of social welfare. In these circumstances national governments may need to direct relevant economic reforms towards the preferred local social maximum - which may also be the global maximum.

These remarks allude to the public authorities being faced with a complex economic policy-implementation problem - a problem made complex by the almost certain fact that the detailed, relevant production information, is not available to guide public action. This class of problems is returned to in sub-section 12.3 in the next set of lectures.

4.4A(i)Another production distortion: Some additional alternative special cases could be considered by considering an appropriately expanded version of (4.15) above. These matters are not considered here however.[73] What is emphasised, however, is that while the discussion above is based upon the assumption that the production distortions take the particular form that there are variable scale economies present in the economy, this class of distortion may take alternative forms - and yet the results, presented in propositions 4.7 and 4.8 above, essentially are still valid. To demonstrate this point suppose that, besides variable scale economies being present in the economy, there are distortions in factor markets which cause the price for some factors of production to vary across industries - i.e. now $w_{fi} \neq w_{fj}$ for at least some factors of production, f, in the case of industries producing goods i and j respectively. In this case the result presented in the basic production relationship, set out in (3.7) above, still applies. However, the definition of dY^h, set out in (3.8) above now needs to be altered from

$$dY^h := \sum_{f=1}^{N} w_f \sum_{i=0}^{n} dF_{fi}^h, \text{ for all h,}$$

[73] Related relevant discussions of the case where variable economies of scale are present can be found be found in Kemp and Negishi [1970], Eaton and Panagariya [1979] and the references to be found in Kemp and Schweinberger [1991].

to the following

$$dY^h := \sum_{f=1}^{N} \sum_{i=0}^{n} w_{fi}\, dF^h_{fi}, \text{ for all } h. \qquad (3.8*)$$

This result implies that the argument employed to derive proposition 4.7 and 4.8 above requires no modification. The only modification that is required is that these propositions can be generalised by assuming that there are distortions in factor markets as well. In the case of proposition 4.7 above, for example, the following can be stated:

Proposition 4.7*: The assumptions are exactly the same as in proposition 4.4 above except that now there are additional distortions present; namely, production takes place under conditions of variable scale economies and there are distortions in factor markets (which take the form that $w_{fi} \neq w_{fj}$ for at least one factor of production, f, in at least the industries producing goods i and j respectively). In these circumstances a small reform of the tariff system, offset by changes in the consumption taxes, will always satisfy CPIC iff there is a rise in the level of real national income valued at final international prices; i.e.

$$p_0 dx_0 + \sum_{i \in NT} p_i\, dx_i + \sum_{j \in T} p^*_j dx_j > 0.$$

Proposition 4.8 above could be generalised in a similar fashion.

4.4B <u>Global Consumption Externalities and Missing Markets:</u> The main component in the previous argument that facilitated the derivation of positive results, even though production distortions were present in the economy, was the fact that there is a relatively simple relationship linking the terms representing the production distortions with the rest of the production constraint facing the economy. (This relationship is set out in (3.7) [along with (3.8) and (3.9)] above.) A similar correspondence applies when global consumption externalities are present[74] - that is if a rather special assumption is satisfied.

To demonstrate this assertion, to begin with, the case covered by proposition 4.4 above is extended by allowing for the presence of a global consumption externality in the economy. (This global externality may represent, for example, widespread environmental pollution so that $\lambda\, dg < 0$, where $\lambda < 0$ and $dg > 0$.[75]) In this case it can be shown, by drawing again on (3.24) above, that when the tariff and consumption tax system is reformed the result is the following:

$$dR^{*} + \left\{ \sum_h \lambda^h \left[\sum_i \frac{\partial g}{\partial t_i} dt_i + \sum_j \frac{\partial g}{\partial \tau_j} d\tau_j + \frac{\partial g}{\partial Y^h} dY^h \right] \right\}$$

---

[74] The case where there is a global externality on the production side of the economy has already been discussed in the context of the variable-economies-to-scale case. In that case the scale economies were the result of there being (by assumption) industry-wide production externalities. See the discussion in 3.2 above.

[75] It is explained in the next sub-section that global consumption externalities allude to a wide class of market failures including such matters as the adverse selection (hidden-knowledge) and moral hazard (hidden-action) problems.

$$+ \quad [\sum_{j \in T} p_j^* \, dx_j + \sum_{i \in NT} p_i \, dx_i + p_o dx_o], \qquad (4.17)$$

where λ^h represents that shadow price placed upon the global consumption externality by individual h. The term, g, represents the particular good which creates this consumption externality.[76] Should the set of terms in curled brackets in (4.17) above take a negative value then the reform of the tariff system may result in CPIC not being met. And this is so even if assumption 1 above is satisfied and national production, valued at final world prices, increases in size [i.e. the statement in (4.9) above applies].[77]

One possible solution to this difficulty is simply to impose the assumption that the term in curled brackets in (4.17) above takes a positive value. In this special case minor modifications to the assumptions employed in the last few propositions would still ensure that CPIC is satisfied.

Since this solution lacks generality it is not particularly appealing. An alternative solution lies with first recognising the fundamental source of the difficulty posed by (4.17) above; namely, that a complete and competitive market for the global externality is missing.[78] That this is so can be seen by assuming, to the contrary, that the market for this externality exists.

---

76 If required, the term, g, may also be taken to represent a vector of goods which create global consumption externalities.

77 A similar point has been made by Wong [1991, pp. 59 - 60] in a slightly less general context.

78 For discussions of the theory of missing markets see Newbery [1989] and Laffont [1988, ch 1].

In this case a price is charged to those who consume good, g. (This good, for example, may be the property right to pollute the environment.) But for this market to be complete (as well as exist) the initial owners of good g must also be compensated for transferring the ownership of at least some of this good. This is done by paying these initial owners the revenue generated by the charge imposed on those who use the good.[79] Finally, if this market is not only complete (in that compensation payments are provided), but is also competitive, then the price charged, p_g, on the marginal unit of the good consumed, would match the marginal social costs (represented by $\sum_h \lambda^h = \lambda$) created by utilising this good; i.e. $\lambda = p_g$ at the margin. This implies that in this assumed complete market, competition ensures that no price distortion is present at the margin.

In marked contrast to this assumed market equilibrium, in (4.17) above the situation is represented where the market for the global consumption externality, g, is simply missing. This fact is represented by the market producer price for this good, p_g, just not appearing in that equation; i.e. $p_g = 0$. Due to the absence of this market price, the terms in the curled brackets appear in (4.17) above.

---

[79] Clearly if this compensation is not paid then the initial owners of this good would have no incentive to transfer its ownership. Newbery [1989] has emphasised the need to pay compensation, as well as impose taxes, when attempting to control the level of externalities.

It follows that the most clearcut solution to the failure of the market system represented in (4.17) above is for the government essentially to create an implicit complete, and competitive, market for good g.[80] This is done by imposing the charge for the use of a unit of good g up to the point where $p_g = \lambda$ at the margin. In this implicit market p_g represents the tax-price paid to acquire access to the property right to create the global externality. To complete the market the revenue raised by imposing this charge should be employed to compensate individuals for the social costs (represented by λ^h in the case of individual h) incurred as a result of the unavoidable consumption of the externality created by the existence of good g. The payment of this compensation should be thought of as the price paid to the initial owners of the property right to create (or not to create) the global externality.[81]

The practical matter, of determining the appropriate level of compensating payments, immediately raises certain in-

---

80 An alternative possible solution, first discussed by Coase [1960], is that a private institution is created in which economic agents bargain over relevant property rights. In this case the owners of the property right to good g bargain with potential purchasers over the price of this good. If good g creates a global externality, however, there are bound to be practical difficulties associated with creating such a private market. In addition, in the case where negative externalities are created, there will tend to be production nonconvexities present. As a result the private market for this good may fail to exist. See Starrett [1972] and Laffont [1988, pp. 17 - 18] on this point.

81 The matter of production nonconvexities, mentioned in the previous footnote, does not arise as a problem when the government is providing the implicit market for the consumption externality. The reason is that the tax-price can always be set at a level which ensures that some pertinent local equilibrium is attained. See Laffont [1988, pp. 22] on this point.

centive-compatible problems which will be returned to below. For the present, however, it is simply assumed that the tax (subsidy) imposed on the global consumption externality is applied with marginal efficiency. This implies that (4.17) above (written in a simplified form) becomes the following:

$$dR^* + p_g dg + (\lambda - p_g) dg + [\sum_{j \in T} p_j^* dx_j$$

$$+ \sum_{i \in NT} p_i \; dx_i + p_o dx_o],$$

$$= dR^* + [p_g dg + \sum_{j \in T} p_j^* dx_j + \sum_{i \in NT} p_i \; dx_i + p_o dx_o] \quad (4.18)$$

when all markets are complete and competitive.

Thus (4.18) above confirms a point alluded to at the beginning of this sub-section - namely, if all markets are complete and competitive, and changes in national income are defined slightly differently [compared to that found in (4.9) above], then the analysis proceeds very much as discussed in sub-section 4.4A above. Having said that, this solution to the problem posed by the presence of global consumption externalities does assume that serious incentive-compatibility problems have been solved - an assumption that cannot be too seriously.

To explain this scepticism first it should be noted that if only partial, or no, compensation is paid to those experiencing the social costs created by the consumption externality, then the implicit market is not complete. This fact, in turn, creates the incentive for these individuals to seek, via political action, to have compensation paid to them, or have the property right to exploit good g withdrawn.[82] What is more, the lack of market completeness implies that CPIC may *not* be satisfied by the reform of the tax-tariff system. And this would be so even if the marginal efficiency condition is satisfied in (4.18) above [i.e. $(\lambda - p_g)\,dg = 0$]. Yet should the attempt be made to provide a personal compensating subsidy to all individuals adversely influenced by the production of the global externality (even if produced at an efficient level), any individual, h, clearly has the incentive to provide inaccurate personal information as to the size of the personal marginal cost (assuming that $\lambda^h < 0$) incurred by increases in the level of good g. In other words, essentially the same incentive-compatible problem, discussed in sub-section 4.1 above, arises in the present case.

These comments imply that a solution to the particular version of the incentive-compatibility problem of concern here may be found by first assuming that Assumption W above is satisfied. That being the case, in the process of reforming the tariff-tax system the consumption taxes need to be altered in a differential manner. By so doing, this will contribute towards completing the market for the global consumption externality by

---

82 See Newbery [1989, pp. 316 - 317] on this point.

providing compensation to those adversely affected by this externality.

But even if this compensation is provided, the previous remarks also indicate that, because of the considerable demands made on relevant personal information, it is quite possible that any implicit market created for the consumption externality will not satisfy the marginal efficiency condition referred to above. To cover this reasonable possibility, the following is assumed:

<u>Assumption 2 (A2):</u> An implicit market exists and is complete (but may not be competitive) for the good which creates a global consumption externality. The price charged in this market, and the non-lump-sum taxes applied elsewhere in the economy, are altered such that:

$$(\lambda - p_g)\, dg \geq 0.$$

This assumption allows for the possibility that if $(\lambda - p_g) < 0$ (> 0) then

$$dg = \frac{\partial g}{\partial p_g} dp_g + \sum_i \frac{\partial g}{\partial t_i} dt_i \leq 0 \ (\geq 0).$$

This line of argument could naturally be generalised to allow for the presence of many goods which create global, or local, consumption externalities. This is not done here, however. Instead the following is stated:

Proposition 4.9: Initial Assumptions: Given (BA) [upon which (3.24) above is based] it is also supposed that the following distortions are present in the economy: (i) production takes place under conditions of variable scale economies; (ii) there are distortions in factor markets (which take the form that $w_{fi} \neq w_{fj}$ for at least some factors of production, f, in at least the industries producing goods i and j respectively); (iii) a global consumption externality exists; (iv) non-prohibitive tariffs and consumption taxes are in place. Taxes on consumption are employed to finance compensating income transfers and, if required, the production of a good which creates a positive global consumption externality. Incentive-compatible income transfer systems are employed to distribute this compensation. Additional Assumptions: (A1) and (A2) are satisfied. It follows that a small reform of the tariff system, offset by changes in the consumption taxes in the consumption sector of the economy, will always satisfy CPIC iff there is a rise in the level of real national income valued at final international prices so that

$$[\sum_{j\in T} p_j^* \, dx_j + \sum_{i\in NT} p_i \, dx_i + p_o dx_o + p_g \, dg] > 0.$$

Similarly a more general version of proposition 4.5 above can be stated:

Proposition 4.10: The assumptions are the same as those stated in proposition 4.9 above. However, in this instance the tariffs are fixed in size but there is an exogenous change in real national income. It follows that CPIC is satisfied iff there is a rise in the level of real national income valued at final international prices.

The measure of changes in national income, measured in terms of final world prices, on this occasion must include the term $p_g dg$. [See the derivation of (4.18) above.]

These last two propositions, while comparatively general, are based upon the relatively strong assumption 2 above - an assumption which imposes considerable demands on being able to obtain personal information. Nevertheless, the inclusion of that assumption serves the purpose of reminding one that when the markets for consumption externalities in the economy are incomplete, or not completely competitive (and this is quite likely to be the case in reality), then some care needs to be taken when assessing if taxation reform, or/and exogenous increase in real national income, have indeed raised the level of social welfare - and this is so even if suitable compensation income transfers have been provided. This point takes on added importance when it is realised that the basic economic problem, associated with global consumption externalities, alludes to a wide class of failures in the market system. This matter, amongst others, is discussed in the next sub-section.

4.4C Concluding Comments: To conclude this sub-section, it is noted that the assumption 1 [i.e. $(\partial R/\partial Y) > 0$], imposed in propositions 4.4 through to 4.9 above, implies that there is always enough government revenue available to finance additional compensating income, or implicit income, transfers - no matter from what relevant initial position the economy moves from. Thus the propositions just referred to can be generalised, via integrating pertinent functions, to consider large changes in social states.

Nevertheless, some caution needs to be shown when assessing such changes in economic states in situations where comparatively complex compensation systems may need to be provided. This is particularly so in situations where adequate information is probably not available. For example, it still needs to be determined if *all* individuals in the community have not experienced an economic loss from this large change in economic states. The personal information required to determine if this is indeed the case (even if this information is not required to determine the level of personal compensation to be provided) almost certainly will not be available. This point will be returned to in section 5.1 below.

What is more, one should also be cognizant of a point made at the end of sub-section 4.2 above; namely, that when the level of compensating lump-sum income transfers loom large in the government budget, limits may be imposed by the authorities on the amount of compensating income transfers provided. If this is in fact the case, this may well prevent the implementation of relatively large reforms of a distorted economic system - such as moving an economy from a situation where international trade is severely limited to one of complete free trade - which also satisfy CPIC.

4.5 Taxation Reform Directed at Partially Offsetting Markets Which Are *Not* Complete and Competitive.

4.5A The General Structure of a Solution: The previous two sub-sections were mainly concerned with broad reforms of the taxation system in an economy distorted in various ways. The direction of reform can take alternative routes, however. For example, instead it may be directed at first reducing the size of the social costs associated with the presence of particular economic distortions in the economy, while the taxation system is employed to provide additional revenue, if required, to finance these reforms. This matter will be briefly dealt with here by considering in more detail the topic touched upon in sub-section 4.4B above; namely, the distortions created by the absence of complete and/or competitive markets for goods which create global consumption externalities. As indicated below, a considerable literature has explicitly, or implicitly, dealt with this general topic - although not quite in the same way as it is discussed here. This point will be explained below.

Consider the case where the market for the public good (bad), g, is not complete and competitive. In this case the subsidy (tax) on good g is altered in the attempt to ensure that CPIC is satisfied. If the shadow price on good g takes a positive value then a subsidy would need to be applied to encourage the production of this good. But to finance this subsidy a set of non-lump taxes will also need to be applied. Alternatively, if this shadow price takes a negative value, then a tax-price will need to be applied to good g (assuming this good to be a normal good). But even in this instance additional revenue probably will also need to be raised to finance the compensating income transfers required to ensure that CPIC is satisfied.[83] Thus, in this case, non-lump-sum taxes will probably still need to be applied in the attempt to curb the production of the public bad.

This set of observations is applied to (3.24) above. It is also assumed, for the sake of simplicity, that there are no distortions on the production side of the economy and the economy is closed. In these special circumstances CPIC is satisfied if, and only if:

$$\frac{dv^h}{v^h} = [\lambda^h - p_g^h]\left[\frac{\partial g}{\partial p_g} + \sum_i \frac{\partial g}{\partial t_i} dt_i\right]$$

$$-\sum_i \left[c_i^h \, dt_i - \frac{\partial R^h}{\partial t_i} dt_i\right] + \frac{\partial R^h}{\partial p_g} dp_g$$

$$+\sum_i \frac{\partial Y^h(g)}{\partial t_i} dt_i + \frac{\partial Y^h(g)}{\partial p_g} dp_g \geq 0, \qquad \text{for h individuals} \quad (4.19)$$

83 See the relevant part of the discussion in sub-section 4.4B above.

where

$$[\lambda^h - p_g^h] \neq 0 \qquad \text{for at least some individuals,}$$

and (4.19) takes a positive value for at least one individual in the community. In addition, the term $dY^h(g)^*$ is defined as follows [drawing on (3.7) above]:

$$dY^h(g) := p_0 dx_0^h + \sum_{i=1}^{n} p_i\, dx_i^h + p_g^h dg.$$

This last result implies that, much as before, a good deal of information needs to be acquired before it can be determined if changes in the tax (transfer) system, aimed at altering the level of supply of public goods (bads), have satisfied CPIC. One reason why this is so is because potentially there are numerous cross-substitution effects between relevant groups of variables - which will be so even if some of the terms in (4.19) above take a value of zero. [For example, the supply of a public good may be completely under the control of the government (eg. national defence and security) . In this case the term $(\partial g/\partial t_i)$ takes a value of zero for all i (= 1 to n) goods. [84]] In certain circumstances, therefore, it will be comparatively difficult to determine if CPIC

---

84 The supply of the good, creating the global consumption externality, need not always be under the direct control of the government, however. For example, in the case of environmental pollution, altering the level of the taxes imposed on petrol and motor vehicles, in the process of raising government revenue, will certainly tend to have the (perhaps unintended) consequence of also altering the level of production of atmospheric pollutants.

has been satisfied as the community attempts to move towards the social optimum (by altering the level of supply of goods producing consumption externalities in distorted economies). This is especially so as the community moves closer to the social optimum, and the exact size of the terms set out in (4.19) above become more important in determining the sign of that equation. On the other hand, should the community initially be well away from the social optimum, the sign of (4.19) above will be self-evident - especially after appropriate compensating transfers have been provided.

The result in (4.19) above also allows the analysis of a problem first posed by Pigou [1947]; namely, the influence of the presence of non-lump sum taxes on the level of supply of public goods. This particular problem subsequently has been analysed by a number of authors, the relevant literature having been surveyed and extended in various ways by, for example, Atkinson and Stiglitz [1980], King [1986], Starrett [1988], Tuomala [1990, p. 176 ff] and Wilson [1991]. These matters will not be considered in any detail here, however. [85,86] Rather a number of general ob-

---

[85] The particular case considered by Wilson [1991], for example, is that where the authorities, at the margin, are able to raise a small amount of additional revenue by employing restricted lump-sum taxes. In this case all the terms with dt_i attached to them can be omitted from (4.19) above in the main text. It is now possible, with the aid of the resulting equation, to analyse the particular problem considered by Wilson. This matter is left to the interested reader to consider.

[86] The particular assumption, employed by Wilson [1991], will be briefly commented upon towards the end of section 12 - to be found in the second set of lectures.

servations will be made in the context of that literature and the result stated in (4.19) above.

First, the main results presented in that literature essentially draws upon a version of (3.25) above - not (3.24) above - where the cross-compensated substitution and income effects are explicitly identified.[87] The result presented in (4.19) above, however, helps to simplify any pertinent analysis by only considering the relevant consequences, flowing from these various price and income effects, for the levels of government revenue and personal incomes. Second, (4.19) above is not concerned with the properties of the social optimum (which is the sole concern in the literature just cited), but covers the more general problem where the community attempts to move from a non-optimum initial position towards the social optimum by altering the supply of the good(s) (bads) creating the global consumption externalities. In the process non-lump sum taxes (subsidies) are altered in size as required to ensure that CPIC is satisfied. This line of enquiry could be extended further by allowing for the presence of various distortions on the production side of an open economy. But, as indicated in sub-section 4.4A above, these complications are relatively easily dealt with when a suitable measure of changes in production levels is employed in the analysis.

The final, and most important, observation that is made with respect to (4.19) above is that that equation in fact alludes

---

[87] In this instance the Slutsky equation is applied in (3.25). Also see, for example, King [1986] where these cross-price and income effects are discussed in some detail.

to a wide class of problems which are not just concerned with the matter of the increased provision of public goods (or reduction in the level of public bads). Rather that equation is concerned with more general information problems which are reflected in markets which are incompletely competitive, or just missing. So, for example, that equation (or versions thereof) could also be employed to analyse situations where markets are incomplete due to the presence of moral hazard and adverse selection. These matters will be turned to next.

4.5B The Moral-Hazard (Hidden-Action) Problem: The moral hazard - or hidden-action[88] - problem arises where individuals, as a result of purchasing insurance against some uncertain future event, take less care to prevent this event occurring (compared to a situation where this insurance is not available). If insurers cannot observe this change in behaviour (in other words, this behaviour is hidden from the insurer), and it is widespread in the community, then the increased incidence of the event insured against actually occurring would result in an rise in the marginal costs of providing this insurance. To ensure economic survival in a competitive insurance market, the profit-maximizing insurer will therefore need to raise the insurance premium charged for this insurance. (This point will be explained further below)

This change in the premium charged for this insurance would not create externality effects if the markets for all goods

88 The term 'hidden action problem' is taken from Arrow [1986].

were complete and competitive, there were no distortions present in the economy and personal income distributive effects (resulting from this price change) could be offset by applying lump-sum taxes and transfers. But this will not be the outcome if the moral hazard (or hidden action) problem is present in a distorted market system and only non-lump-sum taxes (subsidies) are in place and available for use. Indeed in these circumstances there are at least three channels along which changes in the price of insurance may influence individual utility levels.[89]

This point can be demonstrated by first setting out a relevant revised version of (4.19) above; namely,

$$\frac{dv^h}{v_y^h} = \left[\lambda(MH) \frac{\partial g^h}{\partial p_g} + \frac{\partial R^h}{\partial p_g} + \frac{\partial Y^h(g)}{\partial p_g} \right] dp_g,$$

for h individuals, (4.20)

where dp_g (> 0) represents the increase in the price of insurance resulting from increased levels of moral hazard behaviour. The second term in square brackets on the right-hand side (4.20) above refers to that change in the amount of government revenue (raised from individual h due to the imposition of consumption taxes) resulting from the increase in the price of insurance. The third term in square brackets in that equation refers to the altered level of individual real income resulting from the insurance price increase. As for the inclusion for the first term in

---

[89] These matters are also discussed in Arnott and Stiglitz [1990].

square brackets in (4.20), that term represents the direct cost, to individual h, of a marginal increase in the amount of moral hazard behaviour.

To explain this last point, first it is assumed that as more insurance is provided by an insurance firm, the total cost of insurance claims made against this firm, and which are the direct result of unobservable (or hidden) moral hazard behaviour, will tend to rise. (This assumption is based upon the more fundamental assumption that the greater the number of insurance contracts entered into by this insurance firm the more costly it will be for this firm to monitor the relevant behaviour of those insured.) In this case the profit (π) earned by this firm can be represented as follows:

$$\pi = p_g\, g - TNC(g) - MHC(g),$$

where TNC refers to the total normal costs associated with providing insurance, while MHC denotes the total cost of the insurance claims, brought against the insuring firm, which are the result of unobservable moral hazard behaviour.

Assuming that this firm has no direct influence over the price charged for insurance, this profit-maximizing firm will set the producer price of insurance (insurance premium) at the equilibrium level where

$$p_g = \frac{\partial TNC(g)}{\partial g} + \frac{\partial MHC(g)}{\partial g} = MNC + \lambda(MH) > 0, \qquad (4.21)$$

where, by assumption, $\lambda(MH) > 0$.

The term MNC denotes the marginal normal cost of providing insurance. The term $\lambda(MH)$ (>0), on the other hand, reflects the assumption, stated earlier, that as the insurer enters into more insurance contracts, this firm finds it increasingly difficult to monitor the hidden, careless, behaviour of those it has insured. Consequently the marginal, 'moral-hazard', costs of insurance take a positive value. The statement in (4.21) above also indicates that the more severe this latter problem, the higher is the producer price that needs to be charged for this insurance by profit-maximizing insurance firms - that is if they are to survive in a competitive insurance market.

As for the price that all consumers now have to pay for additional units of insurance, at the market equilibrium, it is equal to the profit-maximizing producer price; i.e. [90]

$$q_g = p_g = MNC + \lambda(MH).$$

This actual situation next needs to be compared with the ideal market circumstances where the market for relevant infor-

---

[90] The statement stated in (4.21) above in the main text implies the possibility that if the moral hazard problem is severe enough the price, at which the private insurance firm incurs no losses, is only that where no insurance would be demanded. (Such a situation seems to apply, for example, in the instance of agricultural crop insurance and income insurance.) Where the market does exist, this market may be unstable since small changes in behaviour may induce sharp changes in the price of insurance. What is more, this insurance industry may need to be uncompetitive for it to exist at all. These issues are discussed in detail in Arnott and Stiglitz [1988], Rees [1989, pp. 70 - 77], Newbery [1990,] and Eisen [1990].

mation, relating to potential moral hazard (or hidden) behaviour, is complete and competitive. In this ideal world adequate penalties will be imposed on individuals attempting to practise moral hazard behaviour. Hence this behaviour would be non-existent. As a result $p_g(f) = MNC$, where $p_g(f)$ refers to the producer price of insurance where full information is available concerning all relevant individual behaviour.

On combining this last set of observations it follows that

$$q_g - p_g(f) = \lambda(MH),$$

where $\lambda(MH)$ is exactly the term which appears on the right-hand side of (4.20) above. This term, in turn, essentially represents the marginal cost to any individual, h, resulting from the community not possessing a complete and competitive market for information relating to hidden moral hazard behaviour. [The absence of this market could also be interpreted as having the same consequences for individual welfare as a special consumption tax being imposed on the good g - although in this instance all markets are complete and competitive.]

A benefit to be derived from this line of argument is that it clearly indicates that even if this particular information market is incomplete, or just missing, it may still be possible for compensated Pareto improvements to take place as a consequence of the implementation of appropriate public action.[91] The public authorities may, for example, facilitate the collection of relevant information, or subsidise the consumption of goods which encourage individuals to take greater care to prevent accidents occurring. So, for example, the public legal system may be empowered to assist private insurance companies investigate suspected cases of arson and fraud. In addition the price of anti-theft devices, and fire prevention equipment, may be subsidised out of general government revenue.[92]

{ It should also be noted, in passing, that this type of public action may still be warranted even though profit-maximizing private insurers have taken action in the attempt to offset the moral hazard problem - such as introducing a system of co-payments into insurance contracts. The essential reason why this so is that this private action would not completely offset the particular public economic problem posed by the absence of the relevant market for information.[93] This point has been emphasised by Greenwald and Stiglitz [1986] and Arnott and Stiglitz [1990].}

But whether such action will ensure that CPIC is satisfied would need to take account of a wide range of pertinent con-

---

91 This point has been emphasised by Greenwald and Stiglitz [1986, pp. 245 -247] and Arnott and Stiglitz [1986, 1990].

92 Since evidence of moral hazard behaviour is to be found in various insurance markets, a number of particular additional examples could be provided. Some of these examples are discussed, for example, in Arnott and Stiglitz [1986, pp.13 - 16].

93 This point is clearly indicated by the relevant analysis to be found in Rees [1989, p.71 ff].

siderations - and which are alluded to in (4.19) above.[94] And matters could be made more complicated than indicated there by allowing for the presence of various types of insurance and cross-insurance effects.[95] Nevertheless, if assumptions of an appropriately general form are satisfied, then government intervention will ensure that CPIC is satisfied when attempts are made to offset the moral hazard (or hidden action) problem.

4.5C The Adverse-Selection (Hidden-Knowledge) Problem: The problem, posed by adverse selection (or hidden knowledge) [96], is also associated with the lack of a market for relevant information. Specifically, pertinent knowledge, known to the insured prior to entering into, and during the term of, an insurance contract, is *not* available to the insurer. Again, in this instance, essentially a global consumption externality is created by the absence of a complete and competitive market for relevant information.

To explain this point attention returns to (4.19) above were the term $\lambda^h(g)$ is now assumed to represent, by way of example, the price individual h would be prepared to pay, at the

---

[94] Greenwald and Stiglitz [1986, p. 236] derive an equation similar to (3.25) above in the main text. They do not, however, deal in much detail with the matter of how various appropriate forms of government action are to be financed, and how compensating income transfers are to be provided - although they emphasise that lump-sum transfers are not feasible. They also state explicitly that the matter of compensating transfers is to be ignored in their discussion. See Greenwald and Stiglitz [1986, p. 241 and fn. 16].

[95] These complicated matters are discussed in Arnott and Stiglitz [1990].

[96] The term 'hidden-knowledge problem' was first coined by Arrow [1986].

margin, for health insurance (g).[97] This price is assumed to reflect the risk that this individual may need to seek a certain level of medical services within a given future period. However, this personal information is only known to individual h, and not the insurer - in other words, this information is hidden from the insurer. Due to this lack of detailed personal information, the insurer sets a uniform insurance premium, $\bar{p}_g$, based on the risks associated with providing insurance to some average individual. A consequence is that individuals with a relatively low risk of requiring future medical services [i.e. those for which [$(\lambda^h(g) - \bar{p}_g) < 0$] will tend to leave this insurance market, while high risk individuals [i.e. those for which [$(\lambda^h(g) - \bar{p}_g) > 0$] will tend to enter this market and seek additional insurance. In these circumstances, where the insurer tends to insure only relatively high risk individuals, this market will tend to be unstable and may, as result, not exist - or if it exists, is not competitive.

This particular outcome may also be thought of as the result of the hidden knowledge problem.[98] Flowing on from this implied absence of a market for relevant information, which is both complete and competitive, is the creation of a consumption externality. This externality, in turn, is reflected in the fact

97 The argument being developed in the main text could equally apply, say, to the unemployment insurance market.

98 This term was first coined by Arrow [1986].

that the price for insurance is set at $\bar{p}_g \neq \lambda^h(g)$ for at least some h individuals - instead of being at the market equilibrium where $p_g^h = \lambda^h(g)$ for all individuals - in the community.

Again in this instance compensated Pareto-improving public action is possible. For example, compulsory health and unemployment insurance systems, financed out of general public revenue raised by imposing non-lump-sum taxes, could be imposed.[99] The unit cost of providing either of these insurance systems could be represented by the term $\bar{p}_g$. On applying these assumptions to (4.19) above it is clear that the algebraic symbols, representing this adverse selection case, is, in all relevant respects, essentially the same as that for the Pareto-improving provision of public goods - the case represented in (4.19) above.

But whether such compulsory insurance systems, aimed at avoiding the social costs created by averse selection, will satisfy CPIC will naturally depend on the particular circumstances which apply. Certainly there are no apparent a priori reasons why such compulsory insurance systems should not satisfy CPIC - especially if carefully implemented. And even if they do not satisfy this criterion, it may be argued that these compulsory insurance systems should still be employed for they satisfy more important social values - such as equity considerations -

---

[99] Alternative, private market solutions, to the adverse selection problem as discussed in Rees [1989].

than those implied by the compensated Pareto-improvement criterion. This general class of argument becomes pertinent in section 5 below.

4.5D Concluding Comments: The discussion in this sub-section has attempted to demonstrate that the general information problems, created by the presence of global consumption externalities, in fact allude to a wide class of market failures where the market of pertinent information is absent. What is more, in the instance of each one of the cases discussed above, it is not difficult to think of ways in which public action might be formulated, and implemented, such as to improve the operation of the market system - and also ensure that CPIC is satisfied. Having said that, the qualification should be added that there appear to be major practical difficulties [as indicated by (4.19) above] associated with determining if the community has, in fact, satisfied CPIC as a result of some pertinent economic reform.

4.6 Sufficient Conditions to Ensure Pareto Improvement.

The results presented in the previous sub-sections provided only limited guidance as to how tax rates should be altered to ensure that Pareto improvements take place. Providing more detail in this regard implies, however, a reduction in the level of generality attainable for now only sufficient conditions, required to ensure that CPIC is satisfied, can be determined. This point will become apparent below. The present discussion will also indicate that results, which apply to the case where there is just a single individual in the community, do not simply carry over to the many-person case. The main reason why this is so is that whereas there are income distributional issues that need to be allowed for in the many-person case, this complicating matter just does not arise in the single-person case. It will also be indicated below that the results which emerge are also dependent on the classes of taxes/transfers which are available for use by the public authorities.

4.6A The single-person case with changes in the level of consumption taxes offset by lump-sum taxes.

To begin with a simple case will be considered; namely, there is just a single individual in the community, only consumption taxes are imposed in a closed, competitive, economy which are reduced in size while lump-sum taxes are available for use and are partially substituted for the consumption taxes such as to keep the level of government revenue constant (i.e. $dR = 0$). In addition, aggregate factor supplies are fixed ($dY = 0$), there are no variable scale economies present and any consumption externalities are fixed in size. [100] In this case (3.24) and (3.25) above respectively reduces to the following (remembering that there is just a single person in the community):

$$\frac{dv}{v_y} = -\sum_j c_j \, dt_j \ , \qquad (4.22)$$

[100] A similar list of assumptions is employed, for example, by Auerbach [1985] - although he also assumed that producer prices are fixed.

and

$$\frac{dv}{v_y} = \sum_j \sum_i t_i \frac{\partial c_i}{\partial t_j} dt_j$$

$$= \sum_j \sum_i t_i s_{ij} dt_j - \sum_i t_i \frac{\partial c_i}{\partial y} \sum_j c_j dt_j, \qquad (4.23)$$

where use has been made of the Slutsky equation in deriving (4.23) and s_{ij} refers to the compensated substitution terms between goods i and j. Making use of (4.22) in (4.23) results in the latter equation becoming

$$\frac{dv}{v_y} = \frac{\sum_j \sum_i t_i s_{ij} dt_j}{r}, \quad \text{where } r := \sum_{i=0}^{n} p_i \frac{\partial c_i}{\partial y}. \qquad (4.24)$$

The definition of r is found by noting that, for all i (=1 to n) goods, $t_i := (q_i - p_i)$, $t_o = (p_o - q_o) = 0$, and making use of Engels aggregation - i.e. $\sum_{i=0}^{n} q_i \ (\partial c_i / \partial y) = 1$,

where $y := \sum_{i=0}^{n} q_i \ c_i$.[101]

---

[101] This definition of y is implicitly employed in the budget condition set out in (3.19) above.

The result presented in (4.24) above indicates that given that

$$\sum_j \sum_i t_i s_{ij} dt_j \neq 0, \qquad (4.25)$$

and that $r > 0$ (< 0), then setting $dt_i = t_i d\alpha$ for all i goods, where $d\alpha$ takes a negative (positive) value, will ensure that an improvement in social welfare takes place.[102,103] [This is so since the assumed quasi-concavity of the indirect utility function ensures that the quadratic form, $\sum_j \sum_i t_i s_{ij} t_j$, is negative semi-definite. The assumption in (4.25) above ensures that this quadratic is negative definite.] It follows that in this rather special case a proportionate (or radial) reduction (increase if $r < 0$) of the consumption taxes is sufficient to ensure an increase in the level of social welfare. This result is to be found in Dixit [1975], Hatta [1977a], Auerbach [1985] and Turunen-Red [1991].

102 In this case the condition that $r \neq 0$ is not required to ensure the existence of a welfare-improving consumption tax change. This point was first noted by Turunen-Red [1991, p. 258],

103 The condition that $r \neq 0$ is called the Hatta condition by Turunen-Red [1991] since this condition is discussed in a little detail in papers by Hatta [1977a, 1977b]. However, the use of this condition is is to be found in articles which pre-date the Hatta papers. See, for example, Lloyd [1974].

4.6B <u>The many-person case with changes in the level of consumption taxes offset by lump-sum taxes.</u>

Turning to the case where there are many individuals in the community, but maintaining all the other assumptions listed above, again (3.24) and (3.25) above can be exploited to give:

$$\frac{dv^h}{v_y^h} = -\sum_i c_i^h \, dt_i + dY^h, \quad \text{for all } h, \qquad (4.26)$$

and

$$\frac{dv^h}{v_y^h} = \sum_j \sum_i t_i s_{ij}^h \, dt_j + \sum_i t_i \frac{\partial c_i^h}{\partial Y^h} \left[-\sum_j c_j^h \, dt_j + dY^h \right]$$

$$+ \, dY^h, \quad \text{for all } h, \qquad (4.27)$$

where

$$dY^h = \sum_j \frac{\partial Y^h}{\partial t_j} dt_j + \frac{\partial Y^h}{\partial b^h} db^h, \quad \text{for all } h. \qquad (4.28)$$

In the process of deriving these results it has been noted that, since personal lump-sum taxes are available to be applied to each individual, these lump-sum taxes (subsidies) are altered such as to ensure that $dR^h = 0$ for all h individuals when the consumption taxes are altered in size.

The main difference between these last sets of results and those presented in (4.22) and (4.23) above is that whereas in those former equations it was reasonable to assume that aggregate factor supplies are fixed, in the case of (4.26) and (4.27) respectively above allowance has to be made for the reasonable possibility that the allocation of factor supplies, required to satisfy the demand for goods by any individual, h, may well need to alter as price changes. This implies that allowance must be made for the possible variation of the distribution of total real income in the community as consumption taxes are altered in size.

Making use of (4.26) in (4.27), the manipulation of the resulting equation follows a similar path to that employed to derive (4.24) above. The end result is the following:

$$\frac{dv^h}{v_y^h} = \frac{\sum_j \sum_i t_i s_{ij}^h dt_j}{r^h} + \frac{dY^h}{r^h}, \tag{4.29}$$

where $r^h := \sum_{i=1}^{n} p_i \ (\partial c_i^h / \partial Y^h)$ for all h.

The first point to note in the context of (4.29) above is that even if all compensated substitution terms take a value of zero for all h individuals [i.e. an extension of the condition stated in (4.25) above is not satisfied], there is still room for Pareto-improving tax-transfer reforms if the pertinent changes work through income effects. To ensure that this is possible at least some of the r^h terms need to take non-zero values. Thus in this case the condition that $r^h \neq 0$ for at least some h individuals is necessary for the existence of a Pareto-improving tax-cum-transfer reform. This point was first demonstrated by Turunen-Red [1991, p. 259].

The next observation is that, since aggregate factor supplies are assumed to be fixed (so that $\sum_h dY^h = 0$) this implies that the income effects just referred to must be offsetting across individuals. This observation implies that Pareto-improving changes in the tax-cum-lump-sum-transfer system are possible in these circumstances if and only if the r^h terms do not take the same sign for all h individuals. Finally, given that this is the case, Pareto-improving alterations to the tax-cum-transfer system are possible by leaving the consumption taxes unaltered and altering the distribution of the lump-sum income transfers in the required direction. Again this point was first discussed by Turunen-Red [1991, p. 259].

Finally, and perhaps most important of all, the result set out in (4.29) above indicates that, unlike in the single-person case, a simple radial reduction of the consumption tax rates will not be sufficient to ensure a Pareto improvement.[104] In the present case such a reduction of the commodity tax rates will only

104 This point was not made by Turunen-Red [1991].

be sufficient to ensure that the first term on the right-hand side of (4.29) above takes a positive value - that is given that $r^h > 0$ for all h individuals. But there is still the influence of this tax change, on the distribution of income within the community, to be taken into account. This matter is alluded to in the second term on the right-hand side of (4.29) above.

An additional assumption, sufficient to ensure that a radial reduction of consumption tax rates results in CPIC being satisfied, is the following [after drawing on (4.28) and (4.29) above]:

$$\left[\frac{dY^h}{r^h}\right] = \frac{\sum_j \frac{\partial Y^h}{\partial t_j} dt_j + \frac{\partial Y^h}{\partial b^h} db^h}{r^h} \geq 0, \quad \text{for all h.}$$

While this assumption is stronger than is required, nevertheless it serves to emphasise that it is not a foregone conclusion that a simple tax-reform rule - such as that all consumption taxes should be reduced simultaneously by the same small proportionate amount - will definitely result in CPIC being satisfied.

4.6C <u>The many-person case with changes in the level of tariffs offset by consumption taxes</u>: The unsatisfactory assumption employed in the previous sub-sections - that personal lump-sum taxes (subsidies) are available to offset the alteration in the level of consumption taxes - is now replaced with the more realistic assumption that changes in the level one set of non-lump-sum taxes are matched by changes in another set of non-lump-sum taxes. More specifically it is assumed, as in the previous sub-section, that the economy is open to international trade, is small and that tariffs and consumption taxes are in place. The tariffs are now varied in size, but in a restricted fashion - above all, these tariffs cannot be altered in a differential manner. In these restricted circumstances the consumption taxes are altered in such a way as to provide the required compensation necessary to ensure that CPIC is satisfied.

The restrictive nature of the way in which tariff rates may be altered is reflected in the following assumption (which will be exploited below):[105]

Assumption 3 (A3):

$$\left[\sum_{j \in T} \frac{\partial Y(g)^*}{\partial \tau_i} a_j\right] d\alpha > 0, \qquad \text{where}$$

$$d\tau_j = a_j \, d\alpha, \text{ for all } j \in T, \text{ and } d\alpha < 0, \qquad (4.30)$$

and where

$$dY(g)^* := p_0 dx_0 + \sum_{i \in NT} p_i \, dx_i + \sum_{j \in T} p_j^* dx_j + p_g \, dg > 0. \quad (4.31)$$

105 The line of argument in the main text is following that to be found in Diewert *et al.* [1989, pp. 210 -211].

The term in (4.31), representing the change in real national product valued at final international prices, includes the value of the supply of the good(s) which creates (create) the global consumption externality. It also noted that since tariffs can only be altered according to the conditions set out in (4.30) above, this implies that an assumption, stronger than assumption W above, may need to be applied if CPIC is to be satisfied. Hence the following is assumed:

Assumption W*: If there is an exogenous increase in national production valued at final international prices, such that $dY(g)^* > 0$, then consumption taxes can be altered to ensure that

$$-\sum_{j\in T} c_j^h \, dt_j - \sum_{i\in NT} c_i^h \, dt_i + dR^{h*} + dY^h(g)^* > 0,$$

for all h individuals.

The term, R*, defined in (4.11) above, refers to the tax revenue derived from applying taxes on the consumption of traded and non-traded goods alone.

The following proposition can now be stated - a proposition which also allows for the possible (probable) presence of variable scale economies and incomplete, or missing, consumption markets in the economy:

Proposition 4.11: Given (BA) upon which (3.24) above, it also assumed that non-prohibitive tariffs, consumption taxes and variable economies of scale are present in the economy. (A2) is also satisfied if global consumption externalities exist. Taxes on consumption satisfy assumption W*, while (A3) is satisfied when tariff rates are altered in size by a small amount. In these circumstances CPIC is satisfied. This conclusion also applies if: (i) $a_j = \gamma\tau_j$ for all $j \in T$, where $\gamma > 0$, γ being a scalar, or (ii) $a_j = \gamma_j \tau_j$, where $\gamma_j = 0$ for all $j \in T$ except for good k where $\gamma_k > 0$, $k \in T$.

Proof: Attention turns to (3.24) above where it is assumed that tariff rates are altered in size, while consumption taxes and variable scale economies are present. On aggregating the relevant version of (3.24) over all h individuals, the result is that

$$- \sum_{j \in T} c_j \, d\tau_j + dR^{h*} + \sum_{j \in T} \left[\frac{\partial Y(g)}{\partial \tau_j} + \frac{\partial S}{\partial \tau_j} - \tau_j \frac{\partial x_j}{\partial \tau_j} \right] d\tau_j + \lambda \, dg.$$

Following the same line of argument to be found in the proof for proposition 7 above, the previous equation reduces to

$$- \sum_{j \in T} c_j \, d\tau_j + dR^{h*} + \sum_{j \in T} \frac{\partial Y(g)^*}{\partial \tau_j} d\tau_j + (\lambda - p_g) \, dg, \qquad (4.32)$$

where dY(g)* is defined in (4.31) above. In deriving this equation allowance has been made for the possible creation of an implicit market for the global consumption externality. [This assumption is allowed for by the presence of (A2) in proposition 11 above.]

The assumption set out in (A3) above is now applied to (4.32) so that, in that equation,

$$\sum_{j \in T} \frac{\partial Y(g)^*}{\partial \tau_j} d\tau_j = \left[\sum_{j \in T} \frac{\partial Y(g)^*}{\partial \tau_i} a_j \right] d\alpha > 0,$$

$$\text{where } d\alpha < 0. \qquad (4.33)$$

The statement in (4.33) implies that assumption W* is now relevant. Applying this assumption, as well as (A2), to (4.32) means that there is a set of consumption taxes such that

$$\frac{dv^h}{v_Y^h} = - \sum_{j \in T} c_j^h dt_j - \sum_{i \in NT} c_i^h dt_i - \sum_{j \in T} c_j^h a_j d\alpha + dR^{h*}$$

$$+ (\lambda - p_g) dg + \sum_{i \in NT} \frac{\partial Y(g)^{h*}}{\partial t_i} dt_i + \sum_{j \in T} \frac{\partial Y(g)^{h*}}{\partial t_j} dt_j$$

$$+ \sum_{j \in T} \frac{\partial Y(g)^{h*}}{\partial \tau_j} a_j d\alpha > 0, \quad \text{for all } h. \qquad (4.34)$$

Thus CPIC is satisfied.

In addition, the conditions stated in points (i) and (ii) in proposition 4.11 above, if applied to (4.34) above, would assist in ensuring that CPIC is satisfied. For example, when point (i) is applied to the term $- \sum_{j \in T} c_j^h a_j d\alpha$, the result is that $- \gamma \sum_{j \in T}$

$c_j \tau_j d\alpha > 0$ when $d\alpha < 0$ since $\gamma > 0$ by assumption. This is as required. ||

The results stated in proposition 4.11 above are a variation of results to be found in Diewert *et al.* [1989, p. 210], although the result stated in the previous proposition are in some respects more general in that allowance has been made for the presence of variable scale economies and the provision of goods which produce global consumption externalities.

Compared to the results outlined earlier (where lump-sum taxes are available and there is just a single individual in the community) proposition 4.11 above indicates that relatively stringent conditions need to be satisfied before it is safe to suggest that a radial reduction of tariff rates will satisfy CPIC.[106] Similar remarks apply when the tariff on just a single good, k, is altered. In this latter case a reduction in the size of the tariff on this good satisfies CPIC if assumption W* is satisfied and good k is, on weighted average, a substitute in production for all other goods. [107] This particular result can be extended in various ways but this matter is ignored here.

---

106 Analyses of tariff reform in a single-person community, where variable economies of scale and public goods are absent, are to be found in Foster and Sonnenschein [1970], Bruno [1972], Lloyd [1974], Hatta [1977b] and Fukushima [1979].

107 A similar point is made in Diewert *et al.* [1989]. In this case:

$$\left[p_o(\partial x_o/\partial \tau_k) + \sum_{i \in NT} p_i(\partial x_i/\partial \tau_k) + \sum_{j \in T} p_j^*(\partial x_j/\partial \tau_k) \right] d\tau_k < 0 .$$

It is also noted that proposition 4.11 above does allow for the influence of changes in consumption taxes, and tariff rates, on the untaxed numeraire good. This is so since the measure of changes in national product, valued at final international prices, includes the numeraire good. [See (4.31) above.] This point is of some importance for the impression might be gained from proposition 4.11, point (ii), above that CPIC may be satisfied if all tax rates are altered to the point where they all take the same, uniform, rate. This is not necessarily so, however - even if distributional concerns are put to one side. The reason is that the influence of tax rate changes on the untaxed numeraire good also need to be taken into account.[108] This is a theme which will be returned to, and discussed in some detail, in section 13 (and sub-section 13.1) in the second set of lectures below.

4.6D Concluding Comments: The increasing level of complexity of the cases considered in this sub-section provides a useful insight; namely, for the application of some, apparently simple, tax-reform rule to satisfy CPIC, almost certainly the size of other sets of taxes and subsidies will need to be altered as well. This is a theme which will be returned to in the next section. In addition, the previous discussion demonstrated that results, which apply to the case where there is just a single individual in the community, do not simply carry over to the many-person case. This general theme, in turn, will be returned to in the second set of lectures presented below. Indeed, in those lectures (which are

[108] A similar point has been made by Gordon [1991].

concerned with the matter of the implementation of socially optimal piecemeal taxation policy) much of the general theoretical framework, which has been employed in this sub-section, will be exploited there as well.

5 Non-Pareto Distortion Reform - Application of the Marginal Welfare Dominance Criteria.

The discussion in this section draws on the results presented in sections 2, 3 and 4 above to assess economic reform in circumstances where the marginal welfare dominance criteria (as devised in section 2 above) are applied, instead of the compensated Pareto-improvement criteria, to the task of ranking social states.

5.1 Information Problems and Economic Reform.

The present discussion returns to the information problems discussed (or alluded to) in sub-section 4.1, 4.2, 4.4B and 4.5 in the context of applying the compensated Pareto-improvement criterion. To begin with in sub-section 4.1 it was pointed out that if the attempt is made to provide compensating personal lump-sum income transfers (along with some suitable reform of the taxation system) then, because of incentive-compatibility problems, relevant accurate personal information probably would not be available to determine if any pertinent reform of the taxation system has satisfied CPIC, or not. And while this information problem can be avoided by providing compensating non-personal income transfers - a system of transfers based on assumption W [109] - this compensation will not be targeted just at those who need to be compensated to ensure that CPIC is just

[109] The assumption W* may need to be applied on occasions - as was done in sub-section 4.6c above.

satisfied. This fact implies that the scope for economic reform (that also satisfies CPIC) may be limited - compared to the situation where compensation could be more carefully targeted at those who do need to be compensated for losses incurred over some relevant change in economic states. These limited degrees of freedom, to implement economic reform, are likely to impose particularly pressing constraints on public action if the authorities also place binding upper limits on the budgets available to finance compensating income transfers. (For reasons indicated in section 4.2 above, this does not seem to be an unrealistic possibility.)

Finally, there is still the practical task of determining if all individuals have indeed satisfied CPIC after any relevant reform of the distorted economic system. This requirement would be difficult to satisfy in practice - even if incentive-compatible problems, associated with lump-sum transfers, did not arise. One reason why this would be so is that if at least some markets, on the consumption side of the economy, are not complete and competitive (which is probably the case), then relevant non-market, shadow-price, information would need to be available - information which probably would be difficult to determine with any reasonably degree of accuracy.

In contrast, the results presented in section 2 above indicate that if the social welfare function (swf), W(v), possesses certain general equity-regarding properties, then a rise in the level of social welfare is still possible, as a result of some economic reform, even though all those individuals in the community, who have suffered a loss as a consequence of this reform, have *not* been compensated. The second degree marginal welfare dominance criterion (SDMWDC) stated in proposition 2.1 above, for example, indicates that should the community subscribe to a swf with the property that $W(v) \in \Omega$ [i.e. W(v) is strictly S-concave], then if, as a consequence of some reform of the taxation system,

$$\left[\sum_{h=1}^{k} dv^{h*}\right] > 0, \qquad \text{for all } k \ (= 1 \text{ to } H),$$

then the community will have experienced a rise in the level of social welfare.[110] And this would be so even though some individuals may have experienced an uncompensated fall in the level of utility (as a result of this economic reform). [In this instance all individuals are ranked from those receiving the smallest, to those receiving the largest, individual equivalent income at the initial set of equilibrium prices.]

The need to provide compensation would tend to be reduced even further if the community is assumed to adopt a swf with the stronger equity-regarding property reflected in the assumption that $W(v) \in \Omega^T$. This is so because reductions in the level of utility, experienced by the comparatively better off in the community, would receive relatively little weight in any

110 The term dv^{h*} is defined in (2.19) , and the term Ω is defined just above proposition 1, earlier in the main text.

change in any swf, W(v) to by found in the set Ω^T.[111] In this case the third degree marginal welfare dominance criterion (TDMWDC), set out in proposition 2.2 above, could be applied to determine if the community gained from some reform of the distorted economic system.[112]

If compensating income transfers do need to be paid to ensure that, say, the SDMWDC is satisfied, then this criterion also indicates where in the community these transfers should be directed (to ensure that this compensation has a relatively substantial impact on raising the level of social welfare). Specifically, these lump-sum income transfers should be provided to those groups receiving relatively small equivalent incomes. This is so even if these income groups experience no loss of utility as a result of some economic reform. Thus the compensating lump-sum income transfer system should also be viewed as part of the community's attempts to redistribute total community income towards the social optimum distribution of income.

Naturally, if these compensating income transfers are too precisely targeted at particular income groups in the community, this transfer system is likely to become plagued by incentive-compatibility problems. On the other hand, if the income transfers are too broadly targeted, then possibly this will place relatively severe limitations (of the sort discussed in sub-sec-

---

[111] This may be so even if the community adopts a comparatively mild view of distributive justice. This matter is discussed in section 2.3 above in the main text.
[112] See section 2.3 above.

tion 4.2 above) on the attempts to reform the economic system. It follows that the compensating lump-sum income transfer system needs to attempt to strike a reasonable compromise. Such a compromise might be the payment of a general lump-sum income transfer to, say, the poorest twenty per cent of the community - the rest of the community receiving no, or a diminishing rate of, compensation. While such a system of income transfers probably would not completely eliminate the incentive-compatibilty problem,[113] the use of this compromise system of income transfers would be targeted at those whom the community regards (on grounds of distributive justice) as those most in need of income assistance.

An obvious additional advantage, which naturally flows from the application of the marginal welfare dominance criteria, in place of CPIC, is that it does not need to be determined if every individual in the community has, in fact, not suffered a loss from some pertinent economic reform. Thus the application of MWDC considerably reduces the demand for personal information, relative to what is required when CPIC is applied to rank social states. On the other hand, application of either of the marginal welfare dominance criterion does require some knowledge of the properties of the swf. But these demands on information are comparatively small - all that needs to be know is whether the swf is to be found in the set Ω, or in the set Ω^T.

---

[113] Some individuals (especially those at the margin) may attempt to understate the size of their equivalent incomes in the attempt to be counted as part of the group receiving compensation.

To summarise the argument to this point in the sub-section, it is being suggested that given the results presented in propositions 2.1 and 2.2 above, when combined with the sort of examples of economic reform discussed in section 4 above, it is quite likely that only partial (and possibly no) compensating lump-sum income transfers are required to ensure a rise in the level of social welfare resulting from some pertinent reform of a distorted economic system. If compensation is required, it should only be directed at those receiving equivalent incomes to be found at the lower end of the distribution of individual equivalent incomes. A consequence flowing on from this use of partial compensation is that, compared to the situation where CPIC is applied, it seems reasonable to suggest that difficulties associated with providing suitable compensating lump-sum income transfers are diminished. Above all, it also seems reasonable to assert that the application of marginal welfare dominance criterion, in place of CPIC, reduces (possibly by a sizable amount) the demands for relevant information.

Against these benefits there is a cost, however, and that is that measures of individual equivalent income (not actual income), and individual equivalent expenditures on goods, are required before either of the marginal welfare dominance criterion can be applied satisfactorily.[114] And this information may be difficult to determine accurately.[115]

As part of an answer to these real empirical difficulties it is pointed out that an acceptable ranking of social states, based on either marginal welfare dominance criterion, can possibly be determined by employing approximate, or error-ridden, information. To explain this point consider the following equation:

$$\left[\sum_{h=1}^{k} dv^{h*}\right] = \sum_{h=1}^{k}\left[dv_T^{h*} + \varepsilon^h\right], \text{ for all k (= 1 to H)}, \quad (5.1)$$

where, for any individual h, the term dv^{h*} denotes the *observed* measure of the adjusted change in this individual's level of utility, dv_T^{h*} denotes the *true* measure and ε^h represents the *measurement error* associated with the attempted measurement of dv_T^{h*}. Now suppose that the following statements are satisfied in reality:

$$\left[\sum_{h=1}^{k} dv^{h*}\right] > 0, \text{ for all k (= 1 to H)}, \quad (5.2)$$

114 An explanation of why there is a need to use individual equivalent incomes, when applying the dominance criteria, is provided in sub-section 2.1 above in the main text.
115 The practical difficulties associated with measuring equivalence scales is discussed, for example, in Deaton and Muellbauer [1980], King [1983], Blackorby and Donaldson [1989] and Lewbel [1989].

and

$$\sum_{h=1}^{k} \varepsilon^h \leq 0 \quad \text{for all } k \ (= 1 \text{ to } H). \qquad (5.3)$$

It follows immediately from (5.1), (5.2) and (5.3) that

$$\sum_{h=1}^{k} dv_T^{h*} > 0, \quad \text{for all } k \ (= 1 \text{ to } H).$$

Hence, in this case, a valid welfare rank-ordering of social states has been achieved. This is so even though error-ridden information was employed to determine this ranking.

Whether the assumption in (5.3) above will be satisfied in reality is a matter of fact. But certainly it is reasonable to suggest that valid welfare rank-orderings of social states may be possible even though only approximate information is employed in such a comparison.

A slightly modified line of argument also applies if the third degree dominance criterion is applied.

To keep the analysis presented in the next two sub-section comparatively simple, the argument just outlined will not be formally allowed for in that discussion. All that is stated here is that, in the context of the results to be presented below, the presence of pertinent measurement errors does not necessarily invalidate those results.[116]

Finally, even if the empirical problems, associated with the measurement of individual equivalent incomes, are not satisfactorily resolved, this does not mean that the theoretical application of marginal welfare dominance criteria should be abandoned. As the previous discussion has indicated, the use of MWDC implies that a community may well experience a gain in social welfare as a result of some reform of the economic system, even though CPIC has not been satisfied. Thus the theoretical application of marginal welfare dominance criteria serves the useful purpose, at least, of reminding one that CPIC should not be viewed as the only criterion that should be employed to rank social states in communities in which matters of distributive justice are of concern.[117]

5.2 A Simple Application of Marginal Welfare Dominance Criteria.

The first application of the general marginal welfare dominance criteria set out in section two above is based upon the simple case discussed in section 4.1 above. It is assumed that the economy is closed and is free of distortions except for the presence of consumption taxes. [In the present case it turns out,

---

116 There is an alternative approach to the measurement problem discussed in the main text; namely, to apply restrictive assumptions - of the form stated in (2.11) above in the main text - on the the swf In this case, as explained in sub-section 2.1.1 above in the main text, measures of individual equivalent income are no longer required in the rank ordering of social states. For reasons explained in that section, however, these assumptions are not attractive.

117 A related, but not identical, point has be made by Turunen [1987].

however, that it is of no importance whether, or not, the aggregate supply of factors of production and the technology are fixed.] These assumptions are now applied to the basic reduced-form equation set out in (3.26) above - the equation corresponding to (3.24) above for individual h, except that in that equation all relevant terms have been converted into equivalent terms. The equation which results is the following:

$$[\, dv^h / v^h_{y_e} \,] = -\sum_i c^h_{ei}\, dt_i + dR^h_e + dY^h_e, \text{ for all individuals.} \qquad (5.4)$$

This result, in turn, is now combined with SDMWDC set out in proposition 2.1 above.

<u>Proposition 5.1:</u> Suppose that the Basic Assumptions (BA) are satisfied, the economy is closed and there are no distortions present in the economy, except for the presence of consumption taxes. In these circumstances a small reform of the consumption taxation system, along with the provision, if required, of compensating income-group lump-sum transfers, will always ensure that $dW > 0$ for all $W[\, v(q,y_e) \,] \in \Omega$ iff

$$\sum_{h=1}^{k} [\, -\sum_i c^h_{ei}\, dt_i + dR^h_e + dY^h_e \,] > 0, \quad \text{for all } k = 1, 2, \ldots, H, \qquad (5.5)$$

where, at the initial set of prices, $y^1_e \le y^2_e \le y^3_e \le \ldots \le y^H_e$, and where a strict inequality lies between at least two individuals.

<u>Proof</u>: In the instance of individual 1 - the individual in the community receiving the smallest equivalent income (measured at the initial set of prices) - the change in the level utility (adjusted for the measure of the marginal utility of equivalent income for this individual), resulting from the small change in the consumption taxes, is the following [after drawing on (5.4) above] :

$$dv^{1*} := [\, dv^1 / v^1_{Y_e} \,] = [\, -\sum_i c^1_{ei}\, dt_i + dR^1_e + dY^1_e \,]$$

$$= -\sum_i c^1_{ei}\, dt_i + \sum_i \left[\frac{\partial R^1_e}{\partial t_i} + \frac{\partial Y^1_e}{\partial t_i} \right] dt_i$$

$$+ \left[\frac{\partial R^1_e}{\partial b^\rho} + \frac{\partial Y^1_e}{\partial b^\rho} \right] db^\rho, \qquad (5.6)$$

where b^ρ refers to the compensating lump-sum income transfer only paid to income group ρ (say the poorest twenty percent of the community). If this lump-sum income transfer does not need to be paid, to ensure that the condition stated in (5.5) above is satisfied, then the third set of terms on the right-hand side of (5.6) above is omitted from that equation.

Given the assumptions listed in proposition 5.1 above, the formula for measuring a small change in the level of adjusted utility, dv^{h*}, for any individual, h, is essentially the same as that for individual one represented in (5.6) above. [If the group-lump-sum income transfer is not paid to any individual, h, then the relevant terms representing compensating group income transfers can be omitted from a suitable version of (5.6) above.] That being the case, the rest of the proof is that provided for proposition 2.1 above. ||

Proposition 5.1 above allows for the possibility that compensating group income transfers are provided. For the sake of the present argument it is now assumed, however, that no compensating income transfers are provided to any (income) groups in the community. It is also assumed that, as a consequence, the condition stated in (5.5) above is not satisfied. Nevertheless, it may still be possible to rank relevant social states if the community is concerned enough about matters of distributive justice to the point that this community subscribes to some swf, W(v), that is in the set Ω^T.

<u>Proposition 5.2</u>: Suppose that the Basic Assumptions (BA) are satisfied, the economy is closed, and there are no distortions present in the economy except for the presence of consumption taxes - assumptions which imply that if there is a small reform of the consumption taxation system, but no compensating lump-sum transfers are provided, then [on drawing on (5.4) above]

$$dv^{h*} := [\, dv^h / v_{y_e}^h \,] = -\sum_i c_{ei}^h \, dt_i + \sum_i \left[\frac{\partial R_e^h}{\partial t_i} + \frac{\partial Y_e^h}{\partial t_i} \right] dt_i \, ,$$

for all h.

Given this formula for measuring dv^{h*} for all h, $dW > 0$ for all $W[\, v(q,y_e)\,] \in \Omega^T$ iff

$dv^{1*} > 0$, $\sum_{h=1}^{k} dv^{h*} \geq 0$ for all k=1 to P, and $\sum_{h=P+1}^{m} dv^{h*} \leq 0$ for all m=P+1 to H, and

$$\left| \sum_{h=1}^{k} dv^{h*} \right| \geq \left| \sum_{h=P+1}^{m} dv^{h*} \right| \quad \text{for all k, m,}$$

where k=1, 2, ... , P and m = P+1, ... , H, where $P \geq [H - (P+1)]$, and where $y_e^1 < y_e^2 < \ldots < y_e^H$ at the initial set of prices.

The result stated in proposition 5.2 above is simply a consequence of combining proposition 4.1 with proposition 2.2 above. If the necessary and sufficient conditions stated in proposition 5.2 are not satisfied, then possibly the provision of a relatively small compensating group-lump-sum income transfer (directed at groups receiving comparatively low equivalent incomes at the initial set of prices) may be adequate to result in these conditions being satisfied.

5.3 More Complex Applications of Marginal Welfare Dominance Criteria.

The results presented in the previous section imply that the marginal welfare dominance criteria presented in propositions 2.1 and 2.2 above can also be applied, in place of CPIC, in each one of the propositions set out in sub-sections 4.3 and 4.4 above - that is given that the community is concerned to some degree about matters of distributive justice and that certain other, suitably modified, assumptions are satisfied.

To demonstrate this assertion attention turns to devising a revised version of proposition 4.9 above - the proposition concerned with the reform of the tariff system in an economy where distortions are to be found on both the production and consumption sides of the economy. In the context of that proposition the following definition will be required below:

$$dY_e^{h*} := \left[p_g^r dg + \sum_{j \in T} p_j^* dx_{ej}^h + \sum_{i \in NT} p_i \, dx_{ei}^h + p_o dx_{eo}^h \right], \text{ for all h.} \tag{5.7}$$

This definition refers to the changes in real income for individual h measured using world prices.[118] The term p_g^r denotes the uniform price charged (subsidy provided) for the provision of the public bad (good) g.

---

[118] As before the domestic prices for the non-traded goods are taken to be world prices.

In addition the following assumptions are also required below:

Assumption 1*(A1*): Taxed goods are normal in the sense that

$$\sum_{h=1}^{k} \frac{\partial R_e^h}{\partial Y_e^{h*}} dY_e^{h*} \geq 0, \quad \text{if} \quad \sum_{h=1}^{k} dY_e^{h*} \geq 0, \qquad \text{for all k,}$$

where $y_e^1 \leq y_e^2 \leq y_e^3 \leq \ldots \leq y_e^H$, at the initial set of prices, and consumption tax rates remain unaltered.

As before, the presence of markets, which are not complete and competitive on the consumption side of the economy, requires the imposition of a comparatively specialised assumption. In the present context the following is assumed:[119]

Assumption 2* (A2*): An implicit market exists and is complete, but may not be competitive, for the good which creates a global consumption externality. The price charged in this market, and the non-lump-sum taxes applied elsewhere in the economy, are altered such that:

$$\sum_{h=1}^{k} (\lambda^r - p_g^r)\, dg = k\, [\, (\lambda^r - p_g^r)\, dg \,] \geq 0, \qquad \text{for all k,}$$

---

119 The reason for imposing this assumption is discussed in a little detail in subsection 4.4b above.

where $y_e^1 \leq y_e^2 \leq y_e^3 \leq \ldots \leq y_e^H$ at the initial set of prices.

The term λ^r denotes the reference shadow price for the public good (bad) which is common to all individuals in the community. In the attempt to provide a completely competitive market for good g, a uniform tax-price (subsidy), p_g^r, is applied in this market for good g. Finally, assumption 2* allows for the possibility that if $\sum_{h=1}^{k} (\lambda^r - p_g^r) < 0 \; (> 0)$ then lump-sum taxes and subsidies are altered such as to ensure that the inequality stated in (A2*) is satisfied.

Drawing on these assumptions the following is now stated:

<u>Proposition 5.3</u>: <u>Initial Assumptions</u>: Given (BA) upon which (3.26) above is based, it is also supposed that the following distortions are present in the economy: (i) production takes place under conditions of variable scale economies; (ii) there are distortions in factor markets (which take the form that $w_{fi} \neq w_{fj}$ for at least some factors of production, f, in at least the industries producing goods i and j respectively); (iii) a global consumption externality exists; (iv) non-prohibitive tariffs and consumption taxes are in place. If required, taxes on consumption are employed to finance compensating income transfers and the production of a good which creates a positive global consumption externality. <u>Additional Assumptions:</u> (A1*) and (A2*) are satisfied.

Within this context, if a small reform of the tariff rates is offset by changes in the consumption taxes in the consumption sector of the economy, it follows that:

(i) Given that $W[v(q,y_e,g)] \in \Omega$ then $dW > 0$ iff

$$\sum_{h=1}^{k} \left[p_g^r dg + \sum_{j \in T} p_j^* dx_{ej}^h + \sum_{i \in NT} p_i\, dx_{ei}^h + p_o dx_{eo}^h \right] > 0, \quad \text{for all } k, \qquad (5.8)$$

where, at the initial set of prices, $y_e^1 \le y_e^2 \le y_e^3 \le \ldots \le y_e^H$, and where a strict inequality lies between at least two individuals;

(ii) If the statement in (i) is not satisfied, but $W[v(q,y_e,g)] \in \Omega^T$, then still $dW > 0$ iff the necessary and sufficient conditions set out in proposition 2.2 are satisfied - although the dv^{h*} terms referred to in that proposition are replaced by $dY_e^h{}^*$ terms, where $dY_e^h{}^*$ is defined in (5.7) above.

<u>Proof</u>: (i) The initial assumptions listed in proposition 5.3 above, and the assumption that the changes in the tariff rates are offset in the consumption sector of the economy by changes in the con-

sumption taxes, are applied to (3.26) above. The end result is that: [120]

$$dv^{h*} = dR_e^{h*} + (\lambda^r - p_g^r)\,dg + dY_e^{h*}, \text{ for all } h, \qquad (5.9)$$

where dY_e^{h*} is defined in (5.7) above and

$$R_e^{h*} := \sum_{i\in NT} t_i\, c_{ei}^h + \sum_{j\in T} \tau_j\, c_{ej}^h + \sum_{j\in T} t_j\, c_{ej}^h. \qquad (5.10)$$

Next, on applying assumptions (A1*) and (A2*) to all relevant aggregated versions of (5.9), it follows that if

$$\sum_{h=1}^{k} dY_e^{h*} = \sum_{h=1}^{k}\left[p_g^r dg + \sum_{j\in T} p_j^* dx_{ej}^h + \sum_{i\in NT} p_i\, dx_{ei}^h + p_o dx_{eo}^h \right] > 0,$$

for any k, then it must be that $\sum_{h=1}^{k} dv^{h*} > 0$ for any $k = 1$ to H, where $y_e^1 \leq y_e^2 \leq \ldots \leq y_e^H$ at the initial set of prices.

This result implies that the rest of the proof can be provided by applying the proof for proposition 2.1. above.

---

120 The derivation of (5.6) draws on the discussion to be found in sub-section 4.4A above - i.e. that concerned with the presence of distortions on the production side of the economy.

(ii) It has just been established that, given the initial assumptions stated in proposition 5.3 above, along with (A1*) and (A2*) that

$$\text{if } \sum_{h=1}^{k} dY_e^h{*} > 0\ (<0) \text{ then } \sum_{h=1}^{k} dv^{h*} > 0\ (<0) \text{ for any}$$

k, where $y_e^1 \leq y_e^2 \leq \ldots \leq y_e^H$ at the initial set of prices. It follows that if the dv^{h*} terms are replaced by dY^{h*} terms in proposition 2.2 and, and given that $W[v(q,y_c,g)] \in \Omega^T$ then $dW > 0$ iff the modified necessary and sufficient conditions set out in proposition 2.2 are satisfied.||

The result presented in this last proposition is a relatively general statement of the gains-from-more-trade argument. However, in sharp contrast to the case where CPIC is applied (i.e. the case covered by proposition 4.9 above), the payment of some form of compensating lump-sum transfers may not be required to ensure that the necessary and sufficient conditions set out in propositions 5.3 above are satisfied. If compensating transfers are required (to ensure that, say, part (ii) of the last proposition is satisfied) then, as pointed out in sub-section 5.1 above, they will have most impact, on raising the level of social welfare, if they are directed towards those receiving relatively low equivalent incomes (at initial prices).

The previous proposition provides no guidance, however, as to how tariff rates should be altered. The following proposition addresses this matter.

<u>Proposition 5.4:</u> The assumptions are the same as those stated in proposition 5.3 above except that here (A1*) is omitted, and all non-lump-sum taxes remain fixed except that either : (i) all tariff rates, or (ii) groups of tariff rates are reduced in size by a small amount. It follows that:

(i) Given that $W[v(q,y_e,g)] \in \Omega$ then $dW > 0$ iff

$$\sum_{h=1}^{k} [\, dY_e^h* + dR_e^h* \,] > 0, \qquad \text{for all } k, \qquad (5.11)$$

where, at the initial set of prices, $y_e^1 \leq y_e^2 \leq y_e^3 \leq \ldots \leq y_e^H$, and where a strict inequality lies between at least two individuals.

(ii) Given, instead, that $W[v(q,y_e,g)] \in \Omega^T$ then $dW > 0$ iff the necessary and sufficient conditions set out in proposition 2.2 are satisfied - although the dv^h* terms referred to in that proposition are replaced by $[\, dY_e^h* + dR_e^h* \,]$ terms, where dY_e^h* is defined in (5.7) above and dR_e^h* is simply found by totally differentiating (5.10) above.

(iii) These conclusions also apply if $d\tau_j = a_j \; d\alpha$, for all $j \in T$, and $d\alpha < 0$ and (a) $a_j = \gamma \tau_j$ for all $j \in T$, where $\gamma > 0$, γ being a scalar, or (b) $a_j = \gamma_j \tau_j$, where $\gamma_j = 0$ for all $j \in T$ except for good k where $\gamma_k > 0$, $k \in T$.

<u>Proof:</u> (i) The statement in (3.26) above implies that, after the initial assumptions listed in proposition 5.3 above are employed, and the assumption that the tariff rates alone are reduced in size by a small amount:[121]

$$dv^{h*} = -\sum_{j \in T} c^{h}_{ej} \, d\tau_j + dR^{h}_{e}* + (\lambda^r - p^{r}_{g})\, dg$$

$$+ dY^{h*}_{e}, \qquad \text{for all h.} \qquad (5.12)$$

Due the assumption that all, or groups of, tariff rates are reduced in size

$$-\sum_{j \in T} c^{h}_{ej} \, d\tau_j > 0, \qquad \text{for all h.}$$

This fact implies that

121 As in the case of (5.9) in the main text, the derivation of (5.12) draws on the discussion to be found in sub-section 4.4A above.

$$\sum_{h=1}^{k}\left[-\sum_{j\in T} c_{ej}^{h}\, d\tau_j \right] > 0. \text{ for all } k. \qquad (5.13)$$

Applying the statement in (5.13), along with assumption (A2*), to any suitably aggregated version of (5.12), it follows that if

$$\sum_{h=1}^{k} [\, dY_e^{h}* + dR_e^{h}* \,] > 0, \qquad \text{for all } k,$$

then it must be that $\sum_{h=1}^{k} dv^{h*} > 0$ for any k = 1 to H, where $y_e^1 \leq y_e^2 \leq \ldots \leq y_e^H$ at the initial set of prices.

Hence the rest of the proof for part (i) of this proposition can be provided by exploiting that for proposition 2.1. above.

The rest of the proof is omitted except to note that, in the case of part (iii) of the proposition, if the conditions stated in points (a) and (b) are applied to (5.12) above this would ensure that the relevant marginal welfare dominance criterion is satisfied. For example, when point (a) is applied the result is that

$$-\sum_{j\in T} c_{ej}^{h}\, d\tau_j = -\sum_{j\in T} c_{ej}^{h}\, a_j\, d\alpha = -\gamma \sum_{j\in T} c_{ej}^{h}\, \tau_j\, d\alpha > 0,$$

for all h,

when $d\alpha < 0$ since $\gamma > 0$ by assumption. This is as required. ||

The result stated in this last proposition is an alternative version of proposition 4.11 above (which in turn is a variation of results to be found in Diewert *et al.* [1989, p. 210]) - the latter proposition being based on CPIC. Amongst other things, proposition 5.4 indicates that a radial reduction of tariff rates will, under certain circumstances, ensure that the relevant marginal welfare dominance criterion is satisfied.

This last proposition can also be modified to take account of alternative situations such as: (i) consumption taxes, but not tariff rates, or both consumption taxes and tariff rates, are reduced in size; (ii) the consumption tax (instead of the tariff rate) on just a single good, k, is reduced in size. In fact this latter case comes nearest to that considered by Yitzhaki and Slemrod [1991, pp. 483 - 4]. An extension of the particular case they considered will be discussed below. But before dealing with that case, it is noted that a natural extension of the results presented in propositions 5.3 and 5.4 above is the following:

<u>Proposition 5.5</u>: The assumptions are the same as those stated in proposition 5.3 above. However, in this instance all non-lump sum taxes remain fixed but there is an exogenous change in real national income. It follows that: (i) given that $W[v(q,y_e,g)] \in \Omega$ then $dW > 0$ iff

$$\sum_{h=1}^{k} \left[p_g^r dg + \sum_{j \in T} p_j^* dx_{ej}^h + \sum_{i \in NT} p_i \, dx_{ei}^h + p_o dx_{eo}^h \right] > 0, \quad \text{for all}$$

k, where, at the initial set of prices, $y_e^1 \leq y_e^2 \leq y_e^3 \leq \ldots \leq y_e^H$, and where a strict inequality lies between at least two individuals;

(ii) given that $W[v(q,y_e,g)] \in \Omega^T$ then $dW > 0$ iff the necessary and sufficient conditions set out in proposition 2.2 are satisfied - although the dv^{h*} terms referred to in that proposition are replaced by dY_e^h* terms, where dY_e^h* is defined in (5.7) above.

This proposition provides a relatively general statement of the gains-from-real-economic-growth argument. Again compensating income transfers may not be required in this case where the second, or third, degree marginal welfare dominance test is applied - and if required it should be directed at those receiving relatively low equivalent incomes. Put another way - and as noted in the previous sub-section - the compensating income transfer system should also be utilised to redistribute total community income in the attempt to move the community towards a socially optimal distribution of income.

What should also be mentioned, concerning proposition 5.5 above, is that it extends still further the Atkinson-Dasgupta-Sen-Starrett-Shorrocks propositions concerning the ranking of generalized Lorenz curves. While, as pointed out in section 2 above, proposition 2.2 allows for the situation where individuals in the community possessing different tastes, it was not clear exactly how changes in individual utility levels were to be measured - especially in economies distorted in various ways. The result in proposition 5.5 indicates under what circumstances suitable proxy measures of changes in individual utility levels may be generated.[122] Applying these proxy variables in that proposition allows a generalization of the main result to be found in Shorrocks [1983], for example. [There the ranking of social states was based upon non-intersecting generalized Lorenz curves, based on individual income information, in a community where each individual possessed identical tastes. Proposition 5.5 clearly generalises that result in a number of dimensions - not only does it allow for taste variations and the influence of economic distortions on individual utility levels, it also takes into account the possibility that the generalised Lorenz curves may intersect.]

It might also be pointed out that the statement in proposition 5.5. above may be employed to provided an analytical framework within which to measure changes in the level of economic and social advancement (level of social welfare) in developing countries. Mention of this possibility alludes to a vast topic which cannot be discussed here.

---

122 This is not to say that it is an easy task to generate these variables. On the contrary, as proposition 5.5 in the main text indicates, strong assumptions have to satisfied before these proxy variables can be regarded as being satisfactory.

Finally, to conclude this sub-section, the previous three results are generalisations of the corresponding results presented in propositions 4.9, 4.10 and 4.11 above, a number of the remarks, made with respect to these latter three propositions, apply equally to proposition 5.3. 5.4 and 5.5 above. (See the remarks made at the end of sub-sections 4.4 and 4.6 respectively above.) Those remarks, therefore, need not be repeated here.

5.4 A Generalization of the Yitzhaki-Slemrod Case

To conclude this section attention returns to consider a generalisation of a particular case, mentioned above, considered by Yitzhaki and Slemrod [1991]. In this case two consumption tax rates are altered in size by a small amount in a closed economy such that the level of aggregate government revenue remains unaltered. There are no other distortions present in the economy. The generalisation of this particular case considered here is that where the economy is open, and there are distortions on both the production and consumption sides of the economy.[123] In these circumstances the result presented in (5.12) above can be exploited by restating that equation in a slightly modified form:[124]

$$dv^{h*} = -c^{h}_{ej}\,dt_{j} - c^{h}_{ei}\,dt_{i} + dR^{h}_{e}{}^{*} + (\lambda^{r} - p^{r}_{g})\,dg + dY^{h*}_{e},$$

---

[123] It was pointed out in sub-section 2.1.1 above that Yitzhaki and Slemrod [1991, p. 482] also place comparatively strong restrictions of individual and social preferences. For reasons explained earlier, these restrictions are not employed in the discussion in the main text.

[124] The derivation of (5.11), as in the case of (5.9), in the main text, draws on the discussion to be found in sub-section 4.4A above - i.e. that concerned with the presence of distortions on the production side of the economy.

$$\text{for all } h. \qquad (5.14)$$

The various terms referred to in this equation have been defined above.

With the aggregate level of government revenue remaining fixed [i.e. $\sum_h dR_e^{h*} = dR^* = 0$] it can be shown that

$$dt_i = -\frac{c_j}{c_i}\varphi_{ji}\, dt_j, \qquad (5.15)$$

$$\text{where } \varphi_{ji} := \varphi_j/\varphi_i \text{ and } \varphi_j := 1 + \sum_k \left[\frac{t_k}{c_j}\right]\left[\frac{\partial c_k(p,g,y)}{\partial t_j}\right]$$

where $[\partial c_k(p,g,y)/\partial t_j]$ refers to an uncompensated change in the level of demand for good k as a result of a change in the level of the consumption tax rate imposed on good j.[125] Substituting (5.15) into (5.14) above results in the following:

$$dv^{h*} = \left[\frac{c^h_{ei}}{c_i}\phi_{ji} - \frac{c^h_{ej}}{c_j}\right] c_j\, dt_j$$

$$+ dR_e^{h*} + (\lambda^r - p_g^r)\, dg + dY_e^{h*}, \qquad \text{for all } h. \qquad (5.16)$$

---

125 At the aggregate level, ordinary (not equivalent) measures of the level of demand for any good apply.

Based on this result the following can now be stated:

Proposition 5.6: The initial assumptions are the same as those stated in proposition 5.3 above. The consumption taxes of two goods are altered such as to keep the level of aggregate government revenue fixed. In these circumstances, and given that $W[v(q,y_e,g)] \in \Omega$, then $dW > 0$ iff the conditions stated in proposition in 2.1 above are satisfied, where dv^{h*} is defined in (5.16) above.

This result generalises that provided by Yitzhaki and Slemrod in a number of respects. Firstly, allowance is made for the presence of markets which are not complete and competitive.[126] Secondly, reference is also made, in (5.16) above, to the possibility that $[\, dR_e^h* + dY_e^h* \,] \neq 0$ for at least some h individuals; in other words, allowance is made for the possibility that the assumed changes to the consumption taxes may influence individual utility levels via changes in the the real income received, and the amount of government revenue paid, by any individual h. Yitzhaki and Slemrod, on the other hand, implicitly assume that all markets are complete and competitive and that $[\, dR_e^h* + dY_e^h*]$ $= 0$ for all h individuals in the community. Applying these two

126 As pointed out in section 4.5 above, such market situations are probably widespread in any reasonably sophisticated economic system. Also see, for example, Arnott and Stiglitz [1986] on this point.

assumptions to (5.16) above results in exactly the measure of dv^{h*} which is employed by Yitzhaki and Slemrod.[127] It is, therefore, this special case which is considered in some depth by Yitzhaki and Slemrod.

The assumption that $[\, dR_e^h* + dY_e^h* \,] = 0$, for all h individuals in the community, essentially rules out of consideration a set of variables which may have an influence on the distribution of individual utility in the community. These changes in the distribution of individual utility, if they occur, in turn will have an influence on the level of social welfare, W(v) - that is if, at least, $W \in \Omega$.

5.5 Marginal Welfare Dominance Tests and Partially Offsetting Incomplete Markets.

In sub-section 4.5 above the topic was considered where economic reform takes the form of attempting to mitigate, to some degree, the social costs created by the distortions created by markets which are not complete and competitive. Most of what was said there applies equally in the present case. What can now be added to that discussion is that SDMWDC, or TDMWDC, certainly could be applied, in place of CPIC, to analyse the particular problems discussed there. Such an exercise will not be

---

127 See Yitzhaki and Slemrod [1991, p.483, equation 6].

carried out here, however - although the interested reader might wish to pursue this matter.[128]

What is noted here, however, is that the use of MWDC probably will tend to reduce the demand for relevant personal information - which returns the present discussion to a theme discussed in sub-section 5.1 above. In considering this topic a little further, attention returns to consider briefly the particular case represented in (4.19) above. In the context of that equation the point was made that the application of CPIC implies that, in certain situations (particularly those comparatively near to the social optimum), relatively large amounts of detailed personal information will need to be known before the sign of (4.19) can be determined for all individuals in the community. In contrast, if either of the marginal welfare dominance criterion are applied, in place of CPIC, then, for the sort of reasons outlined in sub-section 5.1 above, approximate personal information may be adequate to determine if the community has gained from some pertinent reform of the economic system (aimed at attempting to reduce the extent of market failures created by the absence of certain complete and competitive markets). This is more likely to be the case if this economic reform could be combined with some suitable group-lump-sum income transfers which were directed at the less well off in the community.

---

128 It is worth pointing out that such an exercise could be applied to a range of issues relating to the general case where markets are not complete and competive.

6. Conclusions.

Taking account of numerous distortionary cross-price and income effects is fundamental in any analysis of some general problem in the theory of economic reform. What is not so common (although the situation is now changing) in discussions of this class of problem is recognition of the need to allow for the influence of these distortionary cross-effects on the level of utility for each individual in the community. In this way any distributional concerns that the community may possess, can be allowed for.[129] This particular perspective on the general problem of economic reform is reflected in most of the discussion presented in the previous two sections.

One insight that emerges from that discussion is that, in an economy where there are numerous distortionary and distributional cross effects to be taken into consideration, altering only one set of economic distortions alone is not certain to satisfy any one of the three social-welfare-ranking criterion employed above. This is likely to be so even if this set of distortions is altered in a coordinated manner - as would be the case if, for example, there was a small, radial, reduction of a set of consumption taxes. Rather what needs to occur, to ensure that at least one of these three welfare ranking criterion is satisfied, is that this particular economic reform is combined with changes in

---

[129] Even the application of CPIC implies the adoption of some implicit value judgement concerning changes in the distribution of individual utility levels with the community.

other sets of relevant policy instruments - policy instruments aimed mainly (but not solely) at ensuring that undesirable secondary distortionary cross-effects are mitigated. So, for example, a reform of the consumption tax system needs to be combined with changes in other sets of non-lump taxes (subsidies) [remembering that the application of lump-sum taxes and subsidies is not feasible] aimed mainly at offsetting any undesirable consequences arising from changes in the distribution of individual utility, the presence of other types of non-lump taxes, and the presences of markets that are not complete and competitive.

This perceived need to employ a carefully coordinated approach to economic reform[130] creates, by implication, considerable demands for relevant accurate personal information. But the discussion in the previous two sections explicitly argued, the need for this detailed information tends to decline as the community comes to adopt more egalitarian social preferences - although the exact form of the swf is not known. Thus, at one extreme, probably any, and every, application of CPIC (to assess some relevant change in social states) will require the availability of relevant and accurate personal information for every individual in the community influenced by such a change. Only after all this information has been assessed will it be possible to say, with any certainty, if CPIC has been satisfied.

---

130 This general principle in fact will be exploited again in the latter part of the next set of lectures where consideration is given to the matter of setting socially optimal taxation structures.

At the other end of the spectrum, application of the third degree marginal welfare criterion[131] indicates that the need for accurate personal information for every individual, affected by some relevant change in economic states in the community, almost certainly will not always arise - and may arise only rarely. (Whether this is in fact the case naturally is a matter which can only be settled by relevant empirical research.[132])

Flowing on from this last point, the application of the marginal welfare dominance criteria implies that the application of relevant policy instruments do not need to be so carefully coordinated - compared with the situation where CPIC is employed to judge changes in social states.. Thus, whereas the application of CPIC implies that compensating income transfers must be applied throughout the community, the application of TDMWDC, for example, indicates that this compensation, if it needs to be provided at all, should be directed solely towards the lower end of the distribution of individual equivalent incomes - although one needs to be mindful, as pointed out sub-section 5.1 above, of incentive-compatibility problems. These observations, in turn, imply that the application of this particular rule, for providing compensating income transfers (if required), clearly would ease the task of implementing economic reform.[133]

---

131 As pointed out in section 2.3 above in the main text, social preferences do not necessarily need to be extremely egalitarian for the application of TDMWDC to be valid.

132 Empirical research along these lines has already begun, as evidenced by the pertinent empirical finding presented in Yitzhaki and Slemrod [1991].

133 This point is also hinted at by Yitzhaki and Slemrod [1991, p. 492].

Finally, besides the numerous results presented in sections 4 and 5 above with respect to closed and open economies, that discussion has by no means exhausted all the possible applications of the theoretical framework developed in sections 2 and 3 above above. Since that theoretical framework is based upon such fundamental and general principles, there would seem to be numerous applications for that theoretical framework inside, and outside, the field of economic reform. For example, the two main propositions set out in section 2 above should have applications in all situations where the basic problem being considered is just the welfare rank-ordering of one social state relative to another - such as whether the level of poverty has risen or fallen as the community moves from one social state to another. It is true that, to some extent, this matter was addressed in the context of propsition 5.5. above. [As pointed out at the end of sub-section 5.3 above, that proposition does apply to situations where there have been exogenous small changes in the generalised Lorenz curve - a matter which does have a bearing on the measurement of changes in the level of poverty.] Nevertheless, more work, concentrating on measuring the bare economic situation facing poorer members of the community, could be performed.[134] As for the general theoretical framework set out in section 3 above, one additional application of that theory is in the attempt to determine the socially optimal application of piecemeal economic policy. This broad topic is discussed in the next set of lectures.

---

134 Work, along the lines envisaged, would be an extension of that to be found in Atkinson [1987].

References.

Arnott, R. and Stiglitz, J. E. [1986], "Moral Hazard and Optimal Commodity Taxation", Journal of Public Economics, Vol. 29, pp. 1 - 24.

Arnott, R. and Stiglitz, J. E. [1988], "The Basic Analytics of Moral Hazard", Scandinavian Journal of Economics, Vol. 90, pp. 383 - 413.

Arnott, R. and Stiglitz, J. E. [1990], "The Welfare Economics of Moral Hazard", in Loubergè, H. (ed.), Risk, Information and Insurance (Dordrecht: Kluwer).

Arrow, K. J. [1986], "The Economics of Agency", in Pratt, J. and Zeckhauser, R. (eds) Principles and Agents: Structure of Business (Boston: Harvard Business School Press).

Atkinson, A. B. [1970], "On the Measurement of Inequality", Journal of Economic Theory, Vol. 2, pp. 244 - 63.

Atkinson, A B. [1987], "On the Measurement of Poverty", Econometrica, Vol. 55, pp. 749 - 764.

Atkinson, A. B. and Bourguignon, F. [1982],"The Comparison of Multi- Dimensioned Distributions of Economic Status", Review of Economic Studies, Vol 49, pp. 183-201.

Atkinson, A. B. and Bourguignon, F. [1987], "Income Distribution and Differences in Needs", in Feiwel, G. R. (ed.), Arrow and the Foundations of the Theory of Economic Policy (New York: University Press), pp. 350 - 370.

Atkinson, A. B. and Stiglitz, J. E. [1980], Lectures on Public Economics (New York: McGraw-Hill).

Auerbach, A. J. [1985], "The Theory of Excess Burden and Optimal Taxation", in Auerbach, A. J. and Feldstein, M. (eds), Handbook of Public Economics, Vol. 1 (Amsterdam: North-Holland).

Bhagwati, B. [971], "The Generalised Theory of Distortions and Welfare", in Bhagwati, J. *et al.* (eds), Trade, Balance of Payments and Growth: Papers in International Economics in Honor of Charles Kindelberger (Amsterdam: North Holland).

Bhagwati, J. N. and Hansen, B. [1973], "Should Growth Rates be Evaluated at International Prices?", in Bhagwati, J.N. and Eckaus, R. (eds), Development and Planning: Essays in Honour of Parl Rosenstern-Rodan (Cambridge, Mass.: MIT Press).

Blackorby, C.
and Donaldson, D. [1989] ,"Adult-Equivalence Scales, Interpersonal Comparisons of Well-Being, and Applied Welfare Economics", University of British Columbia, Discussion Paper no.: 89-24.

Bruno, M. [1972], "Market Distortions and Gradual Reform", Review of Economic Studies, Vol. 39, pp. 373 - 383.

Coase, R. H. [1960], "The Problem of Social Cost", Journal of Law and Economics, Vol. 3, pp. 1 - 44.

Corden , W. M. [1984], "The Normative Theory of International Trade", in Jones, R. W. and Kenen, P. B. (eds), Handbook of International Economics(Amsterdam: North-Holland).

Dasgupta, P., Sen, A. and Starrett, D. [1973], "Notes on the Measurement of Inequality", Journal of Economic Theory, Vol. 6, pp. 180 -187.

Davies, J. and Hoy, M. [1991], "Making Inequality Comparisons When Lorenz Curves Intersect", University of Guelph, Discussion Paper, no. 1991 - 12.

Deaton, A. S. and Muellbauer, J. [1980], Economics of Consumer Behaviour (Cambridge: Cambridge University Press).

Diewert, W. E.,
Turunen-Red, A. H. and Woodland, A. D. [1989], "Productivity- and Pareto-Improving Changes in Taxes and Tariffs", Review of Economic Studies, Vol. 56, pp. 199 - 216.

Dixit, A. [1975], "Welfare Effects of Tax and Price Distortions", Journal of Public Economics, Vol. 4, pp. 103 - 123.

Dixit, A. [1985], "Tax Policy in Open Economies," in Auerbach, A. J. and Feldstein, M. (eds), Handbook of Public Economics, Vol. 1 (Amsterdam: North-Holland).

Dixit, A. [1987], "On Pareto-Improving Redistributions of Aggregate Economics Gains", Journal of Economic Theory, Vol. 41, pp. 133 - 135.

Dixit, A. and Norman, V. [1980], Theory of International Trade (Welwyn, U.K.: James Nisbet).

Dixit, A. and Norman, V. [1986], "Gains from Trade Without Lump-sum Compensation", Journal of International Economics, Vol. 21, pp. 111 - 122.

Drèze, J. and Stern, N. [1990], "Policy Reform, Shadow Prices and Market Prices", Journal of Public Economics, Vol. 42, pp. 1 - 45.

Eaton, J. and Panagariya, A. [1979], "Gains From Trade: Under Variable Returns to Scale, Commodity Taxation, Tariffs and Factor Market Distortions", Journal of International Economics, Vol. 9, 481-501.

Eisen, R. [1990], "Problems of Equilibria in Insurance Markets with Asymmetric Information", in Loubergè, H. (ed.), Risk, Information and Insurance (Dordrecht: Kluwer).

Foster, E. and Sonnenschein, H. [1970], "Price Distortion and Economic Welfare", Econometrica, Vol. 45, pp. 1859 - 1869.

Foster, J. E., Majumdar, M. K. and Mitra, T. [1990], "Inequality and Welfare in Market Economies", Journal of Public Economics, Vol. 41, pp. 351 - 367.

Fukushima, T. [1979], "Tariff Structure, Nontraded Goods and the Theory of Piecemeal Policy Recommendations", International Economic Review, Vol. 20, pp. 427 - 435.

Gordon, J. P. F. [1991], "Tax Reform and Uniformity: Explaining the Hatta Result", Journal of Public Economics, Vol. 45, pp. 257 - 261.

Greenwald, B. C.
and Stiglitz, J. E. [1986], "Externalities in Economies with Imperfect Information and Incomplete Markets", Quarterly Journal of Economics, Vol. 100, pp. 227 - 264.

Hadar, J. and Russell, W. [1974], "Stochastic Dominance in Choice Under Uncertainty", in Balch, M. S., McFadden, D. L. and Wu, S.

Y. (eds), Essays on Economic Behaviour Under Uncertainty (Amsterdam: North-Holland Press).

Hammond, P. J. [1990], "Theoretical Progress in Public Economics: A Provocative Assessment", Oxford Economic Papers, Vol. 42, pp. 6 - 33.

Hatta, T. [1977a], "A Theory of Piecemeal Policy Recommendations", Review of Economic Studies, Vol. 44, pp. 1 - 12.

Hatta, T. [1977b], "A Recommendation for a Better Tariff Structure', Econometrica, Vol. 45, pp. 1859 - 1869.

Kemp, M. C. and Negishi, T. [1970], "Variable Returns to Scale, Commodity Taxes, Factor Market Distortions and Their Implications for Trade", Swedish Journal of Economics, Vol. 72 pp. 1 - 11.

Kemp, M. C. and Wan, H. Y. [1986], "Gains from Trade With and Without Lump-Sum Compensation", Journal of International Economics, Vol. 21, pp. 99 - 110.

Kemp, M. C. and Schweinberger, A. G. [1991], "Variable Returns to Scale, Non-Uniqueness of Equilibrium and the Gain from International Trade", Review of Economic Studies, Vol. 58, pp. 807 - 816.

King, M. A. [1983], "Welfare Analysis of Tax Reforms Using Household Data", Journal of Public Economics, Vol. 21, pp. 183-214.

King, M. A. [1986], "A Pigovian Rule for the Optimum Provision of Public Goods", Journal of Public Economics, Vol. 30, pp. 273 - 291.

Kolm, S.-C. [1976], " Unequal Inequalities: I", Journal of Economic Theory, Vol. 12 , pp. 416 - 442.

__________, "Unequal Inequalities: II", Journal of Economic Theory, Vol. 13, pp. 82 - 111.

Laffont, J.-J. [1988], Fundamentals of Public Economics (Cambridge, Mass.: The MIT Press).

Lambert, P. J. [1989], The Distribution and Redistribution of Income (Oxford: Basil Blackwell).

Lewbell, A. [1989], "Household Equivalence Scales and Welfare Comparison", Journal of Public Economics, Vol. 39, pp. 377-391.

Little, I. M. D. and Mirrlees, J.A. [1969], Manual of Industrial Project Analysis in Developing Countries, Vol. 2 (Paris: Organisation for Economic Cooperation and Development).

Lloyd, P. J. [1974], "A More General Theory of Price Distortions in Open Economies", Journal of International Economics, Vol. 4, pp. 365 - 386.

Lloyd, P. J. and Schweinberger, A. G.[1988], "Trade Expenditure Functions and the Gains From Trade", Journal of International Economics, Vol. 24, pp. 275 - 297.

Newbery, D. M. [1989], "Missing Markets: Consequences and Remedies", in Hahn, F. (ed.) The Economics of Missing Markets, Information, and Games (Oxford: Clarendon Press).

Ohyama, M. [1972], "Trade and Welfare in General Equilibrium", Keio Economic Studies, Vol. 9, pp. 37 - 73.

Pigou, A.C.[1947], A Study in Public Finance (London: Macmillan).

Rawls, J, [1971], A Theory of Justice (Cambridge, Mass.: Harvard University Press).

Rees, R. [1989], "Uncertainty, Information and Insurance", in Hey, J. D.(ed.), Current Issues in Microeconomics, (London: Macmillan).

Roberts, K. [1980], "Price-Dependent Welfare Prescriptions", Journal of Public Economics, Vol. 13, pp. 277 - 297.

Roberts, K. [1984], "The Theoretical Limits to Redistribution", Review of Economic Studies, Vol. 51, pp. 177 - 195.

Shorrocks, A. F. [1983], "Ranking Income Distributions", Economica, Vol 50, pp. 3 -17.

Shorrocks, A. F. and Foster, J. E. [1987], "Transfer Sensitivity Inequality Measures", Review of Economic Studies, Vol. 53, pp. 485 - 97.

Sidgwick, H. [1883, 2nd Edition 1887], Principles of Political Economy (London: Macmillan).

Slivinski, A. D. [1983], "Income Distribution Evaluation and the Law of One Price", Journal of Public Economics, Vol. 20, pp. 103 - 112.

Starrett, D. A. [1972], "Fundamental Non-Convexities in the Theory of Externalities", Journal of Economic Theory, Vol. 4, pp. 180 - 199.

Starrett, D. A. [1988], Foundations of Public Economics (Cambridge: Cambridge University Press).

Tuomala, M. [1990], Optimal Income Tax and Redistribution (Oxford: Clarendon Press).

Turunen, A. H. [1987], "Economic Inequality and Public Policy in a Small Open Economy", Scandinavian Journal of Economics, Vol. 89, pp. 405 - 419.

Turunen-Red, A. H. [1991], "On the Hatta Normality Condition and Tax Reform", Journal of Public Economics, Vol. 43, pp. 253 - 262.

Weymark, J. A. [1979], " A Reconciliation of Recent Results in Optimal Taxation Theory", Journal of Public Economics, Vol. 12, pp. 171 - 189.

Wilson, J. D. [1991], "Optimal Public Goods Provision with Limited Lump-Sum Taxation", American Economic Review, Vol. 81, pp. 153 - 166.

Wong, K.-Y. [1991], "Welfare Comparison of Trade Situations", Journal of International Economics, Vol. 30, pp. 49 - 68.

Yitzhaki, S. and Slemrod, J. [1991] , "Welfare Dominance: Application to Commodity Taxation", American Economic Review, Vol. 81, pp. 480 - 496.

The Second Set of Lectures

On Socially Optimal Piecemeal Consumption Taxation Structures – Where Distributive Justice Matters and Various Classes of Distortions are Present

7. Introduction.

In this set of lectures the discussion returns to a theme alluded to in the opening paragraph introducing the previous set of lectures on economic reform; namely, that of determining under what set of circumstances it is socially optimal to impose a taxation system which possesses a relatively simple structure. The more particular task to be attempted below is that of determining under what set of circumstances it is socially optimal to apply a taxation structure in which the tax rates applied to consumption taxes are set at a uniform level in one sector of the economy (the controlled sector), while these tax rates are set at fixed, but non-uniform, levels in the rest of the economy (the distorted sector). Each sector contains at least two goods.[135] This particular problem is generally known as the piecemeal-consumption-taxation-structure problem (hereafter called the piecemeal problem).

It would seem that the central explicit, or implicit, reason why this topic has (or related topics have) been investigated by many authors in the past is that if, indeed, it is socially optimal to apply this simplified taxation structure, then this fact should go some way towards making more tractable the second-

---

[135] In sections 13 and 14 below, in the main text, this assumption is altered to allow consideration of two important special cases. In the one case there is just one good in the distorted sector (section 13), and in the other case there is just one good in the controlled sector (section 14). More will be said about these special cases below in the main text.

best problem initially implicitly identified by Ramsey [1927] and Corlett and Hague [1953], and explicitly discussed by Meade [1955, Ch VII, and the mathematical supplement and Lipsey and Lancaster [1956]. [136] Put slightly differently, if it is socially optimal to employ a piecemeal consumption taxation structure, this fact should assist in simplifying the application of socially optimal taxation policy in distorted economic systems

7.1 <u>The Piecemeal Consumption Taxation Structure Problem.</u>

The first to discuss this problem formally was Boadway and Harris [1977]. The particular case they considered was where there is a single-person community and the only distortions present in the economy are those created by the imposition of consumption taxes. The particular result they derived was that it is socially optimal to impose a piecemeal consumption taxation structure if all the goods in the distorted sector are weakly separable from all the goods in the controlled sector. [137]

---

[136] The second-best problem states that if there exists at least one unmovable distortion in prices in some sector of an economy, it may be socially optimal not to set the prices for all other goods in the economy according to the Pareto-efficiency rule (that the marginal rate of substitution is proportional to the marginal rate of transformation for the good concerned). Rather some more complex (possibly much more complex) rule may need to be determined and applied. This general idea was first (implicitly) recognised by Ramsey [1927], and subsequently by Corlett and Hague [1953], in the context of setting optimal consumption tax rates within a distorted economic system. Later the second-best problem was formally considered by Meade [1955, Ch. VII] in considerable detail (particularly in the mathematical supplement to this book), and Lipsey and Lancaster [1956]. For some interesting comments, concerning the history of economic thought relating to the second-best problem, see those by Gorman [1990, p. 447 and p. 454].

[137] A formal definition of this class of separability is to be found in Boadway and Harris [1977] and Jewitt [1981]. It is defined below in the main text.

Within the framework of the special assumptions employed by Boadway and Harris, it was soon pointed out by Jewitt [1981] that a stronger, necessary and sufficient result could be derived; namely, it is socially optimal to impose a piecemeal consumption taxation system if, and only if, all the goods in the distorted sector are quasi- (or implicit-) separable from all goods in the controlled sector.[138]

It probably comes as no surprise to be told the the just cited results require modification once the special assumptions, employed by Boadway and Harris, and Jewitt, respectively are replaced by more general assumptions. To begin with, if the alternative assumption is imposed that there are many individuals in the community (not just one), and these individuals possess heterogeneous tastes, then the analysis of the piecemeal problem becomes rather more complicated. The extent to which it becomes more complicated depends upon what social values the community adopts with respect to matters of distributive justice in the context of the economic system being distorted. Thus if distributive justice is of *no concern* (i.e. Libertarian social values apply), then aggregate consumption preferences need to take a form which is more restrictive than just being quasi-separable as between all goods in the controlled sector and all goods in the distorted sector. This point has been established by Blackorby, Donaldson and Schworm [1991]. In contrast, if matters of dis-

---

138 A formal definition of quasi- (or implicit-) separability is to be found in Gorman [1976] and Deaton and Muellbauer [1980]. This term is also defined below in the main text.

tributive justice *are of concern* in the community, then it seems reasonable to suspect that the relevant analysis of the piecemeal problem would become even more complicated. This is indeed the case as is indicated explicitly at the beginning of section 12 below, and by implication in the discussion to be found in the rest of sections 12 and 13 below.

More particularly, the analysis in those two sections indicates that, to determine the necessary and sufficient (or even just sufficient) conditions for it to be socially optimal to apply a piecemeal consumption taxation system, marginal alterations of personal lump-sum income transfers need to be carefully applied at the social optimum. If this is indeed the case, then it would seem reasonable to suggest that if there are incentive-compatibility problems associated with the imposition of the marginal changes of personal lump-sum income transfers - and there are good grounds for suspecting that this is the case[139] - then relevant accurate personal information is unlikely to be available with which to determine when the social optimum has been reached.[140] In addition, the necessary and sufficient (or even just sufficient) conditions devised in section 12 below indicate that complex aggregate, socially-weighted, separability conditions need to be satisfied before it is socially optimal to impose

139 The sort of argument developed in section 4.1 above (in the previous set of lectures) in the main text suggest that this would be the case. Also see, in particular, Hammond [1990, p.11] and Roberts [1984] and the references cited there on the incentive-compatibility problem associated with the imposition of lump-sum transfers and taxes.

140 A similar point is made, but within a different context, in section 4.1 in the previous set of lectures.

piecemeal consumption taxation systems. This implies that, to determine if these conditions are actually satisfied, the exact form of the total differential form of the social welfare function needs to be known. And, as Yitzhaki and Slemrod [1991] have recently pointed out, acceptable information of this type is not available for any community at the present time.[141]

The other alternative assumption (compared to those imposed by Boadway and Harris) introduced into the analysis in section 12 below is that not all markets are complete and competitive.[142] There are two reasons for introducing this complication into the analysis. The first is that these market failures may create distortions which are fixed in size. (This point is explained in more detail in section 12 below.) Thus the assumed presence of these market failures goes some way towards explaining why a number of (possibly many) goods may be found in the distorted sector (as defined above) of the economy. The other reason for introducing this complication into the discussion is that it strengthens the general point made in the previous paragraph; namely, that considerable amounts of accurate, personal, information need to be available, and correctly assessed, before it can be determined if it is socially optimal to impose a piecemeal consumption taxation structure.[143] In addition, the need to

---

141 Also see Hammond [1990, p.17 f].

142 The particular circumstances where such a situation would arise is discussed in sub-section 4.4B and 4.5 above (in the previous set of lectures) in the main text.

143 This point should not be over-stated, however. The reason is that the errors, made in the measurement of relevant personal information, may cancel out when

carefully coordinate the application of a range of policy tools (consumption taxes, personal lump-sum transfers and taxes to offset distortions created by market failures) at the social optimum suggests that the abilities of the authorities, to implement socially optimal piecemeal consumption taxation systems, would be tested.

It would seem reasonable to conclude from these various observations, therefore, that the probability would seem to be rather low of its ever being socially optimal to apply piecemeal consumption taxation structures. This general conclusion, it must be emphasised, is not markedly different from that arrived at by Boadway and Harris [1977] in their initial discussion of the piecemeal problem.[144] What is more they observed that:[145]

> "Presumably, adding further complications to the model we have used [where all markets are complete and competitive and there is just a single individual in the community] would make the conditions for piecemeal policy even more stringent."

The discussion presented below could be interpreted as providing evidence supporting this conjecture. Having said that, the various results presented below do provide a range of insights into how governments may best go about attempting to implement

---

aggregated over individuals and goods. This point is discussed in the concluding sub-section of section 12 below in the main text.

[144] It seems reasonable to draw a similar conclusion from the survey provided by Stiglitz [1987] of the optimum taxation literature - this is so even though Stiglitz [1987] does not mention the piecemeal policy problem (at least as this problem is defined in the main text).

[145] See Boadway and Harris [1977, p.187].

socially beneficial public policies. One of these insights was mentioned at the beginning of the previous set of lectures; namely, perhaps governments should devote more of their efforts towards attempting to introduce socially improving economic reforms, and less effort towards attempting to implement socially optimal economic policies.

Equally this insight is not original, for Henry Sidgwick [1887, p. 525], over a century ago, could reasonably be interpreted as recommending that in communities, where distributive justice is of concern and the economic system is distorted in various ways, gradual and careful reforms of this economic system are to be recommended over and above 'any sudden and sweeping' alterations which attempt to take this community directly to some social optimum.

7.2 Special Cases - The Uniform Taxation Structure Problem.

A special version of the piecemeal problem is that where there is just *one* good (instead of there being at least two goods) in the *distorted* sector of the economy. This particular case has (implicitly) received far more attention in the relevant literature than the Boadway-Harris piecemeal problem. The first to formally discuss this problem were Atkinson and Stiglitz [1976] in the context of determining when it is socially optimal to impose uniform non-linear, and linear consumption taxation systems. Subsequently Atkinson [1977] went on to examine further when it is socially optimal to impose a uniform linear consumption taxation system.[146] Both of these cases essentially imply that a single good, with a fixed taxed imposed upon it, is to be found in the distorted sector. This good is the numeraire (or the supply of labour). [This point is explained in a little detail in section 13.1 below.] What is perhaps a little surprising is that the link between the Boadway-Harris piecemeal problem, and the uniform consumption taxation problem, has not been explicitly recognised in the relevant literature - at least as far as the author is aware.

In the time since the Atkinson and Stiglitz [1976] and Atkinson [1977] papers appeared, there have been a number of additions to the relevant literature. [This literature is cited at the beginning of section 13 below.] In that section the main results, to be found in that literature, are derived and extended. Again, to be able to derive these results, careful use has to be made of the application of marginal changes of personal lump-sum income transfers, and it needs to be assumed that all markets are complete and competitive.

But once allowance is made for the reasonable possibility that at least some markets are not complete and competitive, then this suggests that there most likely will be at least *two* goods in the distorted sector of the economy (not just one). If that is indeed the case, then this brings the discussion back to exactly the sort of problem initially sketched out by Boadway and

146 A related discussion, in the context of a single-individual community, is provided by Sadka [1977].

Harris, and discussed in some detail in sections 10 through to 12 below.

Another special case that arises within the context of the piecemeal policy problem is that where there is just *one* good in the *control* sector, and many goods in the distorted sector of the economy The good in the control sector is the individual supply of labour. This particular general case allows a comparatively general derivation of the properties of socially optimal linear income tax rates. This matter is discussed in section 14 below. It is also a little surprising that the link between the Boadway-Harris piecemeal problem, and model that could be usefully applied to the task of determining the properties of socially optimal marginal linear income tax rates, has not been explicitly recognised in the relevant literature - at least as far as the author is aware.

7.3 <u>The Plan of the Discussion</u>

In the next section there is a brief re-statement of the essentials of the model devised in section 3 above (in the previous set of lectures). It is a model which is summarised by two reduced-form equations representing changes in individual utility levels, within a distorted economic environment, and a general, total differential form of the social welfare function. It is this set of equations - and two equations in particular - which provide the basis for all of the subsequent analysis. There are two aspects of this system of equations that are worthy of note. The first is that, because they are disaggregated down to the level of the individual, this model allows for income distributional effects. The other useful property of this model is that it allows the use of unconstrained optimising techniques of analysis. It is this particular property of this model which provides the flexibility which is required to allow the derivation of certain necessary and sufficient (as distinct form only sufficient) results presented in sections 12 and 13 below.[147,148] This equation system also allows the demonstration, by implication at least, of the fact that a close relationship exists between a range of the results to be found in the relevant literature.

In section 10 there is a discussion of how the presence of distortions in the economy, and the imposition of various constraints on the form of the social welfare function, produces a range of special cases which are considered in the next three sections. The simplest is that employed to derive, and extend slightly, the results presented by Jewitt. [The methods employed to derive these results prove to be particularly useful in the subsequent discussion.] In section 11 the case is considered where distributive justice is of no concern in a many-person, non-identical-individual, community. As indicated above, the main results in this set of lectures are presented in section 12. Section

---

147 Without going into a detailed discussion, had constrained (Lagrangean) optimising techniques of analysis been employed in the main text, only rather limited results could have been derived.

148 It is interesting to note that Jewitt [1981, p. 218] indicated that unconstrained optimising techniques can be effectively applied to analyse the piecemeal policy problem.

13 deals with the special case where the consumption taxes on all goods are controlled. Section 14 covers the matter of determining the properties of socially optimal marginal linear income tax rates within distorted economic environments - a topic which arises naturally out of the matters discussed in section 13. Summarising conclusions are made in section 15. There are also two appendices provided which deal with matters which are not germane to the central theme in the discussion. In the appendices to sections 10 and 11 respectively a comparatively brief argument is provided to indicate why particular (separable) demand behaviour implies that individual preferences, and group preferences, must take a particular form.

8. The General Analytical Framework.

In the previous discussion of the theory of economic reform it proved to be helpful first to set out a relatively general equilibrium welfare model to determine the signs of changes in the level of social welfare. Exactly the same general analytical approach will be adopted here. This similarity, between these two approaches, goes even further for the general equilibrium welfare model to be applied below is essentially the same as that presented in section 3, along with some of the initial assumptions to be found in section 2, in the previous set of lectures. [If anything, however, that analytical framework is more general than what is really required in much of the present discussion.] Nevertheless, to focus ideas, the essentials of that model will be re-stated here.

To begin with it is assumed that there is a general social welfare function (swf)

$$W = W(v^1, v^2, \dots, v^H) \qquad (8.1)$$

where there are H (≥ 2) heterogeneous individuals in the community. This swf is assumed to be continuously twice differentiable in all arguments and quasi-concave in individual utility levels. This latter assumption, along with the symmetry of the swf implied by 8.1 above, represents the community's concerns about the matter of distributive justice.

The indirect utility function for any individual takes the relatively general form, for any individual h:

$$v^h = v^h(q, g, y^h), \qquad (8.2)$$

where q denotes a vector of positive prices for n+1 goods facing individual h, g the public good consumed by this individual and y^h the income received by this individual. This function is homogeneous of degree zero in prices and income, increasing in y^h, non-increasing and quasi-convex in p, and continuously twice differentiable in all arguments. The statement in (8.2) above also reflects the assumption that tastes vary across individuals.

Substituting (8.2) into (8.1) above, and totally differentiating the resulting equation, the end result is the following:[149]

$$dW = \sum_{h=1}^{H} \beta^h \, [dv^h / v_y^h] = \sum_{h=1}^{H} \beta^h \, dv^{h\#} \qquad (8.3)$$

where $$\beta^h := \frac{\partial W}{\partial v^h}\frac{\partial v^h}{\partial y^h}, \qquad (8.4)$$

$$dv^{h\#} := [dv^h / v_y^h] := \sum_{i=1}^{n} - c_i^h \, dq_i \; + \lambda^h \, dg + dy^h, \qquad (8.5)$$

and

$$\lambda^h = \left[\frac{\partial v^h}{\partial g} \Big/ \frac{\partial v^h}{\partial y^h}\right].$$

149 The price of the numeraire is kept constant in this manipulation.

As before λ^h represents the shadow price for the public good - a price which varies across the heterogeneous individuals in the community. In deriving these equation use has been made of Roy's identity. This implies that c_i^h [p, g, y^h] refers to the uncompensated level of demand for good i by individual h.

Unlike in the discussion presented in section 2 above (in the previous set of lectures), relatively few constraints are imposed upon the relative values of the set of β^h terms except that:

$\beta^h \geq 0$ for all individuals

and (8.6)

$\beta^h > 0$ for at least one individuals in the community.

In the next section more will be said about the constraints set out in (8.6) above.

The rest of the general model to be employed in the discussion presented below is essentially the same as that to be found in section 3 in the previous set of lectures. That being the case attention moves on more or less immediately to the basic reduced-form equations representing the general equilibrium welfare model. Combining the equations representing the production side of the model with (8.5) above, by applying the budget constraint for any individual h, it is possible to derive various reduced-form equations (as explained in section 3 above in the previous set of lectures.) It turns out that only the following reduced-form equations are required in the analysis presented in subsequent sections [which is (3.25) in the previous set of lectures]:

$$\frac{dv^h}{v_y^h} = -\sum_{i\in NT} c_i^h\, dt_i - \sum_{j\in T} c_j^h\, d\tau_j + dR^h + \lambda^h dg$$

$$+ dY^h + dS^h, \qquad \text{for all } h, \qquad (8.7)$$

and

$$\frac{dv^h}{v_y^h} = \sum_{i\in NT} t_i\, dc_i^h + \sum_{j\in T} \tau_j\, dE_j^h$$

$$+ \lambda^h dg + dY^h + dS^h, \qquad \text{for all } h, \qquad (8.8)$$

where, for all h individuals,

$$dE_j^h := [\, dc_j^h - dx_j^h \,], \quad \text{for } j \in T,$$

$$\sum_{i=o}^{n} p_i\, dx_i^h = dY^h + dS^h, \qquad (8.9)$$

$$dY^h := \sum_{f=1}^{N} w_f \sum_{i=0}^{n} dF_{fi}^h, \tag{8.10}$$

$$dS^h := \sum_{i=0}^{n} p_i \, \varpi_i \, dx_i^h, \tag{8.11}$$

$$dR^h := \sum_{i \in NT} t_i \, dc_i^h + \sum_{i \in T} \tau_j \, (dc_j^h - dx_j^h)$$

$$+ \sum_{i \in NT} c_i^h \, dt_i + \sum_{j \in T} c_j^h \, d\tau_j, \tag{8.12}$$

and where

$q_i = p_i + t_i$ for all $i \in NT$ (except the numeraire)

and (8.13)

$q_j = p_j^* + \tau_j$ and $p_j = p_j^* + \tau_j$ for all $j \in T$.

As before, and since it is relative prices, and not the absolute price level, which influence individual economic behaviour, the numeraire is assumed to be untaxed.[150]

The term x_i denotes the level of production for any good i [which is a non-traded, NT, or traded, T, good], E_j denotes the balance of trade on the traded good $j \in T$, w_f denotes the wage

150 This assumption is modified slightly below, in section 13 in the main text, in order to take account of a special case discussed there and in the subsequent section.

rate paid to the factor of production f, F^h_{fi} denotes the amount of the factor of production, f, employed in the production of good i consumed by individual h, ϖ_i denotes part of the shadow price of the externality created in the production of good i, p_i denotes the producer price for good i, t_i the consumption tax imposed on this good, and τ_j the tariff rate imposed on the traded good $j \in T$.

One other constraint can usefully be re-stated; namely the government budget constraint:

$$\sum_{i \in NT} t_i \, c_i + \sum_{j \in T} \tau_j \, [c_j - x_j] = \sum_h b^h + G, \qquad (8.14)$$

where b^h refers to the personal lump-sum income transfer paid to individual h and G denotes other government expenditure (say on providing public goods). In the discussion presented in section 13 below, the fact that personal lump-sum transfers are available for use takes on some importance.

The analysis which follows essentially is based on manipulating, in various ways, the basic equations (8.3), (8.7) and (8.8) above . If anything the reduced-form equations presented in (8.7) and (8.8) provide more detail than is required for much of the discussion presented below - although this detail is called upon on occasions below.

To summarise the basic assumptions applied in deriving the reduced-form equations set out in (8.7) and (8.8) above the following assumption is re-stated:

Basic Assumptions (BA): (i) There are many non-identical, utility maximizing individuals in the community; (ii) the indirect utility function for any individual is at least continuously twice differentiable in all arguments, increasing in individual income and non-increasing and quasi-convex in prices and homogeneous of degree zero in prices and income; (iii) firms maximize profit and produce private goods in perfectly competitive markets employing production functions which are increasing and once differentiable in the factors of production employed; (iii) all private markets are in equilibrium at the relevant set of equilibrium prices and (iv) there are various price and market distortions present in the economy.

[In passing it is pointed out that in part (iii), of the Basic Assumptions, it is assumed that all markets for private goods are perfectly competitive. Relaxing this assumption would create complications for the analysis presented below. This is so because now individual income, derived from pure profits earned in production, would enter the utility functions for individuals in the community. This fact, in turn, would cause the compensated demand functions for any individual not to be homogeneous of degree zero in all prices.[151] But this homogeneity property needs

---

151 This point is discussed in Munk [1978] and Atkinson and Stiglitz [1980, pp. 464 - 465].

to be applied on some occasions in the discussion provided below. Thus, to avoid the difficulties created by the presence of pure profits, it is assumed that the markets for private goods are perfectly competitive. (An alternative assumption that could have been employed is that one hundred percent profits taxes are imposed.)]

9. The General Form of the Social Welfare Function at the Social Optimum.

Before turning to consider a range of special cases, based upon (8.3), (8.7) and (8.8) above, it is useful to indicate, in general terms, that the various results which emerge in the next three sections are the direct result of altering the assumptions imposed on the form of the swf at the social optimum. The particular assumption imposed, in turn, is a reflection of: (i) the fact that distortions are present in the economy and (ii) the community's views of matters of distributive justice at the social optimum. It is the combination of these two factors which essentially generates the most complicated cases considered below; namely, those set out in sections 12, 13 and 14.

9.1 The Broad Distributive Justice Case.

The starting point in this discussion is (8.3) in the previous section - an equation representing the total differential of the swf which is assumed to be, for the present, quasi-concave and continuously twice differentiable. This swf also represents a community of H (≥ 2) heterogeneous individuals.

It is now assumed that this community is at the social optimum. Hence that equation is set equal to zero so that:

$$dW = \sum_{h=1}^{H} \beta^h \, [dv^h / v_y^h] = 0, \qquad (9.1)$$

where relevant terms are defined in (8.4) and (8.5) above. The main objective set for the present discussion is to determine what factors influence the relative size of the β^h terms - the terms representing the individual marginal social value of income.

To simplify the discussion of this matter it is assumed that the economy is closed, but non-lump taxes are employed to raise the revenue required to finance personal lump-sum income transfers within the community. (This latter assumption will be commented on in sub-section 9.4 below.) There is also a set of other distortions present in the economy in the form of global consumption externalities and variable scale economies.[152] Also, and of particular interest here, the authorities alter the personal lump-sum transfers by a small amount at the social optimum.

This assumed change in economic policy, along with the other assumptions mentioned above, can easily be represented in the reduced-form equation (8.8) above. The resulting equation is substituted into (9.1) above to give the following:[153]

---

152 As indicated in the derivation of the basic model set out in section 3 (in the previous set of lectures), the presence of variable scale economies in the economy (at least in the present model) is due to the assumption that there are externalities on the production side of the economy. See sub-section 3.2 (in the previous set of lectures) in the main text for a discussion of this point.

153 Naturally the basic assumptions (BA) are also assumed to be satisfied.

$$dW = \sum_{h=1}^{H} \beta^h \left[\sum_i t_i \frac{\partial c_i^h}{\partial b^h} + \lambda^h \frac{\partial g}{\partial b^h} + \frac{\partial S^h}{\partial b^h} + 1 \right] db^h = 0, \tag{9.2}$$

where b^h represents the personal lump-sum income transfer paid to individual h. It is also noted that it must be that $(\partial Y^h/\partial b^h) = 1$.

Simple inspection of the first-order optimising condition,[154] set out in (9.2) above, indicates that the term in square brackets in (9.2) above almost certainly will take different values for different individuals in the community. This is so because of (i) the various distortions present in the economy, (ii) the fact that the community is composed of heterogeneous individuals and (iii) the assumed properties of the swf. Only in the unlikely situation where the distortions, facing each individual in the community at the social optimum, take the same value, will the β^h terms also take the same value for all individuals.

It is also worth noting that (9.2) above also indicates that the values of the β^h terms will still vary in value across individuals - even if the authorities were able to impose lump-sum taxes (and no consumption taxes) to raise the government

---

154 Throughout the discussion in the main text it is also assumed that the relevant second-order optimising conditions are satisfied. This assumption needs to be imposed since the various first-order conditions set out in the main text may - without further relevant assumptions being imposed - only refer to a local maximum - or even a local minimum. This general point is discussed in Mirrlees [1986].

revenue required.[155] This is so since, while the first term in the square brackets in (9.2) above will take a value of zero, the value of the second term and third terms (implicitly representing the lack of complete and competitive markets for the global consumption and production externalities) will tend to vary in size across the heterogeneous individuals in the community.

It follows on from this observation that the only set of (unlikely) circumstances where the marginal social value of income will not vary in size across households at the social optimum [without having to impose additional assumptions upon the form of the swf] is that where the authorities have available to them the use of a full set of policy tools, and are in possession of all relevant information. In this (unrealistic) case only lump-sum taxes are imposed (i.e. $t_i = 0$ for all i goods), and tax-cum-subsidies can be applied by the authorities to create a complete and competitive set of markets. In these special circumstances (9.2) above reduces to the following:

$$dW = \sum_{h=1}^{H} \beta^h \, db^h = 0. \qquad (9.3)$$

More will be said about the derivation of this equation in subsection 9.5 below [in the context of (9.8) and (9.9)]. For the present it is simply noted that, given that the swf is quasi-concave,

155 A similar point is clearly alluded to by Atkinson and Stiglitz [1980, pp. 495 -6] The particular additional constraint they imposed was that the size of the lump-sum taxes imposed could not vary across households.

the social optimum in this case would be attained when $\beta^h = \beta$ for all h individuals in the community so

$$dW = \beta \sum_{h=1} dbh = 0$$

where $\sum_{h=1} db^h = \sum_{h=1} dY^h = 0,$

due to the assumption that the aggregate supplies of all factors of production are fixed.[156]

These observations imply that in a community composed of H (≥2) heterogeneous individuals, the swf is continuously differentiable and strictly quasi-concave (which represents the case where the community is concerned about matters of distributive justice) and there is at least one distortion present in the economy, it is reasonable to assume that at the social optimum the individual marginal social value of income will vary in size across the individuals in this community. Thus for at least two individuals - a,b - in the community $\beta^a \neq \beta^b$.

The swf which possesses this property is said to represent the *broad distributive justice* case. It is this general case which is applied in sections 12 and 13 below. The form of the swf which represents this case is set out in (9.2) above.

---

[156] On this point see the discussion below (3.9) (in the previous set of lectures) in the main text.

9.2 A Homogeneous Community.

The inferences drawn from (9.2) above are not necessarily valid once the assumptions imposed on the swf are varied. The first to be altered is the assumption that the community is composed of heterogeneous individuals. It is now assumed that the community is made up of indentical individuals. In this case (9.2) above reduces to the following:

$$dW = H\beta \left[\sum_i t_i \frac{\partial c_i}{\partial b} + \lambda \frac{\partial g}{\partial b} + \frac{\partial S}{\partial b} \right] db = 0,$$

so that

$$\left[\sum_i t_i \frac{\partial c_i}{\partial b} + \lambda \frac{\partial g}{\partial b} + \frac{\partial S}{\partial b} \right] = 0. \qquad (9.4)$$

In deriving this last equation again it is noted that

$$\sum_{h=1} db^h = \sum_{h=1} dY^h = 0$$

due to the assumption that the aggregate supplies of all factors of production, and the production technology, are fixed.

In this case matters of distributive justice just do not arise. This particular case, which is discussed in more detail in the next section, provides a useful benchmark against which all other cases, discussed below, can be compared.

9.3 The Libertarian Community.

Relaxing the assumption that the swf is strictly quasi-concave, by assuming instead that the swf is just quasi-concave, allows the following possibility:

$$dW = \beta \sum_{h=1}^{H} \left[\sum_i t_i \frac{\partial c_i^h}{\partial b^h} + \lambda^h \frac{\partial g}{\partial b^h} + \frac{\partial s^h}{\partial b^h} + 1 \right] db^h = 0, \tag{9.5}$$

which, in turn, reduces to

$$= \beta \sum_{h=1}^{H} \left[\sum_i t_i \frac{\partial c_i^h}{\partial b^h} + \lambda^h \frac{\partial g}{\partial b^h} + \frac{\partial s^h}{\partial b^h} \right] db^h = 0, \tag{9.6}$$

since, as before, the assumption is applied that the aggregate supplies of all factors of production, and the production technology, are fixed.

The statement in (9.6) above alludes to the fact that in this case there are never any social gains to be derived from any pure re-distribution of utility within the community. In other words the community is indifferent to matters of distributive justice. This special case is called the *libertarian case* .

This case will also be considered in more detail in section 11 below.

9.4 The Dictator and Oligarchy Cases.

An alternative possibility is to relax the assumption that the swf is continuously differentiable in the utility functions for all individuals in the community. This case now allows for the situation where the β^h term for each individual in the community, except individual δ, is assigned a value of zero. In this case (9.2) above becomes:

$$dW = \beta^{\delta}\left[\sum_i t_i \frac{\partial c_i^{\delta}}{\partial b^{\delta}} + \lambda^{\delta} \frac{\partial g}{\partial b^{\delta}} + \frac{\partial S^{\delta}}{\partial b^{\delta}} + 1 \right] db^{\delta} = 0. \quad (9.7)$$

This equation represents the situation where the changes in the level of utility for only one individual in the community determines the direction of change of social welfare. Hence this individual may be thought of as being a dictator. However, if the community is concerned about matters of distributive justice, this 'dictator' could be least well-off in the community, in which case individual δ could be thought of as being a positional dictator.

The situation represented in (9.7) above does not, however, indicate all the cases which could apply in the situation where the swf is assumed not to be continuously differentiable in all arguments. An alternative that could equally apply is that where the swf is only continuously differentiable with respect to the utility levels for just some individuals in the community.

This case could be thought of as representing an oligarchy. A relevant form of the total differential of the swf, representing this community at the social optimum, could be the following:

$$dW = \beta \sum_{h=1}^{k} \left[\sum_i t_i \frac{\partial c_i^h}{\partial b^h} + \lambda^h \frac{\partial g}{\partial b^h} + \frac{\partial S^h}{\partial b^h} + 1 \right] db^h = 0, \text{ where } k < H.$$

The particular cases, briefly set out in this sub-section, are essentially special versions of those mentioned earlier. For this reason these cases will not be considered further below.

9.5 Personal Lump-Sum Income Transfers and Complete and Competitive Markets.

Before turning to consider in more detail the various special cases set out above, there are two particular matters raised by the previous discussion which need to be commented upon further for they take on some importance in part of the discussion which follows.

The first point to note is that personal lump-sum transfers were employed to re-distribute income in the community. This is a strong assumption for, as the discussion in sub-section 4.1 (in the previous set of lectures) indicated, such income transfers system is almost certainly not feasible. Having said that, in the context of the discussion provided above, this matter is not of any great importance. However, in sections 12 and 13 below, the application of this assumption becomes much more contentious.

The other matter raised by the previous discussion concerns the assumptions employed to derive (9.3) from (9.2) above. There it was assumed that the authorities possessed the detailed relevant information to create, if they did not exist initially, complete and competitive markets. So, for example, in the context of (9.2) above it was essentially assumed that the authorities possessed the detailed relevant information required to ensure that appropriate taxes and subsidies could be applied to the point where:[157]

$$\sum_h \beta^h [\lambda^h - t^h] = 0, \qquad (9.8)$$

and

$$\sum_h \beta^h \left[dS^h - \sum_{i=0}^{n} \mu_i \varpi_i dx_i^h \right]$$

$$= \sum_h \beta^h \left[\sum_{i=0}^{n} p_i \varpi_i dx_i^h - \sum_{i=0}^{n} \mu_i \varpi_i dx_i^h \right] = 0. \qquad (9.9)$$

---

157 Use is being made here of the definition of S^h set out in (8.11) above in the main text.

The statement in (9.8) above implies that tax-prices (the t^h s) are applied to all individuals to create an implicit complete[158] and competitive market for the public good, g. Equally in (9.9.), the implication is that a complete and competitive implicit market is created for the production externalities [159] by imposing an appropriate set of taxes (subsidies) - which are denoted by the μ_i s.

Much of the discussion in sub-section 4.4B and 4.5 above (in the previous set of lectures) indicates that the assumptions, implied by the previous two equations, are extremely strong. Above all the authorities are unlikely to possess all the relevant information to make it feasible to apply the pertinent taxes and subsidies with the precision required.[160] This matter will take on some importance when attempts are made to considerably simplify the structure of socially optimal taxation systems. This topic is discussed in sections 12 and 14 below.

[158] To complete these implicit markets, individual subsidies also have to be paid. This point was discussed in sub-section 4.4B above.

[159] See the discussion in sub-section 3.2 above (in the previous set of lectures) on the derivation of the the production side of the model representing the economy.

[160] It is possible that by chance that the various market imperfections may offset one another.

10. The Single-Person Case (or the Jewitt Case).

The first special case considered is that which is based upon the assumption that the community is composed of H (≥1) identical individuals Within this context it is also assumed that the aggregate supply of factors, and the production technology, is fixed. To ease the present discussion it is also assumed that the economy is closed and there are no other distortions present in the community except for the imposition of a set of consumption taxes. It is also assumed that the price for good k is altered by a small amount at the social optimum.

Applying these various assumption to (8.7) and (8.8) above, and drawing on the relevant result set out earlier in (9.4), it follows that at the social optimum,

$$- c_k + \frac{\partial R}{\partial t_k} = 0, \qquad (10.1)$$

and

$$\sum_i t_i \frac{\partial c_i}{\partial t_k} = 0. \qquad (10.2)$$

On applying the Slutsky equation to (10.2) above, and assuming that the level of government revenue remains fixed (i.e. dR

= 0) [161,162] it is not difficult to show that the previous two equations can be combined to provide the following result: [163]

$$\sum_i t_i s_{ik} = 0, \tag{10.3}$$

where the term s_{ik} [= $s_{ik}(q,u)$] refers to the compensated change in the level of demand for the good i as a result of a change in the price of good k.

The statement in (10.3) above can now be exploited to indicate more formally the nature of the piecemeal policy problem. To begin with it is assumed that the size of the consumption taxes in the distorted sector (D-sector) of the economy are fixed, while the level of the consumption taxes in the control sector (C-sector) can be altered in size. It is not difficult to think of realistic institutional settings which would result in consumption tax in some sectors of the economy being of a fixed, unmovable, size. For example, a federal system of government, the central government has no control over the level of consumption taxes imposed by the state and local governments.

[In addition the taxes in the D-sector may be fixed as part of the attempt to offset the economic distortions created by

---

161 This assumption is applied in Ramsey's [1926] classic article on the theory of optimum commodity taxation.

162 In these circumstances the level of lump-sum taxes needs to be altered by an appropriate amount - although only at the social optimum.

163 The relevant manipulation is very similar to that required to derive (4.24) above (in the first set of lectures) in the main text.

the presence of markets which are not complete and competitive. Alternatively, these taxes may act as proxies for these economic distortions. In either instance the distortions associated with these goods are left unaltered due to the fact that the public authorities do not possess enough pertinent information. This particular issue is not addressed directly within the context of the simple model considered here, although it is a matter which is returned to in sections 12 and 14 below - a discussion which draws on the observations made in sub-sections 4.4B and 4.5 in the previous set of lectures.]

The previous assumptions imply that good k is from the C-sector and that (10.3) above can be re-written as follows:

$$[\sum_{i \in D} t_i s_{ik}] + [\sum_{j \in C} t_j s_{jk}] = 0, \quad k \in C. \qquad (10.4)$$

The result set out in (10.4) can now be employed to assist with attempting to answer a question similar to that initially posed by Jewitt [1981]: What conditions, if satisfied, are sufficient and necessary to ensure that it is socially optimal to set the tax rates for each good in the C-sector at a uniform level, proportional to its corresponding marginal cost of production (i.e. producer price), even though unmovable consumption taxes are present in the D-sector?

This question represents the nature of the socially optimal piecemeal-taxation-structure problem.

One implication of the question just posed is that if it is socially optimal to apply a piecemeal consumption taxation structure then, at the social optimum, changes in the consumer, and producer,[164] price for any single good in the C-sector - say that for good k - must have no influence in determining the size of the uniform, proportionate, tax in this sector. Thus, while the uniform consumption tax assumption implies that

$$t_j = \Theta p_j, \qquad j \in C, \tag{10.5}$$

the proportionate term, Θ, must be independent of any single consumer, or producer, price in the C-sector. However, it proves useful to note (drawing on the definition of t_j) that (10.5) above can equally be written as follows:

$$t_j = \phi q_j, \qquad j \in C, \tag{10.6}$$

where $\phi := [\,\Theta/(1+\Theta)\,]$ - a term which must also be independent of any single consumer, or producer, price in the C-sector. When (10.6) is substituted into (10.4), the resulting equation implies that, at the social optimum:

---

164 In the present case producers' prices, as well as consumer prices, may be variable. In Jewitt [1981] and Blackorby *et al.* [1991] producer prices are assumed to be constant.

$$\phi^* = \phi(p^D, q^D, u), \tag{10.7}$$

where q^D is the vector of consumer prices, and q^D the vector of producer prices, ruling in the D-sector.

To determine the conditions which are *sufficient* to ensure that it is socially optimal to impose a piecemeal policy it is assumed that it is indeed socially optimal to apply a piecemeal public pricing policy. To represent this assumption (10.6) [along with (10.7)] is substituted into (10.4) above to give:

$$[\sum_{i \in D} t_i s_{ik}] + \phi(p, q^D, u)[\sum_{j \in C} q_j s_{jk}] = 0, \; k \in C. \tag{10.8}$$

This equation is manipulated further by noting that Cournot aggregation, the Slutsky equation and Engel aggregation imply that[165]

$$\sum_{i \in D} q_i s_{ik} + \sum_{j \in C} q_j s_{jk} = 0, \quad k \in C. \tag{10.9}$$

This equation is applied in (10.8) above to provide the result:

$$\phi(p^D, q^D, u) = \frac{\sum_{i \in D} t_i s_{ik}}{\sum_{i \in D} q_i s_{ik}}, \quad k \in C. \tag{10.10}$$

165 These concepts are discussed, for example, in Deaton and Muellbauer [1980].

The statement in (10.10) above implies that the initial presumption - that it is socially optimal to impose piecemeal policies - is valid if, and only if, the right-hand side of that equation is independent of the price of good $k \in C$. There are two trivial cases which ensure that this is so. The one is where there is only one good in the D-sector - the other is where there is only one good in the C-sector. [Both of these special cases will be returned to in sections 13 and 14 below - but in the context of a many-person community where distributive justice does matter. In these circumstances these special cases cease to be trivial.]

As for the non-trivial case, where there is more than one good in each sector of the economy, (10.10) above indicates a number of conditions which are sufficient to ensure that it would be socially optimal to impose piecemeal policies. They are:

(Ci) $$s_{ik} = a_i(q^D, u)\, g_k(q^C, u), \quad i \in D,\ k \in C, \qquad (10.11)$$

or

$$s_{ki} = b_k(q^C, u)\, f_i(q^D, u), \quad i \in D,\ k \in C, \qquad (10.12)$$

where $g = g(q^C, u)$ and $f = f(q^D, u)$.

(Cii) The ratio of the compensated substitution terms for any two goods in the D-sector, with respect to the price of any good in the C-sector, is independent of the price of that good (in the C-sector).

(Ciii) The rank of the block matrix for all the compensated substitution terms referring to substitution across the C- and D-sectors (the across-sector compensated substitution terms) is at most of rank one.

(Civ) The expenditure function for the single individual takes either of the quasi-separable forms:

$$e(q,u) = e[\, q^{D}, u, g(q^{C},u)], \qquad (10.13),$$

$$e(q,u) = E[\, q^{C}, u, f(q^{D},u)]. \qquad (10.14)$$

To demonstrate that these conditions are sufficient, first (10.11), or (10.12), is substituted into (10.10) above. Clearly the k-terms cancel out as is required for it to be socially optimal to impose piecemeal policies. Simple inspection of (10.10) also indicates that (Cii) stated above is also a sufficient condition for it to be socially optimal to impose these policies. Next it noted that the statement in (10.11) above, for example, implies that the s_{ik} terms can be formed into a block matrix of across-sector compensated substitution terms, $[\, s_{ik}\,]$, which can be written in the vector form:

$$[\, s_{ik}\,] = (a_{ig})(g_{k})', \qquad (10.15)$$

where (a_{ig}) refers to a column vector of a_{ig} terms, and $(g_{k})'$ a row vector of g_k terms. The statement in (10.15), in turn, implies that the rows in the matrix $[s_{ik}]$ are linearly interdependent. This fact implies that this matrix, with the form set out in (10.15), must be at most of rank one.

As for the statement in (Civ) above, by making use of the standard properties of the expenditure function,[166] (10.13) above, for example, is partially differentiated with respect to the price of any good $i \in D$, Shephard's Lemma is then applied and the resulting expression is differentiated with respect to the price of good $k \in C$. The result is an equation of the form stated in (10.11) above. By a similar argument, (10.12) can be derived from (10.14) above.

The sufficiency conditions, which have just been presented, are also *necessary* to ensure that the application of piecemeal policy is socially optimal. To demonstrate this assertion first (10.9) above is multiplied through by $\phi(p^D, q^D, u)$. The resulting equation is subtracted from (10.4) above. The result is the following:

---

[166] These properties are that the expenditure function, e(q,u), is continuously twice differentiable and increasing in q and u, strictly concave in q and linear homogeneous of degree zero in q.

$$\sum_{i \in D} [t_i - \phi(p^D, q^D, u) q_i] s_{ik}$$

$$+ \; [\sum_{j \in C} t_i - \phi(p^D, q^D, u) q_i] s_{jk} = 0, \quad k \in C. \quad (10.16)$$

Clearly for it to be socially optimal to impose uniform consumption taxes in the C-sector, the first set of terms on the left-hand side of (10.16) above must take a value of zero; i.e.

$$\sum_{i \in D} [t_i - \phi(p^D, q^D, u) q_i] s_{ik} = 0, \quad k \in C. \quad (10.17)$$

But since there are as many of this last equation as there are goods (at least two) in the C-sector, (10.17) above alludes to a homogeneous-equation system in which the matrix, of across-sector compensation substitution terms, is represented by $[s_{ik}]$. What is more, there must exist a set of prices for which at least two of the $[t_i - \phi(p^D, q^D, u) q_i]$ terms ($i \in D$) take non-zero values. [If this was not so the piecemeal policy problem would become trivial, or just cease to exist.]

It follows that, for a non-trivial solution to exist for this homogeneous-equation system, the matrix of compensated substitution terms, $[s_{ik}]$, must have a rank at most of one.[167] This last result also implies that the rows in this matrix must be

[167] See Chiang [1974, pp. 118-119], for example, for a discussion of the properties of homogeneous-equation systems.

linearly interdependent. This, in turn, requires that any s_{ik} term in the matrix, $[s_{ik}]$, must take the general form :

$$s_{ik}[:= e_{ik}(q,u)] = a^i(q, u)\, b^k(q, u), \quad i \in D, \; k \in C, \qquad (10.18)$$

where $a^i(q, u)$ and $b^k(q, u)$ are functions.

These various observations imply that the sufficient conditions, set out in points (Cii) and (Ciii) set out above, must also be necessary to ensure that it is socially optimal to impose a piecemeal policy in a single-person community.

To demonstrate that the sufficient condition stated in (Civ) [and (Ci)] above is also necessary is, however, a relatively complex, and technical, task - as the analysis of this problem by Blackorby, Donaldson and Schworm [1991, 1990a] indicates.[168] Partly for this reason, this matter is not discussed here. In addition, it turns out that this comparatively difficult theory is *not* required in the analysis of the more complex cases (where matters of distributive justice come to the fore) discussed in section 12 below. Nevertheless, for the sake of completeness, this theoretical matter is briefly discussed in the appendix to this section.

---

168 At this point in the analysis the theory of the integrability of individual consumption behaviour, back to underlying individual preferences, needs to be employed.

Of the four sufficiency and necessary conditions listed above, the one with the most content concerning economic behaviour is that presented in point (Civ). The particular behaviour alluded to in the quasi-separable expenditure functions set out in (10.13) and (10.14) above is that a two-stage budgeting procedure is employed by the single individual in the process of allocating income to consumption expenditure. In the first stage the total budget for the single consumer is allocated between two sets of goods - those in the D-sector and those in the C-sector - with the objective of maximizing utility. Expenditures on goods within a given sector are now only influenced by the prices in that sector and the general level of utility. The prices in the other sector - say the D-sector - will only influence the pattern of expenditure on goods in the C-sector by changing the proportion of the total budget allocated to the C-sector. This consumption behaviour, reflected in the quasi-separable expenditure functions [set out in (10.13) and (10.14) above respectively], in turn implies that if prices in a given sector fall, while the level of utility remains constant, then expenditure on each good in the other sector must fall by the same proportionate amount.[169]

This last observation, in particular, indicates that even within the context of the very limited case considered in this section, the many homogeneous individuals in the community will need to possess extremely restrictive preferences before it be-

---

169 See Gorman [1976, p. 240] on this point.

comes socially optimal to apply a piecemeal consumption taxation structure.

The Appendix for section 10.

Only the broad nature of the pertinent argument - to establish that (10.13) and (10.14) set out necessary and sufficient conditions (that need to be satisfied for it to be socially optimal to apply piecemeal consumption taxation systems) - will be sketched out here.[170]

Attention returns to (10.18) above - an equation derived from the necessary and sufficient condition that the matrix, $[s_{ik}]$, is of rank one. Determining the form of the expenditure function underlying (10.18) above requires that it be shown that relevant functions can be represented by continuous partial differential equations. Here it is simply assumed that all relevant functions possess the properties required. These partial differential equations also need to satisfy the integrability condition that the block matrix, $[s_{ik}]$, is symmetric.[171]

Re-writing (10.18) above as a partial differential equation,

$$e_{ik}(p,u) = \gamma(p,u)\, A_i(p,u)\, B_k(p,u)\,, \qquad i \in D,\ k \in C, \qquad (A1)$$

where the sub-scripts refer to partial derivatives, this equation is

170 Those requiring more details should consult Blackorby *et al.* [1990a,b,1991].

171 This integrability condition must be satisfied to ensure that the system of compensated demand functions, which underlie (10.18) above, are derived from an expenditure function.

also assumed to satisfy the integrability condition mentioned above. This will be so if

$$e_i\,(p,u) = A_i\,(p^D,u)\,g\,(p,u) + c_i^1(p^D,u), \quad i \in D, k \in C, \quad (A2)$$

and

$$e_k\,(p,u) = \alpha(p,u)\,B_k\,(p^C,u) + c_k^2(p^C,u), \quad i \in D, k \in C, \quad (A3)$$

where $g_k(p,u) = B_k(p,u)\,\gamma(p,u)$ and $\alpha_i\,(p,u) = A_i\,(p,u)\,\gamma\,(p,u)$.

(A2) and (A3) are also assumed to be partial differential equations. What is more, if a solution is to exist for the system of partial differential equations alluded to by these last two equations, then they must also satisfy the integrability condition referred to above. That being the case, a possible solution for (A2) above is that

$$e(p,u) = A\,(p^D,u)\,g\,(p,u) + c^1(p^D,u) + c^3(p^C,u). \quad (A4)$$

Based on this equation, and by Young's theorem,

$$e_{ik}\,(p,u) = A_i\,(p^D,u)\,g_k\,(p,u) + A(p^D,u)\,g_{ik}\,(p,u)$$

$$= A_i\,(p^D,u)\,g_k\,(p,u) + A(p^D,u)\,g_{ki}(p,u) = e_{ki}(p,u), \; i \in D, k \in C. \quad (A5)$$

The statement in this last equation implies, however, that the sufficient and necessary conditions, set out in (Cii) and in (Ciii) above, would fail to be satisfied. Hence the expenditure function set out in (A4) is not necessary, nor sufficient, to ensure that it is socially optimal to impose piecemeal policy.

Having said that, (A5) above also indicates that that equation would ensure that the conditions set out in (Cii) and (Ciii) above are satisfied if, and only if, $g_{ik} = g_{ki} = 0$ for all $i \in D$, $k \in C$. This would only be so if (A4) is rewritten as follows:

$$e(p,u) = A(p^D,u)\,\tilde{g}(p^C, u) + c^1(p^D, u) + c^3(p^C, u). \qquad (A6)$$

A similar line of argument, applied to (A3) above, indicates that

$$e(p,u) = \tilde{\alpha}(p^D,u)\,B(p^C, u) + c^2(p^C, u) + c^4(p^D, u). \qquad (A7)$$

These last two equations, in turn, can be re-written in the general, more compact, forms stated in (10.13) and (10.14) above.

Thus the suffiency condition set out in (Civ) above is also a necessary requirement for it to be socially optimal to apply piecemeal policy in a single-person community. That being the case, and given the properties of the expenditure function, the sufficiency condition stated in (Ci) above is also a necessary condition.

11. The Many-Person Case Where Libertarian Social Values Apply.

The point of departure in this section is sub-section 9.3 above [and, in particular, (9.6)] where Libertarian social values are applied to the swf in an economy which is closed to international trade. As indicated in that sub-section, in this particular case at the social optimum the relevant general form of the reduced-form equation (8.8) above [when combined with the required version of (8.3)] is the following:

$$dW = \beta \sum_{h=1}^{H} \left[\sum_{i} t_i \; dc_i^h + \lambda^h dg + dS \right] = 0, \qquad (11.1)$$

where, as before, the assumption is applied that the aggregate supplies of all factors of production, and the production technology, are fixed so that

$$\sum_{h} dY^h = 0. \qquad (11.2)$$

This particular assumption will be briefly returned to at the end of this section. Also there are H (≥ 2) heterogeneous individuals in the community.

As in the previous sub-section, this discussion is kept relatively simple by assuming that the only distortions present in the economy are a set of consumption taxes. The price on good k is also altered by a small amount at the social optimum and the level of aggregate government revenue is assumed to remain fixed (by applying offsetting alterations to lump-sum taxes at the social optimum). Imposing these assumptions to the reduced-form equations set out in (8.7) and (8.8) above, bearing in mind that in the present case all individuals are assigned the same value for the marginal social value of individual income [as indicated in (11.1) above], and applying the Slutsky equation, it can be shown that[172]

$$\sum_h \sum_i t_i s_{ik}^h = 0. \qquad (11.3)$$

The special result represented by (11.3) above is essentially the point of departure in the analysis of the piecemeal policy problem considered in some detail by Blackorby, Donaldson and Schworm [1991]. However, they based their discussion on the concept of Scitovsky sets;[173] namely, sets of goods which are the minimum aggregate quantities required, given market prices, to allow each individual in the community to attain a given level of utility. But for this case to represent a social optimum, the community needs to be indifferent to matters of distributive justice.

The rest of the relevant argument that can be based on (11.3) above is very similar to that to be found in the previous

---

172 Again the relevant manipulation required in this case is similar to that needed to derive (4.29) (in the first set of lectures) in the main text.

173 See Scitovsky [1942], Graaff [1957, pp. 53-54] and Blackorby, Donaldson and Schworm [1990b].

section. First of all (11.3) above is partitioned into C-, and D-, sector sets of goods. Next, based on the supposition that the application of piecemeal policy is socially optimal, (10.6) is substituted into the resulting equation to give:

$$\sum_{h=1}^{H} [\sum_{i \in D} t_i s_{ik}^{h} + \theta(p^D, q^D, u) \sum_{i \in C} p_j s_{jk}^{h}] = 0, \quad k \in C. \quad (11.4)$$

In the present case, however, in the function, $\theta(p^D, q^D, u)$, the term **u** denotes a vector of individual utility levels - $\mathbf{u} = \{u^1, u^2, \ldots, u^H\}$ - not just the utility level for a single individual.

The last equation is manipulated by making use of an appropriately expanded version of (10.9) above. On making the relevant substitutions into (11.4) above, it can be shown that that equation becomes:

$$\theta(p^D, q^D, u) = \frac{\sum_h \sum_{i \in D} t_i s_{ik}^{h}}{\sum_h \sum_{i \in D} p_i s_{ik}^{h}} = \frac{\sum_{i \in D} t_i s_{ik}}{\sum_{i \in D} p_i s_{ik}}, \quad k \in C, \quad (11.5)$$

where $s_{ik} := \sum_h s_{ik}^{h}$ for all $k \in C$.

On comparing (11.5) with (10.10) above it is reasonable to infer that more stringent sufficiency conditions need to be satisfied in the present, many-person, Libertarian case - compared to the single-person case - if it is to be socially optimal to impose piecemeal policy. Specifically, conditions which are sufficient to ensure that the extreme right-hand side of (11.5) above is indeed independent of the price of good k, are the following:

(GCi)

$$s_{ik}(p,u) = a_i(p^D, u)\, g_k(p^C), \quad i \in D,\ k \in C. \qquad (11.6)$$

or

$$s_{ik}(p,u) = b^h_k(p^C, u)\, f_i(p^D), \quad i \in D,\ k \in C. \qquad (11.7).$$

(GCii) The ratio of the simple aggregate compensated substitution terms for any two goods in the D-sector, with respect to the price of any good in the C-sector, is independent of the price of that good (in the C-sector).

(GCiii) The rank of the block matrix for all the simple aggregate across-sector compensated substitution terms is at most of rank one.

(GCiv) The aggregate expenditure function takes either of the following general forms:

$$e(p, u) = A(p^D, u)\, \tilde{g}(p^C) + c^1(p^D, u) + c^2(p^C, u), \quad (11.8)$$

or

$$e(p, u) = B(p^{C}, u)\,\tilde{\alpha}(p^{D}) + c^{3}(p^{D}, u) + c^{4}(p^{C}, u). \quad (11.9)$$

The argument required to demonstrate that these various conditions are sufficient [to ensure that that it is socially optimal to impose piecemeal consumption taxation policy] is essentially the same as that presented just below (10.14) in the previous section. Hence those arguments will not be repeated here. What needs to be emphasised, however, is that in the present context aggregate preferences need to be of a form which are more restrictive than that for the single-person case. [This can be seen by comparing (11.8) and (11.9) with (10.13) and (10.14) above.] The argument required to indicate why this is so is rather technically involved. Partly for this reason a sketched-out argument is assigned to an appendix for this section. The other part of the reason is that this theory also has no direct bearing on the discussion presented in the next section - a discussion based upon the more complex case where matters of distributive justice are of concern in the community.

It should also be noted that the previous discussion has not indicated that any restrictions should be placed on individual preferences. Indeed individual preferences may well not satisfy the rank condition referred to (GCiii) above. All that is required is that aggregate preferences satisfy the restrictions set out in (11.8) and (11.9). Nevertheless these restrictions are comparatively severe and, therefore, it would seem reasonable to conjecture that these conditions are unlikely to be satisfied in reality.

The general conclusion that can be drawn from this last observation is that rarely, if ever, would it be socially optimal to apply piecemeal consumption taxation. Added weight can be given to this conclusion by noting that, in the previous discussion, assumptions were applied which were actually *biased in favour* of the thesis that it is socially optimal to apply piecemeal consumption taxation.

To demonstrate this assertion, it might reasonably be argued that the assumption, that aggregate factor supplies, and the production technology, are fixed when the consumption taxes are varied in size, lacks generality, or credibility.[174] Instead, it could be argued that altering these taxes may influence the rate of investment and technological innovation and invention. (Such a reasonable argument might have been put by Henry Sidgwick [1887], for example. [175]) This argument is given added cogency when it is remembered that, in the economic model applied throughout the present discussion, the prices facing producers are allowed to vary in size.[176]

Accepting this line of argument the assumption, represented by (11.2) above, is replaced by the following:

---

[174] This assumption is represented by the statement in (11.2) above in the main text.

[175] See the general introduction to this book and comments made there on the contribution made by Sidgwick [1883, 1887] to the general theory of taxation. Also see Sidgwick [1883, 1887, book III, Ch. VII].

[176] This point can be confirmed by consulting the derivation of the basic reduced-form equations in sub-section 3.4 (in the previous set of lectures) in the main text.

$$\sum_h \frac{\partial Y^h}{\partial t_k} \neq 0 \text{, for at least some k goods.} \tag{11.10}$$

In this case the relevant form of the basic reduced-form equations becomes (given all the other assumptions applied above):[177]

$$\sum_h \left\{ \sum_i t_i s_{ik}^h + \sum_i t_i \frac{\partial c_i^h}{\partial Y^h} \left[- c_k^h + \frac{\partial Y^h}{\partial t_k} \right] + \frac{\partial Y^h}{\partial t_k} \right\} = 0, \tag{11.11}$$

in the instance of combining (8.8) and (8.3) above (and assuming that Libertarian social values apply), and

$$\sum_h [- c_k^h + \frac{\partial Y^h}{\partial t_k}] = 0, \qquad k \in C, \tag{11.12}$$

in the instance of combining (8.7) and (8.3) above (and assuming that Libertarian social values apply).

On applying the result in (11.12) to (11.11) above, and employing the relevant manipulation to the resulting equation, it can be shown that (11.5) above expands to the following:

177 Besides introducing the Slutsky equation into (8.3) above in the main text, allowance must also be made for the influence of the pure-economic-growth effect on the level of demand for all goods.

$$\theta(p^D, q^D, u) = \frac{\sum_{i \in D} t_i s_{ik}}{\sum_{i \in D} p_i s_{ik}} + \frac{\dfrac{\partial Y}{\partial t_k}}{\sum_{i \in D} p_i s_{ik}}, \quad k \in C. \qquad (11.13)$$

In this case no longer are the conditions, set out above in (GCi) through to (GCiv), sufficient to ensure that it is socially optimal to apply uniform consumption taxes in the C-sector.

What this particular case serves to demonstrate is just how sensitive the solution to the piecemeal problem is to the assumptions imposed. This is a theme which is returned to on a number of occasions in the next two sections.

<u>The Appendix for section 11.</u>

In this appendix an argument is sketched out to indicate why aggregate preferences, in the Libertarian case, need to be of a form which is more restrictive than that for the single-person case.

To begin with it is indicated that the sufficiency condition in (GCiii) above is also necessary to ensure that it is socially optimal to impose piecemeal policy in a many-person community where Libertarian social values apply. This can be done by first noting that, in place of (10.17) above, the following applies:

$$\sum_{h} \sum_{i \in D} [t_i - \theta(p, q^D, u) p_i] s^h_{ik}$$

$$= \sum_{i \in D} [t_i - \theta(p, q^D, u) p_i] s_{ik} = 0, \quad k \in C. \qquad \text{(B1)}$$

As before, this equation alludes to a homogeneous-equation system in which the matrix of simple aggregate compensated substitution terms, $[s_{ik}]$, must be at most of rank one - which implies that the sufficiency condition stated in (GCiii) above is also necessary.

This necessary condition, in turn, implies that

$$s_{ik} \; [:= \sum_h s^h_{ik} \;] = a^i(p,u) \; b^k(p,u) \, , \; k \in C, \, i \in D, \quad \text{(B2)}$$

where $a^i(p,u)$ and $b^k(p,u)$ are functions. This last equation is virtually the same as (10.18) above except that now the vector term, u, appears.

From this point on it is a complex exercise to demonstrate, based on (B2) above, that the sufficiency condition stated in (GCiv) above is also a necessary condition.[178] Nevertheless, the broad nature of the relevant argument is similar to that sketched out in the appendix to section 10 above. There is, however, one important additional element that needs to be allowed for in that discussion; namely, account has to be taken of the fact that the community is composed of many heterogeneous individuals, and the size and composition of this community may change as it moves from one social state to another.

To demonstrate the importance of this point, suppose either that at least one additional, heterogeneous, individual is added to the community, or there is a change in the composition of the community (i.e. some individuals are replaced by other individuals who possess different tastes). Either of these changes in social states is represented by re-writing (B2) above in the change form:

---

[178] Again the relevant detailed discussion of this problem to be found in Blackorby [1990a,b, 1991] indicates that this is the situation.

$$\Delta e_{ik} = e_{ik}(p,u) - e'_{ik}(p,u') \approx [\, a^{i}(p,u) - a^{i\prime}(p,u')]\, b^{k}(p,u)$$

$$a^{i}(p,u)\, [\, b^{k}(p,u) - b^{k\prime}(p,u')], \quad i \in D,\ k \in C,$$

where the dashed terms represent the new social state. On making use of (B2) in the previous equation, the result is that

$$e'_{ik}(p,u') \approx a^{i\prime}(p,u')\, b^{k}(p,u) - a^{i}(p,u)\, [\, b^{k}(p,u) - b^{k\prime}(p,u')], \quad i \in D,\ k \in C,$$

or (B3)

$$e'_{ik}(p,u') \approx a^{i}(p,u)\, b^{k\prime}(p,u')] - [\, a^{i}(p,u) - a^{i\prime}(p,u')]\, b^{k}(p,u), \quad i \in D,\ k \in C.$$

This last result implies that the new aggregate cross-sector Slutsky matrix may now not satisfy the rank condition set out in (GCiii) above. Such a situation can be avoided, however, if (B2) above takes either of the following forms:

$$s_{ik} = a^{i}(p,u)\, \tilde{b}^{k}(p), \quad k \in C,\ i \in D, \tag{B4}$$

or

$$s_{ik} = \tilde{a}^{i}(p)\, b^{k}(p,u), \quad k \in C,\ i \in D. \tag{B5}$$

Should either of these cases apply, the rank condition would now be satisfied.

The broad nature of the rest of the argument is that to be found in the appendix for section 10 above - that is after pertinent changes have been made to (A1).[179] It emerges that the simple aggregate forms of the expenditure functions which are necessary for it to be socially optimal to impose piecemeal policy, when libertarian social values apply, are those stated in (11.8) and (11.9) above.

---

179 That equation, in the present context, now needs to be written as follows:

$$e_{ik}(p,u) = \gamma(p)\, A_i(p,u)\, B_k(p), \quad \text{or} \quad e_{ik}(p,u) = \gamma(p))\, A_i(p)\, B_k(p,u), \quad i \in D,$$

$k \in C$.

12. The Broad Distributive Justice Case and Piecemeal Consumption Taxation Structures.

The community is now assumed to adopt a broad set of social values consistent with distributive justice. As demonstrated earlier in sub-section 9.1, in this case (as defined) at the social optimum $\beta^h \neq \beta^m$ and $\beta^h > 0$ and $\beta^h > 0$ for at least two h,m individuals in the community [180] - given that there are distortions present in the economy and that the H (≥ 2) individuals in the community possess heterogeneous tastes. The following assumption will be employed below to describe this situation:

<u>Distributive Justice Assumption (J)</u>: The community, composed of H (≥ 2) heterogeneous individuals, possesses a social welfare function (swf) of the form stated in (8.1). This swf is continuously differentiable in at least two of the individual utility functions. At the social optimum, in the total differential of this swf [set out in (8.3 and (8.4) above] $\beta^h \neq \beta^m$ and $\beta^h > 0$ and $\beta^h > 0$ for at least two h,m individuals in a community.

This assumption is employed when combining (8.3) above with the reduced-form equations set out in (8.7) and (8.8) above. Applying a range of subsidiary assumptions listed in the previous

---

180 The term β^h - the marginal social value of income for individual h - is defined in (8.4) above in the main text

two sections,[181] altering the consumption tax on good k, and making use of the Slutsky equation the end result is that at the social optimum:

$$dW = \sum_h \beta^h \left\{ \sum_i t_i s_{ik}^h + \sum_i t_i \frac{\partial c_i^h}{\partial y^h} \left[- c_k^h \right] + \frac{\partial y^h}{\partial t_k} \right\} dt_k = 0, \quad (12.1)$$

and

$$dW = \sum_h \beta^h \left[- c_i^h + \frac{\partial R^h}{\partial t_k} + \frac{\partial y^h}{\partial t_k} \right] dt_k = 0, \quad k \in C. \quad (12.2)$$

[In the process of deriving these last two equations it is noted that, since there are no real income effects taking place,[182] no allowance must be made for these effects in (12.1) and (12.2) above. Instead, those equations only allow for the income effects which result from the change in the price of good k - income effects reflected in the Slutsky equation and in the changes in the distribution of individual incomes.]

These particular versions of the basic reduced-form equations indicate that it is no longer possible to combine these equations in the manner exploited in the previous two sections -

---

181 These assumptions are: (i) the basic assumptions (BA) are satisfied; (ii) the economy is closed; (iii) aggregate factor supplies and the production technology is fixed; (iv) second-order optimising conditions are satisfied and (v) there are no other distortions present in the economy except for the imposition of consumption taxes.

182 In the previous footnote it is assumed, amongst other things, that $\sum_h dY^h = dY$.

even when $dR^h = 0$ for all h individuals, and aggregate factor supplies, and the production technology, are fixed at the social optimum. This is so essentially because, in the present case, the values of the β^h terms vary [for reasons explained in section 9 above] across individuals in the community. As a result (12.2), for example, cannot simply be substituted directly into (12.1) above. Hence, the fact that the community is concerned about matters of distributive justice in a distorted economy raise complications for the present discussion.

12.1 Necessary and Sufficient Conditions With Markets Complete and Competitive.

The most general solution to these difficulties begins by assuming that the community has some limited access to personal lump-sum transfers (taxes).[183] Next these personal lump-sum transfers are applied, along with the consumption taxes, with the objective of ensuring that:

$$dW = \sum_h \beta^h \left\{ \sum_i t_i s_{ik}^h + \sum_i t_i \frac{\partial c_i^h}{\partial y^h}\left[- c_k^h\right] + \frac{\partial Y^h}{\partial t_k} \right\} dt_k$$

$$+ \sum_h \beta^h \left\{ \sum_i t_i \frac{\partial c_i^h}{\partial b^h} + \frac{\partial Y^h}{\partial b^h} \right\} db^h = 0, \quad k \in C. \quad (12.3)$$

[183] This apparently strong assumption - especially in the light of the discussion in sub-section 4.1 above in the previous set of lectures - will be commented upon below in the main text on a number of occasions.

The revenue, required to finance these marginal changes in lump-sum transfers, is raised by imposing consumption taxes.

Next it is assumed that these personal lump-sum transfers (taxes) can be applied with the precision required to ensure that the following assumption is also satisfied:

Assumption 2.1 (A2.1): At the social optimum personal lump-sum transfers (taxes) can be applied such that

$$\sum_h \beta^h \left\{ \sum_i t_i \frac{\partial c_i^h}{\partial y^h} \left[- c_k^h \right] + \frac{\partial Y^h}{\partial t_k} \right\} dt_k$$

$$+ \sum_h \beta^h \left\{ \sum_i t_i \frac{\partial c_i^h}{\partial b^h} + \frac{\partial Y^h}{\partial b^h} \right\} db^h = 0, \quad k \in C. \tag{12.4}$$

On applying the assumption set out in (12.4) to (12.3) above, the result is that the latter equation reduces to

$$\sum_h \beta^h \sum_i t_i s_{ik}^h = \sum_i t_i \tilde{s}_{ik} = 0, \quad k \in C, \tag{12.5}$$

where $$\tilde{s}_{ik} := \sum_h \beta^h s_{ik}^h . \tag{12.6}$$

The result stated in that equation is virtually the same as that set out in (10.3) above. [The only point of difference is that the socially-weighted compensated substitution terms in (12.5) above refer to a more complex set of factors - which are alluded to in (12.6) above - than is the case in (10.3) above.] Consequently the manipulation of (12.5) can mirror that to be found below (10.3) above.

As before the taxed goods are partitioned into two relevant sets of goods, while the expanded version of (10.9) above which applies in the present case is the following:[184]

$$\sum_h \beta^h \left[\sum_{i \in D} q_i s_{ik}^h + \sum_{j \in C} q_j s_{jk}^h \right] = 0, \qquad k \in C.$$

or, on making use of the definition set out in (12.6) above,

$$[\sum_{i \in D} q_i \tilde{s}_{ik}] + [\sum_{j \in C} q_j \tilde{s}_{ik}] = 0, \quad k \in C. \qquad (12.7)$$

On multiplying (12.7) by $\Phi(p^D, q^D, \beta, u)$, and combining the result with a suitably partitioned version of (12.5) above, this allows the equations to be derived which are required to establish relevant sufficient and necessary conditions (for it to be socially optimal to apply a piecemeal consumption taxation system). Specifically these equations are:

---

184 In this case essentially the property of the compensated demand functions - namely, that they are homogeneous of degree zero in prices - is being exploited. As pointed out at the end of section 8 above, this assumption is valid only if no excess profits are being earned in the community.

$$\Phi(p^D, q^D, \beta, u) = \frac{\sum_{i \in D} t_i \tilde{s}_{ik}}{\sum_{i \in D} q_i \tilde{s}_{ik}}, \qquad k \in C, \qquad (12.8)$$

and

$$\sum_{i \in D} [\, t_i - \Phi(p^D, q^D, \beta, u)\, q_i \,]\, \tilde{s}_{ik} = 0, \qquad k \in C.$$

$$(12.9)$$

The uniform tax rate, $\Phi(p^D, q^D, \beta, u)$, applied to the consumption taxes in the C-sector, now is a function, amongst other things, of a vector of individual utility levels and a vector of terms representing the marginal social value of individual incomes.

The result in (12.9) - which is a generalised version of (10.17) above - alludes to a system of homogeneous equations. Thus, as before, for a non-trivial solution for this system of equations to exist, the matrix of socially-weighted compensated substitution terms, $[\, \tilde{s}_{ik} \,]$, must have a rank of at most one. This last result also implies that the rows (columns) in this matrix must be linearly interdependent which, in turn, implies that the $\tilde{s}_{ik}$ terms must take the following general form:

$$\tilde{s}_{ik} = \tilde{a}^{i}(q, \beta, u)\, \tilde{b}^{k}(q, \beta, u), \; i \in D,\; k \in C, \qquad (12.10)$$

where $\tilde{a}^{i}(q, \beta, u)$ and $\tilde{b}^{k}(q, \beta, u)$ are functions.

This last necessary result is also sufficient - as can be seen by applying the statement in (12.10) to (12.8) above and cancelling out the k-terms. This observation, in turn, implies that the necessary condition - that the matrix of socially-weighted compensated substitution terms is at most of rank one - is also a sufficient condition. [185]

<u>Proposition 12.1</u>: The assumptions (BA) and (J) are satisfied, as are the assumptions that the economy is closed, aggregate factor supplies and the technology, are fixed, all markets are complete and competitive, second-order optimising conditions are satisfied at the social optimum and (A2.1) is satisfied when attempting to apply socially optimal piecemeal consumption taxation system. In these circumstances (where there are at least two goods in each sector) this taxation system is socially optimal if, and only if, the following equivalent conditions are satisfied at the social optimum:

(a) The rank of the block matrix for all the socially-weighted compensated substitution terms referring to substitution across the C- and D-sectors (the across-sector compensated substitution terms) is at most of rank one.

185 Essentially all these issues were discussed in more detail in section 10 above.

(b) The ratio of the socially-weighted across-sector compensated substitution terms [defined in (12.6) above] in the D-sector, with respect to the price of any good in the C-sector, is independent of the price of that good (in the C-sector).

(c) Any socially-weighted compensated substitution term to be found in the block matrix takes the following general form:

$$\tilde{s}_{ik} = \tilde{a}^{i}(q, \beta, u)\, \tilde{b}^{k}(q, \beta, u), \quad i \in D, \; k \in C.$$

No attempt is made here to determine the unique set of social-individual preferences (if such a unique set of preferences exists) which would generate the compensated aggregate demand behaviour alluded to in (12.10) above. What is emphasised, however, is that proposition 12.1 indicates that a considerable amount of information needs to be acquired before it can be determined if it is socially optimal to apply a piecemeal consumption taxation system. First it could reasonably be argued that the information problems, created by incentive-incompatibility behaviour, are so severe that they prevent the precise application of marginal changes in personal lump-sum transfers (taxes) at the social optimum. [186] If, however, these problems are not serious,

[186] It might be argued that the incentive-compatibility problem could be avoided by assuming that there are goods in the D-sector which also satisfy the Weymark condition. [This condition is discussed in connection with proposition 4.3 in the main text (in the previous set of lectures).] Assuming that this is the case, it is doubtful whether applying such an assumption would allow the community the flexibility (in the application of policy tools) required to attain the social optimum - except by chance.

then next the sizes of the marginal social value of individual incomes need to be determined. But this information is probably impossible, to determine - at least at the present time.[187] These matters will be returned to below.

The methods, employed in the process of deriving (12.5) above, differ from those utilised in the derivation of the main results presented in the previous two sections. Firstly, use was not made of the reduced-form equations set out in (12.2) above. This fact implies that (12.5) above is not based upon the assumption that the level of government revenue remains constant over the relevant change in social states (although it could be). Thus it is possible that, by the tax structure being altered from a consumption, to a piecemeal taxation system, the community may gain by also altering the amount of government revenue raised at the social optimum. Such a change in the level of government tax revenue raised is, however, perfectly consistent with the general equilibrium model being employed here.[188]

The other degree of freedom exploited in the analysis employed above is that it was not assumed that individual incomes were distributed optimally (in the sense discussed in section 9 above). On the contrary, in (12.4) above the marginal social costs, created by the lack of social optimality in the distribution

---

187 See the discussion of this point in Yitzhaki and Slemrod [1991, p.480].

188 In this regard it might be remembered that the amount of government revenue raised was allowed to vary in some (in fact most) of the cases discussed in the previous set of lectures - cases concerned with determining when economic reform is socially beneficial. Yet the economic model employed there was the same, in broad detail, as the model being exploited at present in the main text.

on individual incomes, are assumed to offset some of the marginal social costs created by the other distortions present in the economy. This was made possible by employing changes in personal lump-sum transfers (taxes) in a limited, but precise, manner to ensure that various distortionary social costs offset one another at the social optimum.[189] Put differently, the general principle, implicitly applied in assumption 2.1 above, is that the limited use of personal lump-sum transfers (taxes) can be employed, at the social optimum, to reduce the size of the marginal distortionary and distributional social costs created by the application of non-lump taxes.

It should be pointed out that this particular general principle has been exploited elsewhere in the relevant literature. For example, Wilson [1991] has employed this general principle in the context of determining the socially optimal level of supply of public goods.[190] This general principle has also been exploited elsewhere in the relevant optimum taxation literature - as will be indicated in section 13 below in the context of applying socially optimal, uniform, linear and non-linear consumption tax systems.

[Naturally, the application of the comparatively unconstrained methods of analysis employed above was made possible by utilising the general equilibrium welfare model sketched out in section 8 above (and discussed in more detail in section 3 in

---

189 A variation of this theme is returned to in sub-section 13.5 below.

190 See, in particular, Wilson [1991, p.159].

the previous set of lectures). Given the reduced-form equations which represent that model, it is now possible to exploit assumptions of the type set out in A2.1 above. These unconstrained optimising techniques will be exploited further on a number of occasions below.]

12.2 Necessary and Sufficient Conditions Where Markets are Not Complete.

In fact the application of this general principle, in assumption 2.1 above, can be extended to cover the realistic situation where all markets in the economy are not complete and competitive. By drawing on (8.8) above it can be shown that when there are variable economies of scale, and global consumption externalities, present in the economy then (12.3) above becomes:

$$dW=\sum_h \beta^h\left\{\sum_i t_i s_{ik}^h + \sum_i t_i \frac{\partial c_i^h}{\partial y^h}\left[-c_k^h\right] + \frac{\partial Y^h}{\partial t_k} + \frac{\partial S^h}{\partial t_k} + \lambda^h \frac{\partial g}{\partial t_k}\right\}dt_k$$

$$+\sum_h \beta^h\left\{\sum_i t_i \frac{\partial c_i^h}{\partial b^h} + \frac{\partial Y^h}{\partial b^h} + \frac{\partial S^h}{\partial b^h} + \lambda^h \frac{\partial g}{\partial b^h}\right\}db^h = 0,$$

$$k \in C. \qquad (12.11)$$

The various additional terms introduced into this last equation are defined in (8.11), and below (8.13), above.

To illustrate how these complications may be handled in the present context it is assumed that the taxes (subsidies) in the D-sector are employed as part of the attempt to offset the distortions created by the presence of markets which are not complete and competitive. Indeed, part of the explanation of why the taxes (subsidies) in the D-sector are, in fact, fixed, may be due to the fact that these taxes (subsidies) are being applied to the task of attempting to offset economic distortions elsewhere in the economy.

It is also assumed that personal lump-sum transfers are applied in such a manner that the following rather special assumption is satisfied.

<u>Assumption 2.2 (A2.2):</u> At the social optimum consumption taxes and personal lump-sum transfers (taxes) can be applied such that

$$\sum_h \beta^h \left\{ \sum_{i \in D} t_i \frac{\partial c_i^h}{\partial t_k} + \sum_{j \in C} t_i \frac{\partial c_j^h}{\partial y^h}\left[- c_k^h\right] + \frac{\partial Y^h}{\partial t_k} + \frac{\partial S^h}{\partial t_k} + \lambda^h \frac{\partial g}{\partial t_k} \right\}$$

$$dt_k$$

$$+ \sum_h \beta^h \left\{ \sum_{i \in D} t_i \frac{\partial c_i^h}{\partial b^h} + \sum_{j \in C} t_j \frac{\partial c_j^h}{\partial b^h} + \frac{\partial Y^h}{\partial b^h} + \frac{\partial S^h}{\partial b^h} + \lambda^h \frac{\partial g}{\partial b^h} \right\} db^h = 0,$$

$$k \in C. \quad (12.12)$$

Applying the statement in (12.12) to (12.11) above results in the following:

$$\sum_{h} \beta^{h} \sum_{j \in C} t_j s^{h}_{jk} = \sum_{j \in C} t_j \tilde{s}_{jk} = 0, \qquad k \in C.$$

[In the process of deriving this last result it needs to be noted that the summation over the i goods in (12.11) above refers to all goods from both the C-, and D-, sectors.]

In this special case it is socially optimal to apply a piecemeal taxation system without any further restrictions having to be placed upon the economic system.

<u>Proposition 12.2</u>: The initial assumptions are the same as in proposition 12.1 above except that now all markets in the economy are not complete and competitive. Nevertheless, (A2.2) is assumed to be satisfied when attempting to apply a socially optimal piecemeal consumption taxation system. In these circumstances it is socially optimal to apply such a taxation system (without any further restriction being placed upon the economic system).

This last result arises out of the fact that the combined effect of the changes in the various distributional and distortionary effects to be found in the community offset one another perfectly at the social optimum. Such an outcome is most likely the result of luck - rather than judgement.

12.3 Sufficient Conditions Where Markets are Not Complete.

The importance of the positive results presented in the previous two propositions lies, perhaps ironically, rather with the negative implications that can be drawn from them; namely, that it is valid to apply piecemeal consumption taxation systems only if rather strong assumptions are satisfied. Should assumption 2.2 above, in particular, not be satisfied - even just by a marginal degree - then quite different, and weaker, results emerge.

To illustrate this assertion let assumption 2.2 above be replaced with the following marginal variation of that assumption:

Assumption 2.3 (A2.3): At the social optimum personal lump-sum transfers (taxes) can be applied such that

$$\sum_h \beta^h \left\{ \frac{\partial y^h}{\partial t_k} + \frac{\partial S^h}{\partial t_k} + \lambda^h \frac{\partial g}{\partial t_k} \right\} dt_k$$

$$+ \sum_h \beta^h \left\{ \sum_i t_i \frac{\partial c_i^h}{\partial b^h} + \frac{\partial y^h}{\partial b^h} + \frac{\partial S^h}{\partial b^h} + \lambda^h \frac{\partial g}{\partial b^h} \right\} db^h = 0,$$

$$k \in C. \qquad (12.13)$$

Applying (12.13) to (12.11) above results in the following:

$$\sum_h \beta^h \left\{ \sum_i t_i \, [s^h_{ik} - c^h_k \frac{\partial c^h_i}{\partial y^h}] \right\} = \sum_h \beta^h \left\{ \sum_i t_i \; c^h_{ik} \; (q,g,y^h) \right\} = 0, \quad k \in C, \qquad (12.14)$$

where the term c^h_{ik} (q,g,y^h) refers to the uncompensated change in the level of demand for good i by individual h as a result of a change in the price of good k.

In this case it is not possible to take advantage of the relationship [set out in (12.7) above] between changes in the weighted sums of changes in compensated levels of demand. Nevertheless, supposing it is socially optimal to apply a piecemeal consumption taxation system implies that (12.14) can be rewritten as follows:

$$\sum_h \beta^h \sum_{i \in D} t_i \, c^h_{ik} + \Phi(p^D, q^D, \beta, u) \sum_h \beta^h \sum_{j \in C} q_j \, c^h_{jk} = 0, \quad k \in C. \qquad (12.15)$$

This equation indicates that a condition, which is sufficient for it to be socially optimal to apply a piecemeal consumption taxation system, is that all socially-weighted goods in the D-sector are weakly separable from all goods in the C-sector so that [191]

$$\sum_h \beta_h c^h_{ik} := \tilde{c}_{ik} = 0, \qquad k \in C, i \in D. \qquad (12.16)$$

<u>Proposition 12.3</u>: The assumptions (BA) and (J) are satisfied, as are the assumptions that the economy is closed, aggregate factor supplies and the technology are fixed, but all markets are not complete and competitive, second-order optimising conditions are satisfied at the social optimum and (A2.3) is satisfied when attempting to apply a piecemeal consumption taxation system. In these circumstances (where there are at least two goods in each sector) this taxation system is socially optimal if all the socially-weighted goods in the D-sector are weakly separable from all the goods in the C-sector - in the sense defined in (12.16) above.

---

[191] At the level of an individual consumer, preferences are weakly separable for individual h when the direct utility function takes the following form: $u^h = u^h[x^{hC}, \kappa^h(x^{hD})]$. This in turn implies that the expenditure function for this individual takes the form $e^h = e^h[f^h(p^C, U^h), p^D]$. This matter is discussed in more detail in Boadway and Harris [1977] and Jewitt [1981, p. 217 -8).

By way of contrast, in the discussion of the piecemeal policy problem Boadway and Harris [1977] derived the sufficiency condition that, for a single person-community, a piecemeal consumption taxation system is socially optimal when goods in the C-sector are weakly separable from all goods in the D-sector. The result in the previous proposition is a generalisation of the Boadway-Harris result in that here allowance has been made for the presence of (i) many heterogeneous individuals in the community and (ii) distortions created by markets that are not complete and competitive.

This generalisation of the Boadway-Harris result also serves to emphasise a conjecture made by Boadway and Harris [1977, p.187] and cited in the introduction. It seems worthwhile, however, to repeat that conjecture here:

> "Presumably, adding further complications to the model we have used [where all markets are complete and competitive and there is just a single individual in the community] would make the conditions for piecemeal policy even more stringent."

This indeed would seem to be the case. Above all the previous results emphasise, by implication, that considerable amounts of information need to be collated and assessed before it can be determined if it is socially optimal to apply a piecemeal consumption taxation system [192] - that is if this information exists in the first place.

---

192 In the context of determining if rather special consumption taxation structures are socially optimal, Deaton [1987] has provided a discussion of the practical,

In fact the previous discussion does not fully reflect the severity of these information problems. Besides the incentive-compatibility problems alluded to by the need to employ lump-sum transfers, the assumptions in the previous two propositions refer to the situation where variable scale economies are present in the economy - in other words, there are non-convexities in the economy. This particular assumption implies that, even if relevant first-order optimising conditions are satisfied when piece-meal consumption taxation systems are applied, this does not necessarily mean that the community has attained the global social optimum - the community may only be at the local equilibrium - or even at a local minimum. To determine if the global social optimum has been attained, it still needs to be established if the second-order conditions (referred to in propositions 12.2 and 12.3 above) have also been satisfied.[193] The task of determining if this is indeed the case almost certainly would create yet further demands on limited relevant information.

12.4 A Qualifying Remark Concerning Information Problems.

These information problems should not be over-stated, however. It is just possible that the errors, associated with policy implementation, when aggregated over all h individuals,

---

econometric difficulties associated with estimating pertinent parameters. The particular consumption taxation structure Deaton considered is discussed in the next section in the main text.

[193] The comments below proposition 4.8 (in the previous set of lectures) in the main text have a bearing on the present discussion.

offset one another at the social optimum. To illustrate this possibility the statement in (12.4) above is re-arranged as follows:

$$\sum_h \beta^h \left\{ \left[\sum_i t_i \frac{\partial c_i^h}{\partial y^h} \left(- c_k^h \right) + \frac{\partial y^h}{\partial t_k} \right] dt_k \right.$$

$$\left. + \left[\sum_i t_i \frac{\partial c_i^h}{\partial b^h} + \frac{\partial y^h}{\partial b^h} \right] db^h + \varepsilon^h \right\} = 0, \quad k \in C. \qquad (12.17)$$

The terms in square brackets, referred to in (12.17) above, are assumed to represent the true, but unobserved, measures for the pertinent economic variables for individual h. The term ε^h, on the other hand, denotes the errors made in the measurement of these economic variables, and/or errors made in the implementation of economic policy with respect to this individual. Now if, at the social optimum:

$$\sum_h \beta^h \varepsilon^h = 0, \qquad (12.18)$$

it follows that the social optimum has indeed been attained (at least within the context of the assumptions set out in proposition 1 above). This is so even though there have been errors in the measurement of pertinent variables (due, say, to information problems created by incentive-compatible problems) and flaws in the implementation of economic policy.

Determining whether such a situation has been attained would require, however, amongst other things, knowledge about the marginal social values of individual incomes. But reasonably acceptable information for this set of parameters does not seem to be available for any community - as was pointed out above.[194,195]

12.5 Concluding Comments.

The results presented above indicate that in a highly distorted economy, where matters of distributive justice are of concern, there are a number of ways via which the community may attempt to be in a position where it is socially optimal to apply a piecemeal consumption taxation system. There are, however, considerable information problems associated with determining whether the social optimum has been attained. These information difficulties are best illustrated by considering the information that needs to be available to determine if assumption 2.2 above is satisfied.

---

[194] Again the discussion of this point by Yitzhaki and Slemrod [1991, p.480] is relevant.

[195] The argument developed in this sub-section bears a close relationship to part of the discussion presented in section 5.1 (in the previous set of lectures) in the main text. In that discussion, however, information on the marginal social value of income was not required - the individual error terms were simply aggregated over relevant sets of individuals.

Perhaps the result, in the relevant literature, which comes nearest to those presented above in this section is that presented by Deaton [1979, pp. 360-361]. There it was assumed that the community consists of many heterogeneous individuals and matters of distributive justice are of concern. It was also assumed that a uniform consumption tax is applied to one set of goods ($j \in C$) while all other goods ($i \in D$, $i \geq 2$) are left untaxed. From this point on Deaton employed constrained optimising techniques (unlike the comparatively unconstrained optimising techniques employed above) to derive a condition which is sufficient to ensure that the assumed uniform consumption taxation system is socially optimal. [More precisely, individuals need to possess quasi-linear preferences, the taxed goods are weakly separable from the untaxed goods and a particular income distributional condition is satisfied. A special version of this case is considered in more detail in sub-section 13.2C below.]

In contrast, an alternative necessary and sufficient result can be obtained by exploiting the results presented above. Consider, for example, the relatively simple case alluded to in proposition 12.1 above - where it was assumed that all markets are complete and competitive and assumption 2.1 above is satisfied. It is now assumed that all the goods in the D-sector have no consumption taxes imposed upon them. It follows almost immediately from (12.9) above - after making use of (12.7) above - that a uniform taxation system is necessary and sufficient to attain the social optimum. [This result is made possible by the imposition of assumption 2.1 set out above - that is given the other assumptions listed in proposition 2.1 above.]

Again, as was pointed out above, apparently minor alterations in the assumptions made results in quite different results emerging. A similar point has been made by Deaton [1981] - but within the less general context of there being *only one* good in the D-sector, and *at least two* goods in the C-sector. This particular set of assumptions is applied in the next section..

13. Comparatively Simple Cases: The Uniform-Consumption Taxation-Structure Problem

The general theory presented in the previous section can readily be applied to a special case which has received far more attention in the relevant literature (when compared with the matters discussed above) - namely, that of determining when it is socially optimal to apply uniform consumption taxes on all consumption goods in a closed economy.[196] If it is assumed that a full range of consumption taxes are applied in the economy and all markets are complete and competitive, then results are quickly generated by varying the constraints employed in the unconstrained optimising framework exploited in the previous section. And, as in that section, the careful application of lump-sum transfers at the social optimum plays an important rôle in generating results.[197]

In the context of this special case to be considered below there is, however, one small alteration that needs to be made to the general model employed in the previous section. This matter is discussed in the next sub-section. In the sub-sections which follow various special cases are considered. Comments on

---

[196] See, for example, Atkinson [1977], Atkinson and Stiglitz [1976, 1980], Besley and Jewitt [1990], Blackorby *et al.* [1990c], Deaton [1979, 1981, 1987], Deaton and Stern [1986], Kay [1990], Mirrlees [1976], Ray [1988], Slemrod [1990] and Ahmad and Stern [1991, pp. 56 - 59].

[197] A similar point is made by Ahmad and Stern [1991, p. 57] - although within a more particular context than the cases discussed below in the main text.

the strong set of assumptions, upon which all these cases are based, are to be found in the concluding sub-section.

13.1 Normalisation and the Numeraire.

In the situation where all consumption goods have a uniform tax imposed upon them, this implies that the numeraire now essentially has a tax imposed upon it. To demonstrate this point first the following identity is stated:[198]

$$R^h := \sum_{i=1}^{n} t_i \, c_i^h = \phi \sum_{i=1}^{n} q_i \, c_i^h , \qquad \text{for all } h, \quad (13.1)$$

where $t_i = \phi q_i$, and ϕ is the uniform consumption tax imposed on good i (=1 to n). But the identity defining the budget condition facing any individual, h, also requires that

$$y^h := \sum_{i=1}^{n} q_i \, c_i^h + q_o^h \, c_o^h = q_o^h \, T^h + b^h ,$$

so that

$$\sum_{i=1}^{n} q_i \, c_i^h = q_o^h \left[T^h - c_o^h \right] + b^h$$

$$= q_o^h \, L^h + b^h, \qquad \text{for all } h, \qquad (13.2)$$

where y^h refers to the amount of (full) income distributed to

---

[198] It assumed in the main text that the economy is closed to international trade.

individual h, q_o^h denotes the before-tax unit price paid by individual h for the amount of leisure time, c_o^h, consumed. The term L^h denotes the amount of labour time supplied by this individual and T^h denotes the fixed amount of total time available for work. These definitions imply that $T^h := L^h + c_o^h$ for any individual h.

Substituting (13.2) into (13.1) above results in

$$R^h := \sum_{i=1}^{n} t_i \; c_i^h = \phi \sum_{i=1}^{n} q_i \; c_i^h = \phi \; [q_o^h L^h + b^h]$$

$$= \phi \; [y^h(L^h, b^h)], \quad \text{for all h,} \qquad (13.3)$$

where $y^h(L^h, b^h)$ denotes the labour-cum-personal-lump-sum income distributed to individual h.

The last relationship in (13. 3) implies that $t_o^h = \phi \, q_o^h$, where ϕ is the average linear tax rate imposed on the before-tax wage rate paid to individual h. The statement in (13.3) also indicates that ϕ denotes the average, and marginal, linear income tax rate paid by any individual h - where the income for any individual is defined as:

$$y^h(L^h, b^h) := q_o^h L^h + b^h, \qquad \text{for all h.}$$

Thus, as stated above, by imposing a uniform linear tax on the n goods consumed by individual h, this fact can be interpreted as a tax having been imposed on the numeraire (labour) supplied by this individual.

To allow for this special situation the assumption in (3.14) above in the previous set of lectures [and re-stated in (8.13) above] is replaced by the following:

$$q_i = p_i + t_i \quad \text{for } i \in NT$$

and (3.14a)

$$q_o^h = p_o^h + t_o^h \quad \text{for } o \in NT, \text{ where } t_o^h \text{ is fixed for all h.}$$

Since relative prices must always alter, when tax rates are varied, the tax on the numeraire must be fixed.

The rest of the argument to be found in section 3.4 above (in the previous set of lectures) remains virtually unaltered. In place of (3.20), however, the following now appears for all h :

$$dy^h = \sum_{i=1}^{n} [\, q_i \; dc_i^h + c_i^h \, dq_i^h \; - p_i \; dx_i^h]$$

$$+ [\, q_o^h \, dc_o^h - \; p_o^h \, dx_o^h] + dY^h + dS^h. \qquad (3.20a)$$

From this point on the argument is the same as before.

The end results are the reduced-form equations set out in (8.7) and (8.8) above. The only point that needs to be emphasised is that in (8.8) above, the following now applies:[199]

$$\sum_{i \in NT} t_i \, dc_i^h = t_0^h \, dc_0^h + \sum_{i \in NT(i \neq 0)} t_i \, dc_i^h, \quad \text{for all } h,$$

where t_0^h is fixed for all h.

And since it is assumed here that the economy is closed, this means that

$$\left[\sum_{i \in NT} t_i \quad dc_i^h = \right] \sum_{i=0}^{n} t_i \; dc_i^h = t_0^h \, dc_0^h + \sum_{i=1}^{n} t_i \; dc_i^h,$$

$$\text{for all } h. \qquad (13.4)$$

This result will be called upon on a number of occasions below.

Before turning to the main discussion in this section it should be pointed out that the before-tax wage rate paid to any individual, h, for a unit of labour supplied, is allowed to vary across individuals. [This assumption is implied by (13.2) above, for example.] It is also noted that it is being assumed here that factors of production are paid the value of their marginal product.

---

199 The result just stated in the main text naturally implies that the slight generalisation of the normalisation condition, set out in (3.14a) above in the main text, does not have any influence on the relevant results presented in the previous three sections in the main text.

[This assumption was employed in the process of deriving, for example, (3.10), and hence (3.10a), above.] These two assumptions, in turn, imply that, throughout the rest of the discussion presented in this, and the next, section, the abilities of any individual (as measured by the value of the marginal product produced by this individual) can vary from individual to individual.

13.2 Uniform Linear Commodity Consumption Taxation Systems.

Throughout the present discussion a comparatively simple case will be considered; namely, the economy is closed, all markets are complete and competitive, aggregate factor supplies are fixed, and so on - although this list of assumptions is commented upon in the concluding sub-section.

13.2A: A Necessary and Sufficient Result With No Additional Constraints on Behaviour

The point of departure is again (12.3) above. It is assumed, as before, that lump-sum transfers can be applied with precision at the margin so that assumption 2.1 above is satisfied. On applying (12.4) to (12.3) above the result in (12.5) emerges. It is now assumed that a uniform consumption taxation system is applied. This assumption, plus the discussion in the previous sub-section, implies that (12.5) above becomes:

$$\phi \sum_h \beta^h \sum_{i=0}^{n} q_i \, s_{ik}^h = 0, \qquad k \in C.$$

But the symmetry of the Slutsky matrix [i.e. $s_{ik}^{h} = s_{ki}^{h}$],

and the fact that compensated demand functions are homogeneous of degree zero in prices, implies that this last equation must take a value of zero. Hence it is socially optimal to impose a uniform consumption taxation system without any further restrictions being placed upon individual behaviour.

This result implies that all the re-distribution of community total income that the community requires, so that the social optimum is attained, has nearly been achieved by the application of lump-sum transfers and taxes. The setting of uniform commodity taxes takes the community the final step to the social optimum.

13.2 B: Necessary and Sufficient Results With Additional Constraints on Behaviour:

Case 1: Returning to (12.3) above, it is now assumed that lump-sum taxes are applied at the margin so that the following assumption is satisfied:

Assumption 2.4 (A2.4): At the social optimum lump-sum transfers (taxes) can be applied such that

$$\sum_{h} \beta^{h} \left\{ \frac{\partial y^{h}}{\partial t_{k}} dt_{k} + \left[\sum_{i} t_{i} \frac{\partial c_{i}^{h}}{\partial b^{h}} + \frac{\partial y^{h}}{\partial b^{h}} \right] db^{h} \right\} = 0, \quad k \in C. \tag{13.5}$$

Applying the statement in (13.5) to (12.3) above results in

$$\sum_h \beta^h \left[\sum_i t_i c^h_{ik} (q, y^h) \right] = 0, \qquad k \in C, \tag{13.6}$$

which is essentially (12.14) in the previous section. As before the term c^h_{ik} (q, y^h) refers to the uncompensated change in the level of demand for good i by individual h as a result of a change in the price of good k.

Since the present discussion is only concerned with the particular topic of the socially optimal imposition of uniform consumption taxation systems, the remarks in sub-section 13.1 above now become pertinent. Given that it is assumed that a fixed tax is now applied to the numeraire good, the result set out in (13.4) above is applied to (13.6) above to give the following:

$$\sum_h \beta^h \left[\sum_{i=1}^{n} t_i c^h_{ik} (q, q^h_o, y^h) \right] = - \sum_h \beta^h t^h_o c^h_{ok} (q, q^h_o, y^h),$$

$$= - \phi \sum_h \beta^h q^h_o c^h_{ok}, \; k \in C. \tag{13.7}$$

It follows that it is socially optimal to apply a uniform commodity taxation system alone if, and only if, the term on the right-hand side of (13.7) takes a value of zero.

<u>Proposition 13.1</u>: The assumptions (BA) and (J) are satisfied, as are the assumptions that the economy is closed, aggregate factor supplies and the technology are fixed, all markets are complete

and competitive, second-order optimising conditions are satisfied at the social optimum and lump-sum transfers can be applied such that (A2.4) above is satisfied when attempting to apply a uniform consumption taxation system. In these circumstances this taxation system is socially optimal if, and only if, at the social optimum the aggregate socially-weighted sum of the value of uncompensated changes in individual labour supply (demand for leisure) is weakly separable from all other goods in the sense that

$$\sum_h \beta^h \sum_{k=1}^{n} \left[q_o^h \; c_{ok}^h \right] = 0, \qquad k \in C.$$

This result is closely related to proposition 12.3 above. In the present case, however, essentially because there is only one good (instead of at least two goods) in the D-sector of the economy, a necessary and sufficient (not just a sufficient) result can now be obtained. It follows, as a corollary to proposition 13.1 above, that if there are at least two goods with a fixed taxed attached to them, then proposition 13.1 above ceases to be valid.

This last remark alludes to a particular general principle which will be returned to at the end of this section.

The result stated in (13.7) above implies that the optimum linear income tax rate could be one hundred percent since there are no distortionary (or dead-weight) social costs associated with applying a uniform tax on all goods - or a tax just on labour income. In this case, however, the values of individual uncompensated labour supply functions need not all be completely inelastic with respect to the prices of all other goods.

Case 2: An interesting case arises if the following assumption is applied to (12.3) above.

Assumption 2.4 (A2.5): At the social optimum lump-sum transfers (taxes) can be applied such that

$$\sum_h \beta^h \left\{ \sum_i t_i \frac{\partial c_i^h}{\partial b^h} + \frac{\partial Y^h}{\partial b^h} \right\} db^h = 0.$$

The statement in (12.3) above, therefore, reduces to the following:

$$\sum_h \beta^h \left\{ \sum_{i=1}^n t_i \frac{\partial c_i^h}{\partial t_k} \right\} + \sum_h \beta^h \left\{ t_o^h \frac{\partial c_o^h}{\partial t_k} + \frac{\partial Y^h}{\partial t_k} \right\} dt_k = 0 \quad k \in C. \ (13.8)$$

In this last equation use has been made of the argument, presented in sub-section 3.1 above, that a fixed tax has been applied to the numeraire.

Now since all $i \in C$ and and $o \in D$, (13.8) above indicates that a necessary and sufficient condition, for it to be socially optimal to apply a uniform consumption taxation system is if the following condition is satisfied:

$$\sum_h \beta^h \sum_{k=1}^{n} \left\{ t_o^h \frac{\partial c_o^h}{\partial t_k} + \frac{\partial y^h}{\partial t_k} \right\} dt_k = 0. \qquad (13.9)$$

<u>Proposition 13.2</u>: The assumptions (BA) and (J) are satisfied, as are the assumptions that the economy is closed, aggregate factor supplies and the technology are fixed, all markets are complete and competitive, second-order optimising conditions are satisfied at the social optimum and (A2.5) above is satisfied when attempting to apply a uniform consumption taxation system. In these circumstances this taxation system is socially optimal if, at the social optimum, the uniform consumption tax rate satisfies the statement in (13.9) above.

What is particularly interesting about this case is that it provides a relatively simple formula with which to calculate the socially optimal marginal linear income tax rate - given the assumptions imposed in proposition 13.2 above. This is derived from (13.9) above by noting that, since uniform consumption taxation is socially optimal (and, hence, effectively a variable linear tax has been applied to individual labour income), the imposition of such a taxation system implies that (13.9) above reduces to:

$$\sum_h \beta^h \left\{ \phi(.)\ q_o^h \frac{\partial c_{oo}^h}{\partial t_o^h} + \frac{\partial Y^h}{\partial t_o^h} \right\} = 0.$$

This result, in turn, can be re-arranged to give:

$$\phi^* (\beta,\ q_o, Y,\ c_{oo}) = -\frac{\left[\sum_h \beta^h \frac{\partial Y^h}{\partial t_o^h}\right]}{\left[\sum_h \beta^h\ q_o^h \frac{\partial c_{oo}^h}{\partial t_o^h}\right]}, \qquad (13.10)$$

where $\phi^* (\beta,\ q_o, Y,\ c_{oo})$ refers to the socially optimal marginal linear income tax rate.

<u>Corollary 13.1</u>. Given that the assumptions, set out in proposition 13.2 above, are satisfied, then the formula for calculating the socially optimal marginal linear income tax rate is that stated in (13.10) above.

As far as can be determined, the result set out in propositions 13.1 and 13.2 above are not to be found elsewhere in the relevant literature - although Blackorby *et al.* [1990c] have derived a necessary and sufficient result for the case where Libertarian social values apply. In proposition 13.2 above, on the other hand, the imposition of assumption (J) indicates that the community is assumed to have adopted a broad view of distributive justice [as defined earlier].

As for the formula, set out in (13.10) above, it bears a close resemblance to the formula (for calculating the socially optimal marginal linear income tax rate) to be found in Dixit and Sandmo [1977] and Atkinson and Stiglitz [1980, p. 407]. In addition, that formula allows the properties of this marginal income tax rate to be determined comparatively easily. This is a topic which is discussed, for example, by Sheshinski [1972] and Hellwig [1986], and which is returned to in the next section - within the context that individual labour is the only good in the C-sector (not the only good in the D-sector, as in the present case).

13.2C: A Sufficient Result.

Sufficient results can also be derived by imposing more severe constraints on the way (12.3) above is simplified, although the careful application of lump-sum transfers (taxes) at the social optimum is still required. To demonstrate this point the present discussion sets out to establish (by employing the unconstrained optimising techniques employed above) a result first derived by Deaton and Stern [1986] (by employing constrained, Lagrangean, optimising techniques of analysis).

Use is now also made of the alternative reduced-form equation set out in (12.2) above where it is assumed that the level of government revenue remains fixed (i.e. the 'Ramsey' assumption is applied). This means that the statement in (12.2) above can be re-written as follows:

$$\sum_h \beta^h c_k^h = \sum_h \beta^h \frac{\partial y^h}{\partial t_k}, \qquad k \in C. \qquad (13.11)$$

The constraint set out in (13.11) above is now applied to (12.3) above to give, after some manipulation:

$$\phi \sum_h \beta^h p_o^h s_{ok}^h \, dt_k = \sum_h \beta^h \left\{ c_k^h \left[1 - \sum_i t_i \frac{\partial c_i^h}{\partial y^h} \right] \right\} dt_k$$

$$+ \sum_h \beta^h \left\{ \sum_i t_i \frac{\partial c_i^h}{\partial b^h} + \frac{\partial y^h}{\partial b^h} \right\} db^h, \qquad \text{for all } k. \; (13.12)$$

In the process of deriving this last result use was made of the fact that compensated demand functions are homogeneous of degree zero in all prices and that the Slutsky matrix is symmetric.

Now, following Deaton and Stern [1986], it is assumed that:

$$\text{(i)} \quad c_k^h = a_k^h(q) + b_k(q)\, y^h, \qquad \text{for all } h \text{ and all } k,$$ [200]

(13.13)

---

200 Individual preferences in this case are of the quasi-homothetic form; i.e.

$$v(q, y^h) = \alpha^h(q) + \gamma(q)\, y^h.$$

Roy's indentity is then employed to derive (13.12) in the main text.

(ii) for all h individuals leisure is weakly separable from all other goods - i.e.

$$c_{ok}^{h} = 0, \qquad \text{for all } h \quad \text{and all } k,$$

so that, after applying the Slutsky equation, and the symmetry of the Slutsky matrix:

$$s_{ok}^{h} = s_{ko}^{h} = c_{o}^{h} \frac{\partial c_{k}^{h}}{\partial y^{h}}, \qquad \text{for all } h \quad \text{and all } k. \quad (13.14)$$

On applying the assumptions set out in (13.13) and (13.14) to (13.12) the end result is the following:

$$\phi \sum_{h} \beta^{h} p_{o}^{h} c_{o}^{h} b_{k}(q)\, dt_{k} =$$

$$\sum_{h} \beta^{h} \left\{ [\, a_{k}^{h}(q) + b_{k}(q)\, y^{h}] \left[1 - \sum_{i} t_{i} \frac{\partial c_{i}^{h}}{\partial y^{h}} \right] \right\} dt_{k}$$

$$+ \sum_{h} \beta^{h} \left\{ \sum_{i} t_{i} \frac{\partial c_{i}^{h}}{\partial b^{h}} + \frac{\partial y^{h}}{\partial b^{h}} \right\} db^{h}, \qquad \text{for all } k. \quad (13.15)$$

Finally the assumption is imposed that, at the social optimum, marginal changes in lump-sum transfers (taxes) can be applied with the precision required to ensure that the following condition is satisfied:

$$\sum_h \beta^h \left\{ a_k^h(q) \left[1 - \sum_i t_i \frac{\partial c_i^h}{\partial y^h} \right] \right\} dt_k$$

$$+ \sum_h \beta^h \left\{ \sum_i t_i \frac{\partial c_i^h}{\partial b^h} + \frac{\partial y^h}{\partial b^h} \right\} db^h = 0, \text{ for all } k. \qquad (13.16)$$

On applying the assumption in (13.16) to (13.15) above the end result is that, on cancelling terms:

$$\phi = \frac{\sum_h \beta^h \left\{ y^h \left[1 - \sum_i t_i \frac{\partial c_i^h}{\partial y^h} \right] \right\}}{\sum_h \beta^h \, p_o^h \, c_o^h}. \qquad (13.17)$$

Since the terms on the right-hand side of this last equation are independent of k, it follows that it is socially optimal to apply uniform consumption taxes.

As indicated above, the assumptions employed here to constrain the first-order optimisation result set out in (12.3) above [to allow the derivation of the sufficient result stated in (13.17) above] are those to be found explicitly, or implicitly, in Deaton and Stern [1986].[201] What should be emphasised in this regard is that the assumption set out in (13.16) above is not rep-

201 Related discussions are also to be found in Deaton [1979] and Ray [1988]. Also see Stiglitz [1987, p.1027 - 1029].

resenting a particular, single, assumption made by Deaton and Stern. Rather that assumption represents a set of assumptions, employed by Deaton and Stern, which implies a complex system of changes in lump-sum income transfer at the social optimum.[202]

13.3 Uniform Non-Linear Commodity Consumption Taxation Systems.

A Sufficient Result: Up to this point in this section, in the attempt to generate definite results, it has been assumed that lump-sum transfers can be applied with precision at the social optimum. Any information problems, associated with the incentive-compatibility problems, arising from the imposition of these income transfers, are assumed not to exist. This assumption also needs to be invoked when applying the next assumption - which is that non-linear consumption taxes can be applied with accuracy.[203]

In this case the linear consumption taxes referred to in (12.3) above are replaced by the tax function, $t_i(c_i^h)$, for good i.

[204] Thus the average tax rate paid by individual h, on the consumption of good i, varies with the amount consumed of this good by this individual h. This assumption, along with the application of lump-sum transfers, naturally provides the taxing authorities

---

202 Also see Ahmad and Stern [1991, p. 57] on this point.

203 See Deaton [1981, p.1252] on this point.

204 This sort of assumption is employed in Deaton [1981, p. 1251].

with a considerable number of degrees of freedom within which to attempt to maximize the level of social welfare.

The taxation system, implied by this last assumption, is one of considerable complexity. Hence, it is technically a more difficult task to determine the conditions which need to be satisfied before it is socially optimal to impose a uniform non-linear taxation system. Nevertheless, the previous theory does provide a heuristic framework with which to indicate how these conditions may be determined. Specifically, drawing on a suitably revised version of (12.3) above, the flexibility of the non-linear-consumption-tax-cum-lump-sum-subsidy system will allow (given that incentive-compatibility problems are absent) the social optimum to be reached where, for each h individual in the community and for all k goods :

$$\left[\sum_i t_i(c_k^h)\frac{\partial c_i^h}{\partial t_k(c_k^h)} + \frac{\partial Y^h}{\partial t_k(c_k^h)}\right] dt_k(c_k^h)$$

$$+\left[\sum_i t_i(c_i^h)\frac{\partial c_i^h}{\partial b^h} + \frac{\partial Y^h}{\partial b^h}\right] db^h = 0. \qquad (13.18)$$

In addition, this flexible taxation system will also allow the non-linear taxes and lump-sum transfers to be altered to the point where the income distributive effects are exactly offset so that (13.18) above reduces to:

$$\sum_{i=1}^{n} t_i (c_i^h) \frac{\partial c_i^h}{\partial t_k (c_i^h)} = - t_o^h (c_o^h) \frac{\partial c_o^h}{\partial t_k \ (c_k^h)} ,$$

for all h individuals and all k. (13.19)

The final step employed in deriving this last equation has drawn upon the sort of the argument required to derive (13.4) above.

It follows that a uniform non-linear taxation system is socially optimal if, for each heterogeneous individual in the community, leisure is weakly separable from all other goods at the social optimum. As can also be seen, by consulting (13.19) above, this result is completely independent of the form of the social welfare function employed. Hence the result just derived also satisfies a Pareto efficiency condition.

This is just the result first derived by Mirrlees [1976, pp.337-8]. This result was, in turn, a generalisation of a result first derived by Atkinson and Stiglitz [1976, 1980, pp. 416-417]. This class of result is also derived by Deaton [1981, p. 1252] and Tuomala [1990, Ch. 10].

13.4 Qualifications and Concluding Comments.

The advantage of deriving the results, presented in this section, from the general equilibrium welfare model set out in section 8 above, is that it makes relatively clear the range of strong assumptions that need to be imposed before pertinent results begin to emerge. Above all it should now be reasonably clear, that each one of the results presented in this section is dependent on the careful application of lump-sum transfers (taxes) at the social optimum. One could reasonably question this assumption in the light of the sort of analysis of the incentive-compatibility assumption to be found in section 4.1 above (in the previous set of lectures). Although, it should be pointed out that the argument presented in 12.4 above - concerning the matter of errors of measurement and flaws in policy implementation - applies here as well.

The other strong assumption employed above in this section is that there are no markets in the economy which are not complete and competitive. But, on relaxing this assumption, the real possibility now emerges that there may be more than one good with a fixed distortion attached to it - the numeraire and at least one good for which markets are not complete and competitive. This is likely to be so since, due to the almost certain absence of complete and accurate information, the authorities will fail to set the distortions on these goods (for which markets are not complete and competitive) at the uniform level to be found in the C-sector. Hence it could reasonably be argued that the discussion presented in this section is really based upon an inappropriate, or flawed, model. Rather the pertinent model is that where it is assumed (amongst other things) that, due to the lack of perfect information concerning the markets which are not complete and competitive, there are at least two goods to be found in the D-sector. In addition there are, as above, at least two goods in the C-sector of the economy. That being the case, the analysis may now follow the sort of argument (with all its qualifications) developed in the previous section.

An alternative way in which the analysis may proceed is to assume that there is just one good in the C-sector (individual labour), and all other goods are in the D-sector. This particular case is considered in the next section.

14. On The Properties of Socially Optimal Marginal Linear Income Tax Rates.

A revealing way to demonstrate the properties of linear income taxation systems is to begin with a special version of the Boadway-Harris formulation of the piecemeal consumption taxation problem. This particular version is that there is only one good in the Control Sector of the economy - and this single good is individual labour (leisure). All other goods are in the Distorted Sector of the economy. This implies, by definition, that all the taxes, and shadow prices, attached to goods in the D-sector, are fixed or non-existent. This assumption, in turn, implies that on this occasion one of the goods in the D-sector must be the numeraire good.[205]

Based on this set of initial assumptions it is possible to generate a number of results concerning the imposition of linear income tax systems. First, given the assumption that only a linear income taxation system can be applied in the C-sector of the economy, then it can be shown that it may still be difficult to determine the properties of the constrained marginal linear income tax rate in the context of an economy which, due to the absence of all relevant information, is distorted in various ways. What is more, the socially optimal marginal linear income tax rate may take a *negative* value. This general observation is

---

205 In this case labour (or leisure) cannot be the numeraire as the price attached to this good is allowed to vary - relative to the prices of other goods.

consistent with recent results presented by Boadway, Marchand and Pestieau [1991].

Second, along the way to demonstrating this comparatively general finding, the various particular results, initially presented by Sheshinski [1972] and Hellwig [1986], can also be derived, and reconciled.

Third, given the formula for calculating the socially optimal marginal linear income taxation rate - for the initial situation where all markets are complete and competitive and there are no consumption taxes in place - it is now possible to show that on allowing one additional good to be found in the C-sector, it ceases to be socially optimal to impose a linear income taxation system alone - that is if certain separability assumptions are not satisfied. (To demonstrate this result, however, the Envelope Theorem needs to be applied.) This result is really a dual result for those presented in sub-section 13.2 in the previous section.[206]

These various matters will be considered in the subsequent sub-sections.

14.1 <u>The Basic Analytical Framework.</u>

To assist with explaining the general argument to be developed below, it is useful to re-state one of the basic reduced-

---

206 This result is also really an extension, and a generalisation, of the case originally considered by Corlett and Hague [1953] and Meade [1955, Mathematical Supplement].

form equations set out in section 8 above. Before doing so, however, it should be pointed out that to indicate the full extent of the difficulties, associated with determining socially optimal marginal linear income tax rates, the most general version of the basic model is to be re-stated here; namely, the case where (i) there are many taxes applied to goods in both the traded, and non-traded, sectors of the economy, and (ii) markets, which are not complete and competitive, are to be found on both the consumption and production sides of the economy. Finally, but not least, since in the present case a tax is to be applied to individual labour, the argument developed earlier in sub-section 13.1 needs to be taken into account.

Given this general set of circumstances, the elements of the reduced-form equation which is relevant in the present case are the following:

$$dW = \sum_{h=1}^{H} \beta^h \, [dv^h / v_y^h], \qquad (14.1)[(8.3)]$$

where, based on (8.8) above,

$$\frac{dv^h}{v_y^h} = t_o^h \, dc_o^h + \sum_{i \in NT(i \neq 0)} t_i \, dc_i^h + \sum_{j \in T} \tau_j \, dE_j^h$$

$$+ \, dY^h + \lambda^h dg \; + \, dS^h, \qquad \text{for all } h, \qquad (14.2)$$

where $t_o^h = \phi(\,.\,)\, q_o^h$.

and all the other terms referred to in these equations have been defined in section 8 above. In addition, it is assumed, as in the previous two sections, that the Distributive Justice Assumption (J) applies to (14.1) above.

It is now assumed that the economy is at the social optimum and the only good on which the tax can be altered - i.e. the only good in the C-sector - is the individual consumption of leisure (individual labour supply). Altering the tax on this good by a small amount, and substituting the resulting version of (14.2) into (14.1) results in the following reduced-form equation:

$$dW = \sum_{h=1}^{H} \beta^h \left[\phi(\ .\ )\, q_o^h \frac{\partial c_o^h}{\partial t_o^h} + \sum_{i \in NT(i \neq 0)} t_i \frac{\partial c_i^h}{\partial t_o^h} + \sum_{j \in T} \tau_j \frac{\partial E_j^h}{\partial t_o^h} + \lambda^h \frac{\partial g}{\partial t_o^h} + \frac{\partial Y^h}{\partial t_o^h} + \frac{\partial S^h}{\partial t_o^h} \right] dt_o^h = 0. \quad (14.3)$$

From this comparatively general statement of the optimising problem of interest here, it is now possible to consider a number of special cases.

14.2 A Simple Case.

The first case is that where, except for the controllable income tax, all other consumption taxes, tariffs and shadow prices disappear from (14.3) above. This may be due to the fact that either: (i) there has been a careful application of lump-sum transfers (remembering that in the D-sector economic distortions are fixed in size in size); (ii) or relevant sets of goods are weakly separable from individual labour (leisure);[207] (iii) or it is assumed that these consumption taxes etc. are just absent from the economy. Employing any of these assumptions, singly or in combination, ensures that (14.3) reduces, after a little manipulation, to (13.10) above - an equation which is re-stated here:

$$\phi^* (\beta, q_o, Y, c_{oo}) = - \frac{\left[\sum_h \beta^h \frac{\partial Y^h}{\partial t_o^h} \right]}{\left[\sum_h \beta^h q_o^h \frac{\partial c_o^h}{\partial t_o^h} \right]} . \quad (14.4)[(13.\ 10)]$$

This result can now be exploited to reconcile certain results that have been derived concerning the properties of the socially optimal marginal linear income tax rates.[208] To begin with the numerator in (14.4) above is assumed to take a non-positive

---

207 For example, the non-traded and traded goods, which have taxes (tariffs) imposed upon them, are assumed to be weakly separable from leisure. In this case the second and third set of terms, in square brackets in (14.3) above in the main text, would disappear from that equation. A similar argument may be applied to the goods for which the markets are not complete and competitive. The matter of applying the weak separability assumption, in the context of setting socially optimal tax rates - albeit in a slightly different context to that being considered here - is also discussed in Tuomala [1990, Ch, 10].

208 Also see Tuomala [1990, pp. 69 - 75] for a discussion, and a survey, of the relevant literature relating to this topic.

value. This is so since $(\partial Y^h / \partial t_o^h) \leq 0$ for all h individuals, and $\beta^h > 0$ for at least some individuals in the community [by assumption (J)].

As for the denominator in (14.4) above, the term q_o^h (i.e. the consumer price of leisure consumed by individual h) is assumed to take a non-negative value for all individuals in the community.[209] Thus a sufficient condition for the socially optimal marginal linear income tax rate to take a non-negative value is that the uncompensated demand for leisure functions for all h individuals has the following property:

$$\frac{\partial c_o^h}{\partial t_o^h} \geq 0, \qquad \text{for all individuals.}$$

This sufficient requirement implies that all individuals have non-backward-bending uncompensated labour supply functions - i.e.

$$\frac{\partial L^h}{\partial p_o^h} \geq 0 \qquad \text{for all individuals.}$$

This is the result provided by Sheshinski [1972].

---

209 It should be also be noted [as was pointed at the end of sub-section 13.1 in the main text], that since the value of the before-tax price paid , q_o^h, for a unit of labour supplied by individual h is allowed to vary from individual to individual, this implies that the abilities of individuals are also allowed to vary across individuals in the discussion provided in the main text.

More light can be brought to this topic by applying a few additional manipulations to (14.4) above. To begin with, the alternative form of the basic reduced-form equation, set out in (8.7) above, is now made use of. It can easily be shown that (8.7), when combined with (8.3), and applying the simplifying assumptions required to derive (14.4) above, the following emerges:

$$dW = \sum_h \beta^h \left[- c_o^h + \frac{\partial R}{\partial t_o^h} + \frac{\partial Y^h}{\partial t_o^h} \right] dt_o^h . \qquad (14.5)$$

It is now assumed that the community is at the social optimum and that the level of government revenue is held constant - via applying offsetting changes in lump-sum taxes. It follows from (14.5) that

$$\sum_h \beta^h c_o^h = \sum_h \beta^h \frac{\partial Y^h}{\partial t_o^h}, \text{ when } dW = 0 \text{ and } dR = 0. \qquad (14.6)$$

This result provides one of the components that will be substituted back into (14.4) above. The other component, which is concerned with the denominator to be found in (14.4) above, is provided by applying the Slutsky equation for the demand for leisure:

$$\sum_h \beta^h q_o^h \frac{\partial c_o^h}{\partial t_o^h} = \sum_h \beta^h q_o^h \left[s_{oo}^h - c_o^h \frac{\partial c_o^h}{\partial y^h} \right]$$

$$= - \sum_h \beta^h \left[\sum_{i=1}^{n} q_i \; s_{io}^h + q_o^h \; c_o^h \frac{\partial c_o^h}{\partial y^h} \right]. \qquad (14.7)$$

In the process of deriving this last equation use has also been made of: (a) the symmetry of the Slutsky equation [i.e. $s_{oi}^h = s_{io}^h$], and (b) the property that the individual compensated demand functions for labour are all homogeneous of degree zero in all prices.

On substituting (14.6) and (14.7) back into (14.4) above the following emerges:

$$\phi^* (\beta, c_o, .\,.) = \frac{\sum_h \beta^h c_o^h}{\sum_h \beta^h \left[\sum_{i=1}^{n} q_i \; s_{io}^h + q_o^h \; c_o^h \frac{\partial c_o^h}{\partial y^h} \right]}, \qquad (14.8)$$

where $R = \bar{R}$.

The numerator in (14.8) must take a positive value - given the assumption (J) and that all individuals need to consume at least some leisure. The socially optimal marginal income tax rate, therefore, will take a positive value if the following assumptions are satisfied at the social optimum :

(1) Leisure is a non-inferior good for all h individuals - in other words, [$\partial c_0^h / \partial y^h$] ≥ 0 for all h individuals.

(2) For any h individual, the weighted average of the compensated level of demand for all goods (other than leisure) is increasing in the wage rate for this individual. More specifically,

$$\sum_{i=1}^{n} q_i \, s_{io}^h > 0, \qquad \text{for all h individuals.}$$

These are essentially the assumptions employed by Hellwig [1986] in his extension of the Sheshinski result.[210] The Hellwig result is clearly based upon a weaker set of conditions - a result which is made possible by applying the Slutsky decomposition of the individual demand functions for leisure, and that a fixed amount of government revenue is to be raised.

Despite this reconciliation of these two results, both are dependent upon some rather strong assumptions; in particular, those which are required to convert (14.3) into (14.4) above. If these assumptions are relaxed, however, then the nature of the argument changes rather dramatically. Specifically the sign of

---

210 It was also pointed out by Hellwig [1986, p. 168] that assumption 2 is essentially the same as the "agent monotonicity" assumption to be found in Seade [1982].

the socially optimal marginal linear income tax rate becomes far less certain.

14.3 A More Complex Case Where Many Fixed Distortions are Present.

The discussion returns to (14.3) above where now allowance is made for the imposition of consumption taxes on non-trade goods, the imposition of tariffs on traded goods, and the presence of various global externalities to be found in both the production and consumption sectors of the economy. The result in (14.3) above is re-organised, much as that required to derive (14.4) in the previous sub-section. The resulting formula for calculating the socially optimal marginal linear income tax rate is the following:

$$\phi^*(\,.\,) = -\frac{\left[\sum_h \beta^h \frac{\partial Y^h}{\partial t_o^h}\right]}{\left[\sum_h \beta^h q_o^h \frac{\partial c_o^h}{\partial t_o^h}\right]}$$

$$
-\frac{\sum_{h=1}^{H}\beta^{h}\left[\sum_{i\in NT(i\neq 0)} t_i \frac{\partial c_i^h}{\partial t_o^h} + \sum_{j\in T}\tau_j \frac{\partial E_j^h}{\partial t_o^h}\right]}{\left[\sum_h \beta^h q_o^h \frac{\partial c_o^h}{\partial t_o^h}\right]}
$$

$$
-\frac{\sum_{h=1}^{H}\beta^{h}\left[\lambda^h \frac{\partial g}{\partial t_o^h} + \frac{\partial S^h}{\partial t_o^h}\right]}{\left[\sum_h \beta^h q_o^h \frac{\partial c_o^h}{\partial t_o^h}\right]} . \qquad (14.9)
$$

This formula for measuring the socially optimal linear income tax rate is clearly much more complicated than that stated in (14.4) [or (14.8)] above. The reason is that now, at the social optimum, the distortionary influences on individual labour supply, of imposing income taxes, offsets not only the community's concerns about matters of distributive justice. This social efficiency loss may also need to offset a range of various distortions present in the economy.

The result in (14.9) essentially refers to three sets of considerations. The first set of terms in the right-hand side of (14.9) are exactly the same as those to be found in (14.4) above. Consequently this set of terms requires no further comment.

The second set of terms on the right hand side of (14.9) refers to the presence of consumption taxes on non-traded goods, and tariffs on traded goods. These terms may take a positive value. For example, an increase in the linear income tax rate increases the level of demand for goods with taxes and tariffs imposed upon them. Indeed this possibility implies - ignoring for the time being the third set of terms in (14.9) above - that the socially optimal marginal linear income tax rate may take a negative value. Such a situation would occur if the imposition of the fixed taxes and tariffs took the community past the social optimum. Hence, to bring the community back to the social optimum, individuals need to be provided with an income subsidy.[211]

The third set of factors, alluded to in the numerator for the third set of terms on the right-hand side of (14.9) above, is that associated with global externalities on both the consumption and production sides of the economy. But, as was discussed at some length in sub-section 4.5 (in the previous set of lectures), there is a close conceptual relationship between this general class of market failure and that where insurance markets suffer from the information problems created by the presence of adverse selection (the hidden-information problem) and moral hazard (the

211 In this case, perhaps a simpler approach may be to eliminate the income subsidy and reduce the level of the consumption taxes and tariffs. But to do so implies that this set of consumption taxes and tariffs would now be in the C-sector of the economy - which is contrary to what is being assumed at present in the main text. Naturally the question may be asked: Why are these taxes and tariffs rates fixed in the first place? This question was addressed in the introduction to this set of lectures (i.e. section 7 in the main text).

hidden-knowledge problem). That being the case, the failure of relevant insurance markets has special relevance for determining the socially optimal marginal linear income tax rate.

To demonstrate the nature of the issues at stake here, suppose that all individuals in the community cannot purchase private income insurance of any kind - for example, workers cannot purchase private unemployment insurance and entrepreneurs cannot acquire insurance against business risk. In these circumstances the income-tax-personal-lump-sum-income-transfer system provides, at least, a partial public income insurance system - a point that has also been made by Mazur [1989, p. 31].[212] But it is reasonable to suggest that it is unlikely that this publicly provided insurance system will not perfectly offset these private market failures - failures created in private insurance markets essentially because there are (assumed) failures in the markets for relevant information.[213]

This possibility implies that elements in the numerator, in the third set of terms on right-hand side of (14.9) above, will take positive values. [The detailed argument required to support

[212] It has also been emphasised by Barr [1989] that the provision of lump-sum income transfers, in the form of unemployment benefits and public heath schemes for example, are best viewed as attempts to offset failures in relevant private insurance markets. Certainly these personal income transfer systems should not be considered as just attempts by the community to re-distribute income in the process of its attempts to attain satisfactory levels of distributive justice.

[213] This point is discussed in more detail in sub-section 4.5 in the previous set of lectures.

this assertion is essentially the same as that set out earlier in sub-section 4.5 in the previous set of lectures.] The greater the uncertainty facing an individual (i.e. the greater the variance of future income), and the greater the shadow-price placed upon this uncertainty by this individual (i.e. the more risk averse this individual), the larger the size of the elements in the terms to be found in the numerator in the third set of terms to be found on the right-hand side of (14.9) above. This possibility implies, in turn, that the socially optimal marginal linear income tax rate may need to take a negative value. This income subsidy would offset the social costs created by the failure of the private insurance market.

This relationship between the failure of insurance markets and the imposition of a socially optimal marginal linear income tax, was essentially the problem considered by Mazur [1989] and Boadway *et al.* [1991, p. 148 - 159]. The latter authors, for example, considered the case (amongst others) where entrepreneurs bear all the risk flowing from their business decisions. Above all, no pooling of risk was allowed.[214] That being the case, entrepreneurs have to bear additional production and administrative costs - compared to the situation where complete business-risk insurance is available. The rest of the argument can now follow that to be found in the previous two paragraphs. And, just as Boadway *et al.* [1991, p. 155] observed,

---

214 While Boadway *et al.* do not explain why risk pooling is not available, a cogent general explanation would be that, due the hidden-action, and/or hidden-information problems, relevant information markets are not complete and competitive.

due to the lack of complete and competitive private insurance markets, the marginal linear income tax rate may need to take a negative value.

Similar observations apply to the less complicated case considered by Mazur [1989].[215]

Drawing together these various remarks, made in connection with (14.9) above, it is clear that it is a difficult task calculating the socially optimal marginal linear income tax rate in economies where various distortions, of one form or another, are present in the economy. Although, if these distortions could be offset, by the careful application of personal lump-sum income transfers, matters could be made much simpler for the calculation of socially optimal linear income tax rates.[216] But, as the earlier discussion in section 12 indicated, there are a separate set of policy-implementation problems associated with such an action.

Finally, it is noted that the statement in (4.19) above alludes to the possibility that there may be many local solutions to the optimising problem set out in that equation. This fact only adds to the problems of determining the value of the globally optimal value of the marginal linear income tax rate.

---

215 Mazur [1989, p. 45] also alludes to the possibility that the socially optimal marginal linear income tax rates may need to take a negative value.

216 The relevant remarks made in section 13 above in the main text, with respect to the provision of suitable personal lump-sum income transfers, applies here as well.

14.4 Is Applying a Linear Income Tax System Alone Socially Optimal? An Application of the Envelope Theorem

The discussion in the previous two sub-sections is based upon the assumption that the only good in the C-sector of the economy is individual labour (leisure). And only a linear income tax can be applied to this good. The question which may be asked at this point is the following: Should a socially optimal taxation *structure* be composed solely of a linear income taxation *system* - even though the marginal linear income tax rate has been set socially optimally - if, in fact, the authorities *are* free and able to alter a range of (but not all) consumption taxes ?

Given the circumstances just described, the answer to this question is almost certainly no. Indeed the answer is clearly implied by the argument presented in the previous section (section 13). Nevertheless, an alternative method will be employed here to demonstrate the validity of the assertion just made.

To begin with the simple case will be considered where all markets are complete and competitive and, initially, there are no consumption taxes and tariffs in place. It is also assumed that the linear income tax rate has been set socially optimally (given the initial assumption that consumption taxes cannot be altered in size). Next it is assumed that the authorities are now free to alter a range of (but not all) commodity taxes to any level. As a result a small tax on good k is applied at the initial social optimum.

These various assumptions, when imposed on (14.3) above, imply the following:

$$dW = \sum_{h=1}^{H} \beta^h \left[\phi^*(\ .\ )\, q_o^h \frac{\partial c_o^h}{\partial t_k} + \frac{\partial Y^h}{\partial t_k} \right] \quad \text{for some k,} \qquad (14.10)$$

where $\phi^*(\ .\ )$ refers to the socially optimal marginal linear income tax rate at the initial situation. The value of this term does not vary in size, as the small tax is applied to good k, since $\phi^*(\ .\ )$ has already been set optimally.

As the authorities are free to apply any one of a range of consumption taxes, this means that the authorities probably have the degrees of freedom to ensure that the tax that is applied results in (14.10) above taking a positive value. Assuming that $\phi^*(\ .\ )$ takes a positive value, a sufficient set of conditions which would ensure that this is so are the following:

for some k good,

$$\frac{\partial Y^h}{\partial t_k} \geq 0 \quad \text{and} \quad \frac{\partial c_o^h}{\partial t_k} > 0, \qquad \text{for all h.} \qquad (14.11)$$

Thus if leisure is an uncompensated substitute for good k, for all h individuals, and a rise in the tax on good k does not reduce the real income received by any individual in the community, then this fact implies that imposing a linear income tax system alone is no longer the socially optimal taxation structure - the community probably could make itself better off by applying at least one of the consumption taxes it is now free to impose.

This result is essentially the dual of the result stated in proposition 13.1 in the previous section. This point can be demonstrated by noting that, in the context of (14.11) above, if all k goods are weakly separable from individual leisure so that

$$\sum_{h=1}^{H} \beta^h \, q_o^h \frac{\partial c_o^h}{\partial t_k} = 0, \qquad \text{for all k,}$$

and personal lump-sum transfers can be arranged such that

$$\frac{\partial Y^h}{\partial t_k} + \sum_h \frac{\partial Y^h}{\partial b^h} = 0, \qquad \text{for all k,}$$

then it now becomes socially optimal to apply a linear income taxation system alone. This line of argument is a slightly less general version of that result stated in proposition 13.1 above.

Returning to the result, based on (14.10) and (14.11) above, that result was derived by essentially applying the envelope theorem. This point will be returned to below, but for the present it is noted that this case is really the dual of that considered by Corlett and Hague [1953] and Meade [1955, Mathematical Supplement]. Specifically, the case they considered was that where there are consumption taxes imposed on two goods, and no tax is imposed on individual labour (leisure). In the present case the reverse is true - a tax is imposed on leisure alone (at least initially). The present case is, however, more general than the Corlett-Hague-Meade example in that allowance has also been made for the concern the community may have for distributive justice.

The argument based on (14.10) can be generalised by allowing for the presence of markets which are not complete and competitive, and allowing consumption taxes to be imposed on a number of goods. In this case the pertinent form of (14.3) is the following [where it is assumed that personal lump-sum transfers are not altered at the social optimum]:

$$dW = \sum_{h=1}^{H} \beta^h \left\{ \sum_{k=1}^{m \leq n} \left[\phi^*(\;.\;)\, q_0^h \frac{\partial c_0^h}{\partial t_k} + \frac{\partial Y^h}{\partial t_k} \right. \right.$$

$$+ \quad \lambda^h \frac{\partial g}{\partial t_k} + \frac{\partial S^h}{\partial t_k} \Bigg] \Bigg\} dt_k \; . \quad (14.12)$$

In this much more complex case, what is required is that the range of taxes, which are altered by a small amount at the initial social optimum (where only a linear income tax is applied), ensures that (14.12) above takes a positive value.

Proposition 14.1: Assumptions (BA) and (J) are satisfied, and all markets may, or may not, be complete and competitive, and only a linear income tax is applied at the initial social optimum. In these circumstances, if the consumption taxes can be altered in size, and the sum of the terms on the right-hand side of (14.12) above takes a non-zero value, then it is not socially optimal to impose a linear income taxation system alone.

As for the matter of what form the socially optimal taxation structure should take in the new situation - where a number of consumption taxes are now controllable - that particular issue was addressed in section 12 above. Certainly the alternative socially optimal taxation structure could now be one of many possibilities.

As pointed out above the argument, employed to demonstrate proposition 14.1 above, was simply the application of the envelope theorem. This point can be explained a little further by assuming, for the sake of simplicity, that the level of social welfare be solely a function of the linear income tax and the prices facing consumers and producers in the community. The linear income tax rate is set at the socially optimum level. Thus

$$W = F[q, p, t_o^*(q, p)], \tag{14.13}$$

where q denotes a vector of prices facing consumers, and p denotes a vector of prices facing producers.[217] Given that this version of the social welfare function is continuously differentiable, the previous equation becomes, when a small set of consumption taxes are introduced into the economy:

$$dW = \sum_k \frac{\partial F(\,.\,)}{\partial q_k} dq_k + \sum_k \frac{\partial F(\,.\,)}{\partial p_k} dp_k\,, \tag{14.14}$$

where $dt_k = [\,dq_k - dp_k\,]$ for all k.

The linear income tax remains unaltered in this case as it has already been set at the socially optimal level; i.e. $[\,\partial t_o^*/\partial t_k\,] = 0$ for all k. Thus, if the sum of the terms, on the right-hand side of (14.14) above, take a non-zero value, then it is socially optimal to impose consumption taxes (subsidies) - in addition to the linear income tax. This result is just the application of the Envelope Theorem.

217 Clearly a great deal of detail is being omitted from (14.14) in the main text.

15. Conclusions.

The previous discussion has not covered all the special cases that could be considered by drawing upon the basic general model sketched out earlier in sections 8 and 9. The present discussion has gone far enough, however, to satisfy the central objective set for this set of lectures; namely, to justify the assertion [made in the opening paragraph of the first set of lectures] that there appears to be only a small probability that it is socially optimal to apply comparatively simple taxation structures - and, in particular, a piecemeal consumption taxation structure. This is particularly so in a community composed of many heterogeneous individuals, where matters of distributive justice are of concern, and in which all markets are not complete and competitive. This is not to say that there is not a remote chance that pertinent necessary and sufficient (or just sufficient) conditions will be satisfied to ensure that it is socially optimal to impose relatively simple consumption taxation structures. But the reasonably accurate information, required to determine when and where such an event occurs, is not available at the present time. {The pertinent discussions to be found in the papers by Hammond [1990], Yitzhaki and Slemrod [1991] and Deaton [1987], for example, are of particular relevance at this point in this argument.}

It should also be pointed out that these conclusions were arrived at by employing the comparatively general piecemeal taxation model first specified by Boadway and Harris [1977]. Simplifying this model down, by employing models which only have one good in the Control Sector, or only one good in the Distorted Sector, does not seem to be a satisfactory approach to adopt - as parts of the discussion in the previous two sections indicated. Rather a community, attempting to attain the social optimum, will probably face a situation where there are at least two goods in the Control Sector of the economy, and at least two goods in the Distorted Sector of the economy. It was this formulation of the piecemeal problem which was applied, in particular, in section 12 above - the section in which the bulk of the central results, in this set of lectures, were presented.

A natural response to these concluding remarks may take the following form: It is accepted that a community, in which distributive justice matters and where the economic system is complex, is faced with considerable information problems when attempting to apply socially optimal taxation structures - let alone determine the socially optimal values of specific tax rates. Might it not be preferable, therefore, for this community to adopt the strategy of attempting to determine, without placing excessive demands on limited information, the necessary and sufficient (or just sufficient) conditions which need to be satisfied for this community to gain from some general reform(s) of the economic system? It is this particular question which was addressed in the first set of lectures.

References.

Ahmad, E. and Stern, N. [1991], The Theory and Practice of Tax Reform in Developing Countries (Cambridge: Cambridge University Press).

Atkinson, A. B. [1977], "Optimal Taxation and the Direct Versus Indirect Tax Controversy", Canadian Journal of Economics, Vol. 10, pp. 590 - 606.

Atkinson, A. B. and Stiglitz, J. E. [1976], "The Design of Tax Structure: Direct Versus Indirect Taxation", Journal of Public Economics, Vol. 6, pp. 55-75.

Atkinson, A. B. and Stiglitz, J. E. [1980], Lectures in Public Economics (London: McGraw-Hill).

Barr, N. [1989], "Social Insurance as an Efficiency Device", Journal of Public Policy, Vol. 9, pp. 59 - 82.

Besley, T. and Jewitt, I. [1990], "Optimal Uniform Taxation and the Structure of Consumer Preferences", in Myles, G. D. (ed.) Measurement and Modelling in Economics (Amsterdam: North Holland).

Blackorby, C., Donaldson, R.
and Schworm, W. [1990a], "Implicit Separability: Characterization and Implications for Consumer Demand", G.R.E.Q.E., Document de Travail no. 90A16.

Blackorby, C., Donaldson, R.
and Schworm, W. [1990b], "Economics With Two-Sector Representation," G.R.E.Q.E., Document de Travail no. 90A18.

Blackorby, C., Donaldson, R.
and Schworm, W. [1990c], "Use and Misuse of Single-Consumer Results in a Multi-Consumer Economy: The Optimality of Proportional Commodity Taxation", in Myles, G. D. (ed.) Measurement and Modelling in Economics (Amsterdam: North Holland).

Blackorby, C., Donaldson , R.

and Schworm, W. [1991], "The Validity of Piecemeal Second-Best Policy", Journal of Public Economics, Vol. 46, pp. 267 - 290.

Boadway, R. W. and Harris, R. G. [1977], "A Characterization of Piecemeal Second Best Policy", Journal of Public Economics, Vol. 8, pp. 169-190.

Boadway, R., Marchand, M.
and Pestieau, P. [1991], "Optimal Linear Income Taxation in Models with Occupational Choice", Journal of Public Economics, Vol. 46, pp. 133 - 162.

Chiang, A. C. [1974], Fundamental Methods of Mathematical Economics: Second Edition (Tokyo: McGraw-Hill Kogakusha).

Corlett, W. J. and Hague, D. C. [1953], "Complementarity and the Excess Burden of Taxation", Review of Economic Studies, Vol. 21, pp. 21 - 30.

Deaton, A. S. [1979], "Optimal Uniform Commodity Taxes", Economic Letters, Vol. 2, pp. 357 - 361.

Deaton, A. S.[1981], "Optimal Taxes and the Structure of Preferences", Econometrica, Vol. 49, pp.1245-1260.

Deaton, A. S. [1987], "Econometric Issues for Tax Design in Developing Countries", Newbery, D. and Stern, N. (eds), The Theory of Taxation for Developing Countries (Oxford: Oxford University Press).

Deaton, A. S. and Muellbauer, J. [1980], Economics of Consumer Behaviour (Cambridge: Cambridge University Press).

Deaton, A. S. and Stern, N. [1986], "Optimally Uniform Commodity Taxes, Tastes Differences and Lump-Sum Grants", Economic Letters, Vol. 20, pp. 263 - 266.

Dixit, A. K. and Sandmo, A. [1977], "Some Simplified Formulae for Optimal Income Taxation", Scandinavian Journal of Economics, Vol. 79, pp. 417-423.

Gorman, W. M. [1976], "Tricks With Utility Functions", in Artis, M.J. and Nobay, A.R. (eds), Essays in Economic Analysis (Cambridge: Cambridge University Press).

Gorman, W. M. [1990], "Comments" in in Myles, G. D. (ed.) Measurement and Modelling in Economics (Amsterdam: North Holland).

Graaff, J. de V. [1957], Theoretical Welfare Economics (Cambridge: Cambridge University Press).

Hammond, P. J. [1990], "Theoretical Progress in Public Economics: A Provocative Assessment", Oxford Economics Papers, Vol. 42, pp. 6 - 33.

Hellwig, M. F. [1986], "The Optimal Linear Income Tax Revisited", Journal of Public Economics, Vol. 31, pp. 163 - 179.

Jewitt, I. [1981], "Preference Structure and Piecemeal Second Best", Journal of Public Economics, Vol. 16, pp. 215 - 231.

Kay, J. A. [1990], " Tax Policy: A Survey", Economic Journal, Vol. 100, pp. 18 - 75.

Lipsey, R. G. and Lancaster, K. [1956],"The General Theory of Second Best", Review of Economic Studies, Vol. 24, pp. 11 -32.

Mazur, M. J. [1989], "Optimal Linear Taxation with Stochastic Incomes", Public Finance, Vol. 45, pp. 31 - 49.

Meade, J. E. [1955], Trade and Welfare, and Trade and Welfare: Mathematical Supplement (Oxford: Oxford University Press).

Mirrlees, J. A. [1976], "Optimal Tax Theory", Journal of Public Economics, Vol. 6, pp. 327 - 358.

Mirrlees, J. A. [1986], "The Theory of Optimal Taxation", in K.J. Arrow and M.D. Intriligator (eds), Handbook of Mathematical Economics, Vol. 3 (Amsterdam: Elsevier Science Publishers).

Munk, K. J. [1978], "Optimal Taxation and Pure Profit", Scandinavian Journal of Economics, Vol. 80, pp. 1 - 19.

Ramsey, F. P. [1927], "A Contribution to the Theory of Taxation", Economic Journal, Vol. 37, pp. 47 - 61.

Ray, R. [1988],"Optimally Uniform Commodity Taxes in a Non-Linear Demographic Demand Model", Bulletin of Economic Research, Vol. 40, pp. 227 - 233.

Roberts, K. [1984], "The Theoretical Limits to Redistribution", Review of Economic Studies, Vol. 51, pp. 177 - 195.

Sadka, E. [1977], "A Theorem on Uniform Taxation", Journal of Public Economics, Vol. 7, pp. 387 - 391.

Scitovsky, T. [1942], "A Reconsideraration of the Theory of Tariffs", Review of Economic Studies, Vol. 9, pp. 89 - 110.

Seade, J.[1982], "On the Sign of the Optimum Marginal Income Tax", Review of Economic Studies, Vol. 49, pp. 637-643.

Sheshinski, E. [1972], "The Optimal Linear Income Tax", Review of Economic Studies, Vol. 39, pp. 297 - 302.

Sidgwick, H. [1883, 2nd Edition 1887], Principles of Political Economy (London: Macmillan).

Slemrod, J. [1990], "Optimal Taxation and Optimal Tax System', Journal of Economic Perspectives, Vol. 4, pp. 157-178.

Stiglitz, J. E. [1987], "Pareto Efficient and Optimal Taxation and the New New Welfare Economics", in Auerbach, A. and Feldstein, M. (eds), Handbook of Public Economics, Vol. 2, (Amsterdam: North Holland).

Tuomala, M. [1990], Optimal Income Tax and Redistribution (Oxford: Clarendon Press).

Wilson, J. D. [1991], "Optimal Public Goods Provision with Limited Lump-Sum Taxation", American Economic Review, Vol. 81, pp. 153 - 166.

Yitzhaki, S. and Slemrod, J. [1991], "Welfare Dominance: Application to Commodity Taxation", American Economic Review, Vol. 81, pp. 480 - 496.

Vol. 307: T.K. Dijkstra (Ed.), On Model Uncertainty and its Statistical Implications. VII, 138 pages. 1988.

Vol. 308: J.R. Daduna, A. Wren (Eds.), Computer-Aided Transit Scheduling. VIII, 339 pages. 1988.

Vol. 309: G. Ricci, K. Velupillai (Eds.), Growth Cycles and Multisectoral Economics: the Goodwin Tradition. III, 126 pages. 1988.

Vol. 310: J. Kacprzyk, M. Fedrizzi (Eds.), Combining Fuzzy Imprecision with Probabilistic Uncertainty in Decision Making. IX, 399 pages. 1988.

Vol. 311: R. Färe, Fundamentals of Production Theory. IX, 163 pages. 1988.

Vol. 312: J. Krishnakumar, Estimation of Simultaneous Equation Models with Error Components Structure. X, 357 pages. 1988.

Vol. 313: W. Jammernegg, Sequential Binary Investment Decisions. VI, 156 pages. 1988.

Vol. 314: R. Tietz, W. Albers, R. Selten (Eds.), Bounded Rational Behavior in Experimental Games and Markets. VI, 368 pages. 1988.

Vol. 315: I. Orishimo, G.J.D. Hewings, P. Nijkamp (Eds), Information Technology: Social and Spatial Perspectives. Proceedings 1986. VI, 268 pages. 1988.

Vol. 316: R.L. Basmann, D.J. Slottje, K. Hayes, J.D. Johnson, D.J. Molina, The Generalized Fechner-Thurstone Direct Utility Function and Some of its Uses. VIII, 159 pages. 1988.

Vol. 317: L. Bianco, A. La Bella (Eds.), Freight Transport Planning and Logistics. Proceedings, 1987. X, 568 pages. 1988.

Vol. 318: T. Doup, Simplicial Algorithms on the Simplotope. VIII, 262 pages. 1988.

Vol. 319: D.T. Luc, Theory of Vector Optimization. VIII, 173 pages. 1989.

Vol. 320: D. van der Wijst, Financial Structure in Small Business. VII, 181 pages. 1989.

Vol. 321: M. Di Matteo, R.M. Goodwin, A. Vercelli (Eds.), Technological and Social Factors in Long Term Fluctuations. Proceedings. IX, 442 pages. 1989.

Vol. 322: T. Kollintzas (Ed.), The Rational Expectations Equilibrium Inventory Model. XI, 269 pages. 1989.

Vol. 323: M.B.M. de Koster, Capacity Oriented Analysis and Design of Production Systems. XII, 243 pages. 1989.

Vol. 324: I.M. Bomze, B.M. Pötscher, Game Theoretical Foundations of Evolutionary Stability. VI, 145 pages. 1989.

Vol. 325: P. Ferri, E. Greenberg, The Labor Market and Business Cycle Theories. X, 183 pages. 1989.

Vol. 326: Ch. Sauer, Alternative Theories of Output, Unemployment, and Inflation in Germany: 1960–1985. XIII, 206 pages. 1989.

Vol. 327: M. Tawada, Production Structure and International Trade. V, 132 pages. 1989.

Vol. 328: W. Güth, B. Kalkofen, Unique Solutions for Strategic Games. VII, 200 pages. 1989.

Vol. 329: G. Tillmann, Equity, Incentives, and Taxation. VI, 132 pages. 1989.

Vol. 330: P.M. Kort, Optimal Dynamic Investment Policies of a Value Maximizing Firm. VII, 185 pages. 1989.

Vol. 331: A. Lewandowski, A.P. Wierzbicki (Eds.), Aspiration Based Decision Support Systems. X, 400 pages. 1989.

Vol. 332: T.R. Gulledge, Jr., L.A. Litteral (Eds.), Cost Analysis Applications of Economics and Operations Research. Proceedings. VII, 422 pages. 1989.

Vol. 333: N. Dellaert, Production to Order. VII, 158 pages. 1989.

Vol. 334: H.-W. Lorenz, Nonlinear Dynamical Economics and Chaotic Motion. XI, 248 pages. 1989.

Vol. 335: A.G. Lockett, G. Islei (Eds.), Improving Decision Making in Organisations. Proceedings. IX, 606 pages. 1989.

Vol. 336: T. Puu, Nonlinear Economic Dynamics. VII, 119 pages. 1989.

Vol. 337: A. Lewandowski, I. Stanchev (Eds.), Methodology and Software for Interactive Decision Support. VIII, 309 pages. 1989.

Vol. 338: J.K. Ho, R.P. Sundarraj, DECOMP: an Implementation of Dantzig-Wolfe Decomposition for Linear Programming. VI, 206 pages.

Vol. 339: J. Terceiro Lomba, Estimation of Dynamic Econometric Models with Errors in Variables. VIII, 116 pages. 1990.

Vol. 340: T. Vasko, R. Ayres, L. Fontvieille (Eds.), Life Cycles and Long Waves. XIV, 293 pages. 1990.

Vol. 341: G.R. Uhlich, Descriptive Theories of Bargaining. IX, 165 pages. 1990.

Vol. 342: K. Okuguchi, F. Szidarovszky, The Theory of Oligopoly with Multi-Product Firms. V, 167 pages. 1990.

Vol. 343: C. Chiarella, The Elements of a Nonlinear Theory of Economic Dynamics. IX, 149 pages. 1990.

Vol. 344: K. Neumann, Stochastic Project Networks. XI, 237 pages. 1990.

Vol. 345: A. Cambini, E. Castagnoli, L. Martein, P Mazzoleni, S. Schaible (Eds.), Generalized Convexity and Fractional Programming with Economic Applications. Proceedings, 1988. VII, 361 pages. 1990.

Vol. 346: R. von Randow (Ed.), Integer Programming and Related Areas. A Classified Bibliography 1984–1987. XIII, 514 pages. 1990.

Vol. 347: D. Ríos Insua, Sensitivity Analysis in Multi-objective Decision Making. XI, 193 pages. 1990.

Vol. 348: H. Störmer, Binary Functions and their Applications. VIII, 151 pages. 1990.

Vol. 349: G.A. Pfann, Dynamic Modelling of Stochastic Demand for Manufacturing Employment. VI, 158 pages. 1990.

Vol. 350: W.-B. Zhang, Economic Dynamics. X, 232 pages. 1990.

Vol. 351: A. Lewandowski, V. Volkovich (Eds.), Multiobjective Problems of Mathematical Programming. Proceedings, 1988. VII, 315 pages. 1991.

Vol. 352: O. van Hilten, Optimal Firm Behaviour in the Context of Technological Progress and a Business Cycle. XII, 229 pages. 1991.

Vol. 353: G. Ricci (Ed.), Decision Processes in Economics. Proceedings, 1989. III, 209 pages 1991.

Vol. 354: M. Ivaldi, A Structural Analysis of Expectation Formation. XII, 230 pages. 1991.

Vol. 355: M. Salomon. Deterministic Lotsizing Models for Production Planning. VII, 158 pages. 1991.

Vol. 356: P. Korhonen, A. Lewandowski, J . Wallenius (Eds.), Multiple Criteria Decision Support. Proceedings, 1989. XII, 393 pages. 1991.

Vol. 357: P. Zörnig, Degeneracy Graphs and Simplex Cycling. XV, 194 pages. 1991.

Vol. 358: P. Knottnerus, Linear Models with Correlated Disturbances. VIII, 196 pages. 1991.

Vol. 359: E. de Jong, Exchange Rate Determination and Optimal Economic Policy Under Various Exchange Rate Regimes. VII, 270 pages. 1991.

Vol. 360: P. Stalder, Regime Translations, Spillovers and Buffer Stocks. VI, 193 pages . 1991.

Vol. 361: C. F. Daganzo, Logistics Systems Analysis. X, 321 pages. 1991.

Vol. 362: F. Gehrels, Essays In Macroeconomics of an Open Economy. VII, 183 pages. 1991.

Vol. 363: C. Puppe, Distorted Probabilities and Choice under Risk. VIII, 100 pages . 1991

Vol. 364: B. Horvath, Are Policy Variables Exogenous? XII, 162 pages. 1991.

Vol. 365: G. A. Heuer, U. Leopold-Wildburger. Balanced Silverman Games on General Discrete Sets. V, 140 pages. 1991.

Vol. 366: J. Gruber (Ed.), Econometric Decision Models. Proceedings, 1989. VIII, 636 pages. 1991.

Vol. 367: M. Grauer, D. B. Pressmar (Eds.), Parallel Computing and Mathematical Optimization. Proceedings. V, 208 pages. 1991.

Vol. 368: M. Fedrizzi, J. Kacprzyk, M. Roubens (Eds.), Interactive Fuzzy Optimization. VII, 216 pages. 1991.

Vol. 369: R. Koblo, The Visible Hand. VIII, 131 pages.1991.

Vol. 370: M. J. Beckmann, M. N. Gopalan, R. Subramanian (Eds.), Stochastic Processes and their Applications. Proceedings, 1990. XLI, 292 pages. 1991.

Vol. 371: A. Schmutzler, Flexibility and Adjustment to Information in Sequential Decision Problems. VIII, 198 pages. 1991.

Vol. 372: J. Esteban, The Social Viability of Money. X, 202 pages. 1991.

Vol. 373: A. Billot, Economic Theory of Fuzzy Equilibria. XIII, 164 pages. 1992.

Vol. 374: G. Pflug, U. Dieter (Eds.), Simulation and Optimization. Proceedings, 1990. X, 162 pages. 1992.

Vol. 375: S.-J. Chen, Ch.-L. Hwang, Fuzzy Multiple Attribute Decision Making. XII, 536 pages. 1992.

Vol. 376: K.-H. Jöckel, G. Rothe, W. Sendler (Eds.), Bootstrapping and Related Techniques. Proceedings, 1990. VIII, 247 pages. 1992.

Vol. 377: A. Villar, Operator Theorems with Applications to Distributive Problems and Equilibrium Models. XVI, 160 pages. 1992.

Vol. 378: W. Krabs, J. Zowe (Eds.), Modern Methods of Optimization. Proceedings, 1990. VIII, 348 pages. 1992.

Vol. 379: K. Marti (Ed.), Stochastic Optimization. Proceedings, 1990. VII, 182 pages. 1992.

Vol. 380: J. Odelstad, Invariance and Structural Dependence. XII, 245 pages. 1992.

Vol. 381: C. Giannini, Topics in Structural VAR Econometrics. XI, 131 pages. 1992.

Vol. 382: W. Oettli, D. Pallaschke (Eds.), Advances in Optimization. Proceedings, 1991. X, 527 pages. 1992.

Vol. 383: J. Vartiainen, Capital Accumulation in a Corporatist Economy. VII, 177 pages. 1992.

Vol. 384: A. Martina, Lectures on the Economic Theory of Taxation. XII, 313 pages. 1992.